The First-Time Investor

FINANCIAL TIMES
Prentice Hall

In an increasingly competitive world, it is quality of thinking that gives an edge – an idea that opens new doors, a technique that solves a problem, or an insight that simply helps make sense of it all.

We work with leading authors in the fields of management and finance to bring cutting-edge thinking and best learning practice to a global market.

Under a range of leading imprints, including *Financial Times Prentice Hall*, we create world-class print publications and electronic products giving readers knowledge and understanding which can then be applied, whether studying or at work.

To find out more about our business and professional products, you can visit us at www.business-minds.com

For other Pearson Education publications, visit www.pearsoned-ema.com

Pearson
Education

The First-Time Investor

The complete guide to buying, owning and selling shares

Debbie Harrison

FINANCIAL TIMES

Prentice Hall

An imprint of Pearson Education

London • New York • San Francisco • Toronto • Sydney
Tokyo • Singapore • Hong Kong • Cape Town • Madrid
Paris • Milan • Munich • Amsterdam

PEARSON EDUCATION LIMITED

Head Office:
Edinburgh Gate
Harlow CM20 2JE
Tel: +44 (0)1279 623623
Fax: +44 (0)1279 431059

London Office:
128 Long Acre, London WC2E 9AN
Tel: +44 (0)20 7447 2000
Fax: +44 (0)20 7240 5771
Website: www.business-minds.com

First edition published 1998
Second edition first published in Great Britain in 2002

© Debbie Harrison 2002

The right of Debbie Harrison to be identified as Author of this work has been asserted by her in accordance with the Copyright, Designs and Patents Act 1988.

ISBN 0 273 65426 8

British Library Cataloguing in Publication Data
A CIP catalogue record for this book can be obtained from the British Library.

10 9 8 7 6 5 4 3 2

Designed by designdeluxe, Bath
Typeset by Northern Phototypesetting Co. Ltd, Bolton
Printed and bound in Great Britain by Biddles Ltd, Guildford & King's Lynn

The Publishers' policy is to use paper manufactured from sustainable forests.

About the author

Debbie Harrison is an award-winning financial author and journalist. She writes regularly for the *Financial Times* and is the author of five FT reports on retail and institutional investment. Her consumer books include *Personal Financial Planner*, *Pension Power* and *The Money Zone*, published by Pearson Education, and *How to Make it in The City*, published by Virgin Publishing.

Contents

CONTENTS

CONTENTS

Foreword

The millennium is upon us and not far after the 'baby boom' generation starts to retire. That generation, for whom countless flat-roofed secondary schools were built in the late fifties and early sixties, the generation who were the authors of the teenage revolution, the first wearers of the miniskirt and fans of the Rolling Stones and the Beatles, will now provide the retirement bulge. And in so doing they bring with them a demographic change of substantial proportion. Next, the average life expectation of a baby girl born today is over 80 years and, if that is the average, think what the maximum is likely to be. So we are living longer, with an increasing proportion of our active lives being after retirement; in addition, the proportion of the population who are of retirement age is steadily increasing whilst that of those of working age to support them is reducing.

Public policy is also changing, aiming to concentrate social security provision towards an essential safety net whilst encouraging individuals of all incomes to save for their own and their families' future. Saving is essential. Saving means that we have the ability to live more comfortably, buy those things which we would like to buy and not be afraid of the future.

So what has all this got to do with a first-time investor? Well, saving is too often synonymous in peoples' minds with an interest-earning account at either a bank or a building society. Yet saving is much more than just that. As this book so eloquently describes, money saved by investment in stocks and shares and in equities generally (and this book describes what these terms mean) has given a much better return than cash held in the traditional account. This all shows us not just the importance of saving, but also the importance of investing some money at least in shares.

Many people are already part way there as a result of the privatizations of the 1980s and the demutualizations of the 1990s. Best estimates say that some 16 million people now hold shares and so that is one foot on the ladder. But where next? It is not as simple to get involved with shares as it is to buy a lottery ticket, though the returns are generally much better. It can be hard to know where to start and difficult to understand the strange terms that financial people use. So as a first step, read this book. It is a truly definitive and an understandable guide. As a second step, take good independent financial advice. Such advice is essential. For how to find it, what to ask for and where the snags lie, *The First-Time Investor* is again an excellent, readable and comprehensible source.

Angela Knight
Chief Executive, Association of Private Client
Investment Managers
and Stockbrokers

Preface

Share ownership is for everyone. Whether you invest in the stock markets through collective funds such as unit trusts and insurance funds or directly in equities and bonds, the basic decisions you make are the same.

The need for careful and considered private investment is greater than ever before. Strange as it may seem, a different outcome in the May 2001 election would have had little impact on the way we run our personal finances. Behind the scenes both major political parties are united in their view that the state should provide a safety net for the very needy and everyone else should be financially self-sufficient.

This means we should address our financial needs for key areas such as pensions, mortgages and further education for our children. There is no magic one-size-fits-all solution, but despite what the cynics say, a little knowledge goes a very long way towards avoiding expensive mistakes.

The amount of free information available to private investors is unprecedented. The availability of online research, fund supermarkets and execution-only stockbrokers on the Net has revolutionized the way we can invest spare capital. What it hasn't done is made it any less risky.

Indeed, there appears to be an inverse correlation between the ease with which we can part with our money and the jitteriness of world capital markets. Anyone with money invested in equities – and particularly those who went into technology stocks – will have suffered poor and possibly negative returns.

Fortunately – or unfortunately, depending on your point of view – financial institutions and advisers are always coming up with new ways to cushion the impact of volatility. 'With profits' funds, guaranteed funds (backed by financial instruments known as derivatives) and the latest – hedge funds – are all designed to prevent the value of your investment from plummeting when markets go through the floor.

As an investor you need to be aware of the way these black-box products work because they tend to be extremely complicated and have at least one significant drawback that may not be made clear in the sales process. In many cases the salespeople themselves will not understand how the products work.

This book helps you to appreciate the fundamentals of investing so that you can select the right types of assets and the right types of products for your requirements and your risk tolerance.

Caveat emptor – buyer beware – is as important today as it ever was.

Debbie Harrison

Acknowledgements

Many people helped with this book and the source of specific material is provided in the text. I would like to thank in particular the Association of Private Client Investment Managers and Stockbrokers (APCIMS), Barclays Capital, Chiswell Associates, the Council of Mortgage Lenders, the Financial Services Authority, Hendersens, the Institute for Financial Planning, and ProShare.

Introduction

If you are one of the many millions of people who invest directly or through collective funds in the stock market yet do not consider yourself a member of that elite group of 'private investors', this is the book for you.

Your starting point

Most of us start our investments when we join the company pension scheme which is designed to build up a fund to pay for our old age pension. Or we might take out a mortgage and start an individual savings account or possibly an endowment which builds up a fund to repay the debt after 20 years or more.

We tend to associate these types of investments with our employer or our building society, both of which seem a far cry from the risky and volatile stock markets.

This misconception is perpetuated by financial institutions, which encourage us to compartmentalize our investments rather than to create a coherent portfolio. So, we end up with a pension plan for retirement, an endowment for the mortgage repayment, life assurance funds or unit trusts for the children's school fees, and so on.

In addition to these collective funds, you may be one of the millions of investors who own a collection of individual shares which were not chosen because of the companies' long-term profit forecasts or because you wanted to invest in utilities or financials to balance your portfolio's asset allocation. Rather, they were bought because you subscribed to a tempting privatization issue or you are one of the six million people given shares when your building society or life insurance company demutualized.

You may also have a collection of shares bought to take advantage of the now defunct £3,000 annual single company Pep allowance, or you may be one of an increasing number of employees who are encouraged to buy shares in their employer's company at a discount through a share option scheme.

A coherent portfolio

All of these diverse investments may serve you well, but they do not represent an efficient, balanced and properly managed portfolio. Armed with the right information and, in most cases, the right type of professional adviser, you can make your investments work a lot harder for you.

Whatever your starting point, no doubt you would like to manage your existing investments more efficiently, to learn more about the markets and companies in which you invest, and, above all, to feel more confident and informed when you make investment decisions.

Answers, not questions

This book provides in one source the answers to the most important questions for new investors:

■ How do the stock markets work?

■ What are the important characteristics of equities and bonds?

■ How do I find the right investment adviser?

■ How do I set appropriate investment goals?

■ Which are the right savings and investment products for me?

■ Which investments are tax-efficient?

■ How do I select individual shares, gilts and bonds?

■ Will my ethical and environmental views have an adverse effect on my portfolio?

■ Should I change my portfolio to protect against a bear market?

■ Which benchmarks should I use to measure performance and monitor my portfolio?

■ What rights do I have as a shareholder?

■ What do I do if things go wrong?

How this book can help

Section 1 explains in clear language how the UK stock market works. It then examines the two most important asset classes – equities and bonds – and how investing in the right mix of assets will help you meet your short and long-term goals. Armed with this information you will find that the financial papers and specialist publications start to make a lot more sense.

Your financial plan

The next steps, discussed in Section 2, explain how you can apply this knowledge to your personal circumstances in order to find the right type of adviser for your needs and to determine what sorts of investments are appropriate.

This section explains that before you invest a penny you need to know the answer to two simple but crucial questions:

- What state are your finances in now?
- What are your investment goals?

You cannot answer the second question unless you have first examined your current position to determine how much capital, if any, is genuinely spare. To give yourself a financial health check, you should draw up a financial plan which sets out all your income and expenditure, and lists your investments and liabilities.

If you find the prospect daunting it is worth consulting a financial planner (see Chapter 3 for tips on how to find an adviser) who will guide you through this process and will help you build an accurate financial profile – a family profit and loss account, if you like.

Your financial plan should cover the following aspects:

- **Protection insurance:** Do you have the right level of life assurance and disability insurance to protect your family if you die or are too ill to work?

- **Emergency funds:** Are your income and rainy-day savings sufficient to cover your current and future cash requirements?

- **Mortgages and pensions:** Have you made proper provision for your mortgage repayment, pension, school and college costs, and any other long-term savings requirements? These goals – and the investments you choose to meet your targets – should be incorporated into your overall investment plan.

- **Income and capital gains tax planning:** Are you making the most of the government's annual allowances and exemptions? Could you redistribute your assets within your family to lower your tax bill?

- **Estate planning:** Have you made or updated your will? Have you considered ways to pass on your wealth using suitable inheritance tax planning methods?

Your investment goals

Once you have assessed your current financial position and tidied up any loose ends, it is time to identify your investment goals. Whether you need your investments to generate income, capital growth, or a combination of the two, your investment aims will dictate the types and proportion of each asset class (for example, equities, bonds, gilts and deposits) you should hold in your portfolio.

The place for savings and investment products

Section 3 considers the wide range of savings and investment products available. Some are ideal for short-term goals; others are designed for the long term and may be particularly tax-efficient for some or all tax-payers.

For most investors, savings products (for example, building society deposit and National Savings accounts) and collective funds (for example, unit and investment trusts, pension plans and life assurance funds) play an important part in their financial plans.

Even the very wealthy investor will use savings accounts for emergency cash and collective funds to gain access to specialist areas such as emerging markets and more risky sectors such as technology.

Planning your portfolio

Section 4 will help you start and improve on your portfolio of directly held equities and bonds.

Here you will discover the basic asset allocation and stock selection techniques. If you have strong views on armaments or the environment, for example, there is guidance on ethical and environmental investment. The processes involved with buying and selling as a private investor are also explained.

Interpreting economic indicators

If you choose companies which can demonstrate good long-term potential, they should be able to ride out the market cycles and serve you well for many years. After all, if a company was worth investing in two weeks ago, it will still be worth holding even if the stock market as a whole has taken a tumble. But this does not mean you should ignore economic trends, and active investors will want to protect themselves or even improve the performance of their portfolio by keeping one step ahead of the market. Section 4 explains how to interpret the implications of market cycles, and in particular what action you could take to protect your portfolio in the light of recent volatility and low returns.

Monitoring your portfolio

Section 5 concentrates on the mechanics of running your portfolio smoothly and efficiently. You need to know how to monitor the performance of your collective funds and individual shares and how to interpret the information available to you as an existing or prospective investor.

In particular you need to know how to interpret company reports and accounts, and the statistical pages of the *Financial Times*. You also need to know what rights you have as a shareholder.

In addition, Section 5 explains how your investments will be taxed and shows you how to make the most of the annual tax allowances and exemptions in order to minimize or avoid certain taxes altogether. With care, you can slash your tax bill and still pass the Inland Revenue's scrutiny with flying colours.

Finally there is a roundup of useful information about the internet, investment clubs, regulation and making complaints. Chapter 21 lists some sources of information, and there is a glossary to guide you through all the jargon. Terms listed in the glossary are in italic print.

Keep a clear head

Do remember, though, that however much you learn, investment is not a science, no matter how scientific you try to make the process. Things can and do go wrong, simply because the stock markets refuse to behave in a logical way. So, arm yourself with as much useful information as you can, but never fall into the trap of thinking that you have a foolproof system.

How the markets work

The stock markets

- A (very) brief history lesson

- Three key functions of the stock market

A market is a place where buyers and sellers come together for mutual benefit and gain. The London Stock Exchange is no exception but simply represents an important market place where on the one hand companies can raise finance for expansion, and on the other investors can lend spare capital and in return share in the growth of their chosen companies.

London is one of the top three stock markets in the world. The other two you will hear about most frequently are New York and Tokyo.

The London Stock Exchange is also the world's leading international exchange. More international companies are listed, and more international equities are traded in London than on any other exchange.

For the history buffs, there are many books dedicated to the origins and development of the London Stock Exchange, including those available from the Exchange itself.

This chapter covers the essential details, and helps to explain the context in which the Exchange works. Remember that for all its fancy jargon it is, after all, just a market place.

A (very) brief history lesson

History teaches us that wherever there are a seller and a buyer a middle man will emerge and create a market. The Stock Exchange is no exception.

The origins of the stock market go back to the coffee houses of the 17th century where people who wanted to raise money met with those who wanted to invest in the original *'joint stock'* *companies* – the forerunners of today's *public limited companies* (plcs). Joint stock, in this context, referred to a company where partners pooled their stock, or ownership, with that of outsiders. Therefore, the company was jointly owned by the original owners and private investors.

As the volume of trade in joint stock companies grew, the number of dealers expanded. The original traders were the *brokers*, who bought and sold the shares on behalf of clients, and *jobbers*, through whom the brokers made their transactions. In 1986 jobbers were replaced by *market makers*.

The early market was a far cry from the elegant, pin-striped gentleman's club it later became. Some of the original traders were so unruly that in 1760 a group was kicked out of the Royal Exchange, which had largely replaced the coffee houses as a central market place.

About 150 of these financial hooligans formed a club at Jonathan's Coffee House to carry on the business of buying and selling shares. In 1773 the members voted to change the name of their meeting house to the *Stock Exchange*.

Following a tremendous boom in trade and accompanying scandals – most notably the South Sea Bubble (see page 157) – the members of the Stock Exchange agreed on a set of rules and tighter controls. This resulted in the 1812 Deed of Settlement which formed the basis of the rules for the operation of the markets today.

Big Bang

We now skip a century and a half and move to the 1970s, when London's pre-eminent position in international markets was under threat. In particular, in 1979 the abolition of foreign exchange controls made it easier for UK savings institutions to invest money overseas in non-UK securities. As a result, London Stock Exchange member firms were exposed to competition from overseas brokers who were also contending for UK and international company shares.

These were not the only pressures to change. In the early 1980s the government took the Exchange to court, claiming that some of the principles on which the Exchange's rules were based restricted trade. Under an out-of-court settlement the Exchange agreed to abolish its system of minimum commissions by the end of 1986 to encourage greater competition. This in turn was expected to bring down commission rates and the overall cost of share transactions.

Big Bang took place on October 27, 1986. The important changes were as follows:

■ Ownership of member firms by an outside corporation was allowed, enabling member firms to build larger capital bases to contend with overseas competition. Many firms were bought by UK and foreign banks, and by major overseas securities firms.

■ The separation of member firms into brokers and jobbers ended. All firms became broker/dealers able to operate in a dual capacity – either buying securities from, or selling them to, clients without having to go through a third party.

■ Minimum scales of commission were abolished, opening the way for much greater competition on charges and services.

■ Voting rights at the Exchange were transferred from individual members to member firms.

■ Trading moved from the Exchange floor, where it was carried out face to face in a single hall, to separate dealing rooms, where transactions were performed using telephones and computers.

■ Two computer-based systems were introduced – *SEAQ* (Stock Exchange Automated Quotations) and *SEAQ International*. These enabled investment managers to see share price information from anywhere in the UK. In 1993 *SEATS* (the Stock Exchange Alternative Trading System) was introduced for less liquid securities.

Three key functions of the stock market

The Stock Exchange has three key functions:

■ to raise capital;
■ to trade services;
■ to regulate the stock market (see Figure 1.1).

Raising capital

The Stock Exchange provides a range of markets which allow UK and international companies, governments and other entities to raise capital and to gain wide access to investors and borrowers.

How to buy and sell your shares is covered in Chapter 15 but it is worth running through the basic mechanics of the process here.

There are three main ways in which you can buy shares:

1. *The primary market for initial public offerings:* this is when a company first offers shares on the stock market, a process known as a *flotation.* You may be able to buy direct (through newspaper advertisements, for example) to avoid a stockbroker's commission or, in the case of 'windfall' shares, if you are a member of a mutual building society or life assurance society you may receive free shares in exchange for giving up your right to a share in the mutual's ownership.

2. *Further issues:* companies may need to raise more money at a later stage to fund large projects. In this case it may launch a *rights issue* where existing investors have the opportunity to subscribe for the new shares at less than the current market price.

Figure 1.1   The London Stock Exchange

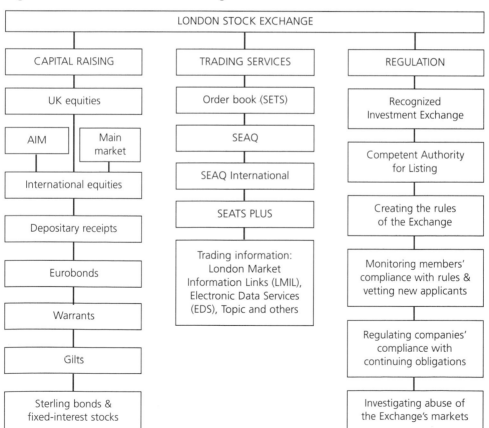

3. *Secondary or trading market:* the most common way of investing in a company's shares is in the secondary or trading market where you buy shares through a stockbroker from existing investors who wish to sell.

So, how do companies 'come to the market' and trade their shares?

The role of the primary market Many UK and international companies come to London to raise new capital or to have their shares more widely marketed and traded. They can raise capital via the main market (known as the *Official List*) or the *Alternative Investment Market* (AIM), which is more suitable for smaller, newer companies.

There are about 1,880 UK companies on the main market, about 490 international companies, and about 500 UK companies on AIM. (See Chapter 18 for more details about listed companies and the *Financial Times* indices.)

Companies can raise capital both at the time of 'going public' and, subsequently, by issuing securities for cash. Access to equity or debt finance gives companies greater flexibility to fund expansion and development programmes or to reduce borrowings.

During a typical year, UK companies might raise more than £50bn, while a further £44bn might be raised by government securities (gilts).

> Access to equity or debt finance gives companies greater flexibility to fund expansion and development programmes or to reduce borrowings.

The main market (Official List) Companies on the main market come from all sectors of business and range from those with a £1m *market capitalization* to those capitalized at £90bn. The market capitalization is calculated by multiplying the current share price by the number of shares in issue.

A company which applies for a listing has to supply the Stock Exchange with a great many details about its trading history, financial records, management and business prospects, as well as information on the securities to be listed, plus the terms of any fundraising. This information is included in the company's *listing particulars* or *prospectus*. The document provides prospective investors with most of the information they need to decide whether to proceed. Clearly an independent assessment is also important.

The company must appoint a sponsor approved by the Exchange to handle its application to join. This can be a member firm, a bank, an investment manager or a firm of solicitors or accountants, among other advisers. There are about 150 approved sponsors.

Trading on the Exchange is carried out through SEAQ for UK companies, SEAQ International for international companies and SEATS Plus for smaller companies.

The companies on the main markets are divided into various categories or *sectors* so that performance can be related to the appropriate peer group. The companies are also divided into different *indices*, based on market capitalization. Sectors and indices are discussed in Chapters 11 and 18.

The Alternative Investment Market AIM was launched in June 1995 and provides a market for young, usually small, but fast-growing companies. Since the eligibility criteria are less stringent than for the main market, companies listed on AIM are generally considered more risky than companies on the Official List, although recently some attempts have been made to disprove this argument.

The majority of AIM companies have a market capitalization of between £5m and £50m, but the range starts as low as about £3m and rises to in excess of £100m.

Trading services

The London Stock Exchange provides a secondary market for trading in more than 12,100 quoted *securities* (the generic term for UK and foreign equities, bonds, gilts and derivatives).

The Exchange provides detailed trading and information services. In October 1997 it introduced a new Stock Exchange Electronic Trading Service (SETS) to speed up order-driven trading, initially in the FTSE 100 equities. *Order book trading* allows sales and purchases to be matched electronically rather than under the old system where quotations were sought by telephone (see page 10).

> Order book trading allows sales and purchases to be matched electronically rather than under the old system where quotations were sought by telephone.

The Exchange offers markets for:

- *UK equities:* the ordinary shares issued by UK companies quoted on SEAQ or SEATS Plus;
- *international equities:* ordinary shares issued by non-UK companies, many of which are quoted on SEAQ International;
- *UK gilts:* securities issued by the UK government;
- *sterling bonds:* securities issued by companies or local authorities;
- *AIM securities:* shares and fixed-interest stocks of companies admitted to AIM;

■ *traditional options:* (a type of derivative, see page 19) traded on SEAQ and SEAQ International.

How the UK market works

Throughout the trading day, market makers display on SEAQ the following details for all the securities for which they are registered to deal:

■ their *bid* (buying) price;

■ their *offer* (selling) price;

■ the *maximum transaction size* to which these prices relate.

The market makers must stick to these prices when dealing with other Exchange member firms. Prices for larger transactions are subject to negotiation.

SEAQ   The Stock Exchange Automated Quotations service is a continuously updated database with market makers' bid and offer prices and sizes of trades. Registered market makers must maintain their prices during the mandatory quote period – 08.30 to 16.20, Monday to Friday. See Figure 1.2 for an example screen.

The information is analyzed to create the SEAQ 'yellow strip' across the screen which identifies for the investor, at any moment of the day, the best bid and offer prices for every SEAQ security, and also identifies up to four market makers quoting this price.

SEAQ International and SEATS Plus operate in a similar way.

SETS   In October 1997 the 'order book' was introduced. This, as previously noted, is known as the Stock Exchange Electronic Trading Service. SETS signals the London equity market's switch from the existing *quote-driven* system of share trading, under which buying and selling of shares are largely conducted by telephone, to an *order-matching* system. See Figure 1.3 for an example screen.

So, instead of market makers placing buy and sell orders by phone, now when bid and offer prices match, orders will automatically pair off.

In theory this should improve efficiency and drive down transaction costs, because it automates the execution of trades and narrows the spread between buying and selling prices, which represents the market maker's 'turn' and adds to the investor's costs.

From the private investor's point of view, if you use an *execution-only* service (where no advice is given – see page 35) you will still telephone your stockbroker and agree a price at which you are willing to buy or sell a

Figure 1.2 SEAQ screen

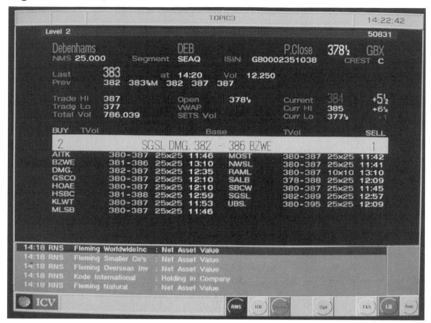

Source: London Stock Exchange

Figure 1.3 SETS screen

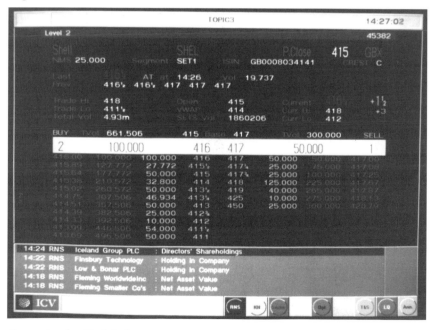

Source: London Stock Exchange

particular share. Alternatively you can place your order via the internet – an increasingly popular method for execution-only investors (see Chapter 15). The broker will enter the order directly into the order book and it will be displayed anonymously to the entire market along with other orders.

Settlement services   After an order has been carried out, the settlement process transfers stock from seller to buyer and arranges for the exchange of money from buyer to seller.

A new electronic share dealing settlement and registration system, Crest (not an acronym), was introduced in 1997. In effect this is an electronic book entry transfer of registered stock, so its aim is to reduce the movement of paper, although investors can still keep share certificates if they wish.

> The point to remember about regulation is that if you ask a stockbroker to provide a discretionary service, they should select the investments that best suit your requirements.

Regulation: The Financial Services Act (1986)

The regulatory system designed to protect investors was completely overhauled with the introduction of the Financial Services Act (FSA) 1986. The Exchange had always been responsible for regulating member firms, but the Act added a new statutory dimension so that it is now illegal for anyone except those authorized or exempted under the Act to carry on investment business.

Under the Act, the Stock Exchange regulates both *capital raising* and *trading markets*. Its activities include:

- to assess the credentials of companies that apply to join the main market (the Official List);
- to monitor listed companies' compliance with the rules;
- to deal with any breaches of the rules;
- to supervise the conduct of the 300 member firms which deal on its markets.

If you want to find a good stockbroker, see Chapter 3, which explains how to check whether a firm has the right regulatory authorization and what other key factors to consider in the selection process. Chapter 21 includes a guide to making complaints, should anything go wrong.

The point to remember about regulation is that if you ask a stockbroker to provide a discretionary service, they should select the investments that best suit your requirements. If, at your initial meeting, you and your broker agree that a portfolio of low-risk collective investments is most appropriate to your needs, and you end up with individual shares listed on AIM, then clearly you have a justified complaint. But if you deal through an execution-only stockbroker and your shares take a tumble, or if your adviser recommends a sensible spread of FTSE 100 shares and the entire stock market crashes, then that's just bad luck.

Summary

- London is one of the top three stock markets in the world.
- Big Bang improved competition on dealing costs and introduced important technology.
- The Stock Exchange's main functions are to raise capital for companies, to trade services and to regulate the stock market.
- There are about 1,880 UK companies on the main market – the 'Official List'.
- The Alternative Investment Market is for young, fast-growing companies.
- Throughout the trading day, market makers display details of the securities for which they are registered to deal on SEAQ (Stock Exchange Automated Quotations).
- In October 1997 the Stock Exchange Electronic Trading Service (SETS) introduced 'order book' trading, which matches sales and purchases electronically for shares in the largest UK companies.

Further information

The London Stock Exchange publishes many useful information leaflets and books. For details contact The Public Information Department, London Stock Exchange, London EC2N 1HP. Tel: 020 7797 1372. Fax: 020 7410 6861. www.londonstockexchange.co.uk

Equities and bonds without tears

- Securities

- The main asset classes

- Comparing equities, bonds and cash (deposits)

- Different styles of institutional fund management

Savings and investment institutions are adept at dressing up what are essentially quite straightforward assets. As a result, it is easy to fall into the trap of investing in 'products' and to end up with a growing number of plans and schemes which, when examined in more detail, represent anything but a co-ordinated, well-balanced portfolio.

This chapter explains the characteristics of the asset classes you will come across in your quest for the best investments for your requirements. Keep this information in mind when you consider the wide range of products discussed later in Section 3. The trick is to keep a co-ordinated approach to the underlying asset allocation and to use the tax-efficient product wrappers only where they can enhance the return of your preferred investments.

To make the best of the available tax breaks, you also need to understand the basics of taxation from the family as well as the individual point of view. For example, if you have a non-working spouse, it makes sense to put income-generating assets in his or her name to make use of the annual income tax allowance.

Equally, you can often eliminate a potential capital gains tax liability by giving some of your assets to your spouse so that he or she can make use of the annual capital gains tax exemption. Taxation is discussed in Chapter 20.

Securities

Investment literature uses a lot of confusing jargon. Commonly used (and misused) terms include 'securities', 'stocks' and 'shares'.

Securities is the general name for all stocks and shares. What we call shares today were known originally as 'stocks' because they represented part ownership in the joint stock companies – the precursors to today's public limited companies or plcs (see Chapter 1). So to some extent the terms stocks and shares are interchangeable, and we still use the terms *stock* market and *stock*broker.

Broadly speaking, stocks are fixed-interest securities and shares are the rest. The four main types of securities listed and traded on the UK Stock Exchange are:

- *UK ('domestic') equities:* ordinary shares issued by about 1,880 UK companies;
- *overseas equities:* ordinary shares issued by non-UK companies;
- *gilts:* bonds issued by the UK government to raise money to fund any shortfall in public expenditure;
- *bonds:* fixed-interest stocks issued by companies and local authorities, among others.

The main asset classes

UK equities

If a company wants to raise finance, it has two main options: it can sell part of the ownership of the company by issuing ordinary shares (equities) or it can borrow money by issuing bonds, which are a sophisticated IOU. Shares and bonds are bought and sold on the stock market.

Equities are the quoted shares of companies in the UK and tend to dominate most private investors' portfolios, whether they are held directly or are pooled through collective funds such as unit and investment trusts or a pension fund.

The return achieved by UK equities, when measured over the long term, has exceeded both price and earnings inflation (see page 22).

As we discovered in Chapter 1, companies 'go public' when they are quoted on the Stock Exchange or Alternative Investment Market. In this way a company can raise the money it needs to expand by issuing shares.

A *share* or equity literally entitles the owner to a specified share in the profits of the company and, if the company is wound up, to a specified

T I P

Your aim is to invest in companies which will achieve a good return for your money in exchange for an acceptable level of risk.

share of its assets. The owner of shares is entitled to the *dividends* – the six-monthly distribution to shareholders of part of the company's profits. The *dividend yield* on equities is the dividend paid by a company divided by that company's share price.

There is no set *redemption date* for an equity when the company is obliged to return your original investment. If, as a shareholder, you want to convert your investment into cash ('to realize its value'), you must sell your shares through a stockbroker. The price will vary from day to day, so the timing of the purchase and sale of shares is critical.

Share classes

There are different classes of shares. Most investors buy *ordinary shares*, which give the holder the right to vote on the constitution of the company's board of directors. Since this is the most common type of share, the term 'ordinary' usually is dropped, unless it is to distinguish the shares from a different category.

Preference shares carry no voting rights but have a fixed dividend payment, so can be attractive to those seeking a regular income. These shares have 'preference' over ordinary shares if the company is wound up – hence the name.

There are several sub-classes of equities or equity-related investments.

Convertibles and warrants Convertibles and warrants are special types of shares with characteristics that make them attractive in certain circumstances.

Convertibles are more akin to bonds (see page 20), in that they pay a regular income and have a fixed redemption date. However, a convertible confers the right to convert to an ordinary share or preference share at a future date. This can be an attractive proposition if the price is favourable on the convertible date.

Warrants confer a right, but not an obligation, on the holder to convert to a specific share at a predetermined price and date. The value of the warrant, which itself is traded on the stock market, is determined by the difference or *premium* of the share price over the conversion price of the warrant.

Derivatives   Derivatives, as the name suggests, derive their value from the price of an underlying security. This is the generic term given to futures contracts and options, both of which can be used to reduce risk in an institutional fund or, in the case of options, even in a large private portfolio.

A *futures contract* binds two parties to a sale or purchase at a specified future date. The price is fixed at the time the contract is taken out. These futures contracts can be used by institutional funds to control risk, because they allow the manager quickly to increase or reduce the fund's exposure to an existing asset class. Futures have also proved

> Some private investors use options as a type of insurance policy to protect their portfolio against a fall in the market.

popular as a cost-cutting mechanism, particularly in index-tracking funds and other funds where there are rapid changes of large asset allocations.

Options allow you, for a down payment, to have the right, but not the obligation, to buy or sell something at an agreed price on a specific date. Some private investors use options as a type of insurance policy to protect their portfolio against a fall in the market. Options are discussed in Chapter 14.

Overseas equities

Overseas equities are similar in principle to UK equities, but there are differences in shareholder rights. Investment overseas provides exposure to the growth in foreign markets, including younger, fast-growing economies. However, these shares also expose you to currency fluctuations. This can be both good and bad, of course, but the point is that it adds an extra layer of risk.

The taxation of foreign shares can be less favourable than UK equities. In particular, some or all of the withholding tax on dividends deducted by the foreign country may not be recoverable.

As a rule of thumb, exposure to the major developed economies – for example the European Union countries, the US, and Canada – is considered important in order to diversify risk in your equity portfolio. Generally this is achieved through collective funds – for example investment trusts (see Chapter 6). Exposure to the emerging economies is high risk and so suitable only for those prepared to take a punt.

Bonds

UK bonds are issued by borrowers, for example the government (these bonds are known as *gilt-edged securities* or just 'gilts') and companies (*corporate bonds*). Bonds are also issued by local authorities, overseas governments and overseas companies.

In return for the loan of your money, the borrower agrees to pay a fixed rate of interest (known as the *coupon*) for the agreed period, and to repay your original capital sum on a specified date, known as the maturity or *redemption date*.

UK domestic bonds are either *secured* on the company's underlying assets – for example the company's property – or *unsecured*, in which case there is no physical asset backing the bond's guarantee to pay interest and to repay the capital at maturity.

Secured bonds are known as *debentures* and unsecured bonds are known as *loan stocks*. Since the security offered by debentures is greater than for loan stocks, the former tend to pay a lower rate of interest.

The point to remember about fixed-interest securities is that the investment return is determined more by the level of interest rates than the issuing company's profitability. Provided the issuer remains sufficiently secure to honour the future *coupon payments* (the regular interest) and *redemption payment* (the return of the original capital) you know exactly what your return will be, provided you hold the bond to maturity. Gilts offer the highest degree of security because they are issued by the UK government.

Traded bonds   If you or a fund manager sells a bond before its maturity date, the value of the future coupon and redemption payments will depend on the prevailing interest rates at the time of sale.

So, if interest rates are rising, the value of the fixed-interest security will fall. This is because for the same amount of capital invested, you could get a better return elsewhere. Conversely, if interest rates are falling, the value of the fixed-interest security will be higher because it provides a greater stream of income than you could get from alternative sources.

This volatile pattern of behaviour is more apparent with fixed-interest securities that have a long period to run to maturity since they are more likely to be traded before redemption date.

To summarize, as a general rule equities are considered more risky and volatile than bonds because they behave in an unpredictable way, whereas provided the company or government backing a bond is watertight, the return on a bond held to maturity is predictable. However, it is not predictable if you decide to sell before maturity.

Eurobonds   UK companies can raise money outside the UK market by issuing 'eurosterling' bonds – that is, bonds denominated in sterling but issued on the Eurobond market. Contrary to the name, the euromarkets are not confined to Europe but are international markets where borrowers and lenders are matched.

The main advantage of eurosterling bonds, from the borrower's point of view, is that they can reach a much wider range of potential lenders. However, this is not a market for private investors in the UK.

Index-linked gilts

Index-linked gilts are issued by the UK government and are guaranteed to provide interest payments (the coupon) and a redemption value which increase in line with annual inflation. For this reason they are one of the lowest-risk assets for income seekers. Having said that, in practice they have not proved particularly attractive compared with other income-generating alternatives.

The return on index-linked gilts in excess of the Retail Price Index varies, but usually it is possible to buy these securities in the market place at a price which guarantees a real rate of return to the holder, assuming that the stock is held to maturity.

> Cash does not refer to stacks of £20 notes stuffed under the mattress, but usually means a deposit account.

Cash

Cash does not refer to stacks of £20 notes stuffed under the mattress, but usually means a deposit account. Deposits have the advantage that the value in monetary terms is known and is certain at all times. What is unknown is the interest that will be received and by how much this will fall short of the rate of inflation.

Property

In investment terms, 'property' usually refers to the ownership of land and buildings that are used by a business or other organization. The owner of the property receives income from the rent charged to the tenant and, over time, this rent is expected broadly to keep pace with inflation. The dominant factor in the value of a property is the desirability or otherwise of its location.

There are several problems with property. First, it is often sold in large blocks which cannot be easily split for investment purposes. As a result, only the larger institutional funds can afford (or are wise) to own property directly.

Second, property is a very illiquid asset and it can take several years for the right selling conditions to arise. Moreover, unless you invest via a collective fund, you cannot dispose of your investment piecemeal to make best use of your annual capital gains tax (CGT) exemption but instead could be landed with a whopping CGT bill.

Comparing equities, bonds and cash (deposits)

It is common practice to compare returns on equities with bonds, and both asset classes with cash (deposits).

However, as Barclays Capital pointed out in its annual *Equity–Gilt Study*, it is important to view equities over the long term. Over a period of just a few years the returns can be volatile and even negative – as happened in 2000 when the total return from equities was –8.6 per cent, after adjusting for inflation. By contrast gilts returned +6.1 per cent in real terms. In 1999 equities performed well, but in 1998 returns on equities fell far short of gilts again.

Barclays pointed out: 'Timing is therefore very important for equity investors. The received wisdom that long-term investors should concentrate their assets in the equity market is an oversimplification. The case for equity investment may be weak if an investor can realize his or her objectives by means of a less risky strategy.'

Investors keen to keep up with the comparative movements of gilts and equities should refer to the *Financial Times*, which publishes the gilt–equity yield ratio. This tracks the yield on gilts divided by the yield on shares. As a rule of thumb the normal range is between 2 and 2.5, so if it dips or soars well out of this range it may indicate that shares are very expensive or that gilts are very cheap. Market analysts use this as one of the signals to indicate that a bull (lower figure) or bear (higher figure) market is imminent. (See Chapter 14 for more details about economic cycles.)

Inflation

It is also important to keep in mind the relationship between inflation and returns. At the time of writing the government's aim was to keep inflation below 2.5 per cent. This is based on a definition of retail price inflation that excludes mortgage interest payments (see Chapter 14).

Barclays' guide points out that inflation is a key determinant of investment returns. Stock markets may not be prepared for an inflation 'shock' (a sudden and unexpected change) but they adjust over time and provide a long-term hedge against price rises. Gilts and cash are not suitable inflation hedges.

Period of investment

Clearly, long-term returns on equities, gilts and cash should be viewed with some caution and certainly should not be treated as a guide to the future. While history indicates that equities should provide a better return than bonds over the medium to long term, there is an important caveat. 'Medium to long term' means a minimum of five years. If you go into the stock markets for shorter periods you are in danger of getting your fingers burned either because the markets take a tumble just before you want to get out or because the fixed costs associated with setting up your investment undermine the return over the short term.

Dividend reinvestment or 'compound growth'

This is important. The Barclays study states: 'Dividends account for nearly two-thirds of total returns to equities over long periods of time. Gilts have been poor long-term investments but income from them has outweighed the reduction in capital values. Since 1990, however, the capital values of gilts have been improving.'

Stock selection

Income from equities or gilts? Chiswell Associates, in its *Compendium of Stock Market Investment*, provided the following succinct argument in favour of equities as a source of income, as well as capital growth (see 'Further information' at the end of this chapter).

Equities represent part ownership of a business. Equity investors provide the core finance for the business and in return they receive dividends paid out of the company's profits. The remainder of the profits are retained by the company for reinvestment in its business, thus building up its assets, earning power and future dividend paying potential.

The value of equities, therefore, rests on the value of the dividend flow which investors receive.

If dividend payments grow over the years then, all other things being equal, the value of shares will rise too since the income stream will be more valuable. Investors may buy and sell shares for short-term gain but in the final analysis equity investment is really about income.

The interest on gilts will look attractive compared with the current income from equities but since gilt income is fixed, the flow of income from the gilt cannot rise over time in the same way as equity dividends (unless the gilt is index-linked – but here the initial income would be quite low).

Eventually the cash value of the rising equity dividend will catch up and exceed the value of the fixed interest payment. Furthermore, the rising dividend flow will have pulled up the value of the shares whereas the capital value of the gilt will not have changed.

This process is accelerated by inflation. By and large companies are able to absorb the costs of inflation by passing on cost increases to customers in the form of higher prices.

This preserves the profitability of the business, whereas with fixed-interest gilts your capital and income are exposed to inflation.

Stock selection refers to the process where the investment manager or private investor chooses individual securities. This topic is covered in Section 4 and in particular in Chapter 11.

At this stage, it is helpful to understand the jargon that investment managers love to use to confuse.

Don't imitate the big boys   It is rarely wise for a private investor to imitate the style of an institutional fund manager. The large pension funds, for example, are worth millions of pounds. Some run into billions. This means they can make money on minor price changes owing to the sheer volume of their transactions.

> It is rarely wise for a private investor to imitate the style of an institutional fund manager.

Moreover, compared with a private client, institutional funds benefit from very low dealing costs and, in the case of pension and charity funds, automatic exemption from capital gains tax and most income tax. This means that what might trigger a buy or sell transaction in the institutional market often should be interpreted as a much more cautious 'hold' position by the private investor.

Different styles of institutional fund management

It is also helpful to understand the tactical and strategic techniques employed by institutional managers. These may not be appropriate for your portfolio, but will certainly be employed by those managing your collective funds.

For dedicated enthusiasts keen to employ suitable strategic investment techniques for private investors, a more advanced book on investment, such as Gillian O'Connor's *A Guide to Stockpicking*, is an excellent guide.

The following descriptions are intended as a broad guide only.

Active managers

Active investment managers aim to increase a fund's value by deviating from a specific benchmark – for example a stock market index. There are two basic techniques used in active stock selection.

The starting point for active managers who adopt a *bottom-up* approach is the company in which the manager may invest. The manager will look at in-house and external research on the company's history and potential prospects. This will include an examination of the strength of the balance sheet, the company's trading history, the management's business strategy and the price/earnings ratio (the market price of a share divided by the company's earnings/profits per share in its latest 12-month trading period).

From the company analysis the manager will proceed to look at the general performance and prospects for that sector (for example oil, retailers and so on) and then take into consideration national and international economic factors.

The *top-down* manager works in reverse, looking first at the international and national economic factors that might affect economic growth in a country, geographic area (for example the 'Tiger' economies of south east Asia) or economic category (emerging markets, for example) and gradually working down to the individual companies.

Among private investors, the *fundamental analyst* focuses almost exclusively on individual companies and would tend to disregard the economic climate and market conditions.

The *technical analyst*, also known as a *chartist*, concentrates on historical price movements and uses these charts as a way of reading future movements in share prices.

Passive managers

Passive managers aim to track or replicate a benchmark. This style is also known as *index tracking*. It may sound simple but in practice this is a complex process based on emulating the performance of a particular stock market index by buying all, or a wide sample, of the constituent shares.

The passive manager does not consider the merits of each stock, of different sectors and economic cycles. If it is in the index then it must be represented in the fund. To date index-tracking funds have done very well compared with actively managed funds, largely because the passive manager's charges are very low in comparison with those of the active manager.

Passive management becomes very complex when the process tries to outstrip the index returns by deviating in a specific way. This is known as *quantitative management*.

Summary

- 'Securities' refers to UK equities, overseas equities, gilts and bonds.

- If a company wants to raise finance it can issue shares, which represent a share in the ownership, or bonds, which are a form of debt and behave like a sophisticated IOU.

- Shares and bonds have sub-classes which have different characteristics and can be used to achieve different investment aims.

- If you want to match or beat inflation, historically you would have had to invest in equities, although this has not always been the case – over the past few years markets have been particularly volatile.

- The higher risk/return characteristic of equities is known as the equity risk premium.

- Inflation has a major impact on the real return provided by your investments.

- Equities are suitable only for the medium to long term owing to their volatility and the cost of investing.

- The reinvestment of dividends increases your return substantially.

- It is important to understand but not to imitate the large institutional fund managers.

Further information

Barclays Capital Equity–Gilt Study 2001: www.barclaysglobal.com

Chiswell Associates, No 4 Chiswell Street, London EC1Y 4UP. Tel: 020 7614 8000. *www.chiswell.co.uk*

Getting started

How to choose your investment adviser

- ■ Which type of advisory service?

- ■ Stockbroker services

- ■ Selecting your adviser

- ■ How to pay for your advice

- ■ Investor protection

In the complex world of investment it is helpful to remember that there are two major factors which affect your return. The first is *performance*, and more is said about this in Section 4. The second is the *level of charges*. This includes purchase costs, the regular charges imposed by fund management groups (for example the annual charge on unit trusts) and, if relevant, your adviser's fees.

Very experienced investors enjoy making their own decisions based on their own research. You can also get a lot of fun if you join an *investment club*, where you can exchange ideas and invest modest amounts as a group. It is cheering to note that the collective wisdom of many clubs enables them to achieve better performance than the experts. These clubs are discussed in Chapter 21.

With or without other private investors to help you, if you are a beginner, you probably need an adviser to guide you or make the investment decisions on your behalf. Even more experienced investors may not have the time to run their portfolio unaided.

This chapter looks at the wide range of advisers authorized under the Financial Services Act. It explains the different levels of advice on offer and highlights some of the main points to consider. The contact details for all the trade associations are set out in Chapter 21. These associations will send you either a complete directory of their members or, in some cases, a list of their members in your area.

Which type of advisory service?

Your choice of adviser will depend to a large extent on the type of service you need and the amount you have to invest. For example, if you want an advisory service for a portfolio of shares you will go to a stockbroker. If you want a unit or investment trust and you are happy to go to just one fund manager, you can buy direct, or go to one of several thousand independent financial advisers.

The term *independent financial adviser* covers many different types and styles of firms ranging from the one-man band with limited resources and qualifications to the well-resourced professional firms of chartered accountants, actuaries and solicitors which specialize in financial services. Even here the boundaries between independence and 'tied' blur, as more and more firms launch their own range of funds.

> **T I P**
>
> Many advisers are not independent. This does not mean that they will necessarily give inferior advice, but it does mean that the range of products on which they can advise is limited.

Step one, therefore, is to know what an adviser can and cannot do. This is determined largely by the way firms are authorized and regulated.

The *Financial Services Act 1986* requires all companies involved in managing and selling investments to be authorized by the Financial Services Authority.

Under the Act advisers are divided into different categories.

Company and appointed representatives

These advisers are not independent. *Company representatives*, as the name suggests, work for just one company. Traditionally, company representatives were paid only when they made a sale. This put them under tremendous pressure to sell the products that preferably paid the best commission rates, but in any event, to sell something.

Clearly, this does not encourage good practice, and today most companies pay representatives a basic salary which is topped up by bonuses related to sales, in a bid to distance themselves from the image of the pushy, foot-in-the-door salesman.

Appointed representatives are companies that have a contract with a financial institution – a life assurance company, for example – under which they agree to sell exclusively one or more of that institution's products in return for an agreed level of sales commission.

Rather confusingly, the appointed representative may act independently in other non-investment-related product lines. For example, a building society will conduct its own lending and borrowing business but might sell the endowments or personal equity plans of only one institution.

The main point to note about company and appointed representatives is that they are authorized only to discuss the products of the company they represent. They are not authorized under the Financial Services Act to tell you whether their products are competitive compared with what you could get elsewhere, in terms of cost and performance.

> It might be convenient to buy all your financial products from one supplier but frankly it's a bit of a gamble.

It might be convenient to buy all your financial products from one supplier but frankly it's a bit of a gamble.

It may be possible in future for sales staff to represent a limited number of companies for certain highly regulated products – which will add to the confusion no end.

Independent financial advisers

Independent advisers in theory should have a thorough knowledge of the whole investment and insurance market and select the most appropriate products for your requirements in terms of risk, investment aims, performance and charges.

One of the encouraging developments in financial services is the increasing emphasis placed on qualifications and training. All advisers must pass at least one basic competence test in order to deal with the public.

In addition there are several associations that require members to undertake specific training and also run some highly professional examinations. Two worth noting are the Society of Financial Advisers, a professional body set up by the Chartered Insurance Institute, and the Institute of Financial Planning.

The professionals

Many firms of professional advisers now offer a complete range of financial services. In addition to stockbrokers, chartered accountants and solicitors are particularly active in financial services (see Chapter 21).

Stockbroker services

If investment management is your primary requirement you should consider a stockbroker.

The *Association of Private Client Investment Managers and Stockbrokers* (APCIMS) represents well over 90 per cent of private client stockbrokers as well as an increasing number of other investment managers. Members have direct access to the stock market for buying and selling shares. The APCIMS directory of members (see page 262) provides a brief guide to the services offered by its member firms and gives you an indication of the minimum size of portfolio accepted by the firm.

In theory there are three types of stockbroker service, although in practice the boundaries between advisory and discretionary blur, and many investors require a combination of the two. The following definitions, therefore, are intended only as a guide.

Dealing or 'execution-only'

This service is designed for investors who do not require advice but who need a stockbroker to buy and sell shares for them. Some stockbrokers specialize in this low-cost, no-frills service and offer competitive rates and a rapid service, particularly those that offer a service via the internet. Do remember though, with an execution-only service you will get information on prices of shares but the broker will offer no comment or opinion on the merits of your choice. So don't expect a phone call even if your broker has a hot tip.

Advisory

With an advisory service, usually you would make the buying and selling decisions yourself based on a combination of your own ideas and the advice of your manager.

In practice there are different types of advisory service. You may want a stockbroker to advise on the sale and purchase of your shares. Alternatively, you may want a more comprehensive service to include advice on capital gains tax and to provide regular valuations of your portfolio.

The main point to remember is that an advisory manager will not take any investment decisions without your authority, although they will give you an opinion. Whether you contact your broker at regular intervals or they phone you with tips is a matter of preference. A mixture of both is probably pragmatic.

Discretionary

If you want your stockbroker to make all the decisions for you then you need a discretionary or portfolio management service.

This does not mean you lose control entirely. You and your manager will have meetings to discuss your current financial circumstances, your investment aims and any ethical views you may have. Your discretionary manager will work with this plan and keep you up to date with changes in your portfolio. Your manager should send you a contract note every time a transaction takes place and regular portfolio valuations.

Comprehensive financial planning

In addition to investment management many stockbrokers offer a broader financial planning service. This can cover tax, pensions, mortgages, life assurance, school fees, inheritance tax, cash and deposits.

Selecting your adviser

Once you have decided on the type of adviser or stockbroker service you require, you need to draw up a shortlist and make the final selection.

The following checklist may help you in your search for a financial adviser or planner, as well as a stockbroker. Before you start, check with the Financial Services Authority (FSA) that the firm is authorized and registered with the appropriate regulator. Also check the adviser's level of qualifications and find out how highly these are rated by the examining body.

- How long has the firm been trading? (New firms should be investigated thoroughly.)
- What is the company's turnover?
- Who are the directors and what relevant experience do they have?
- Does the firm offer the right level of expertise for your requirements?
- How many clients does the firm have?
- What criteria does the firm use to select an investment company?
- How does it assess performance, charges and commercial strength?
- How much will the advice cost per hour, including VAT?
- If your adviser is away, who will look after your business?
- What methods does the firm have for dealing with complaints and disputes?

Points to consider include:

- efficiency in carrying out orders;
- ease of contact by phone;
- dealing with paperwork efficiently;
- prompt settlement;
- low charges;
- real-time dealing;
- good reputation;
- friendliness, helpfulness;
- in-depth market knowledge;
- available outside normal working hours;
- regular newsletters/seminars;
- Internet/online dealing.

Many stockbrokers use their own funds to achieve exposure to specialist markets, smaller companies and foreign investment, for example. This is not necessarily a bad thing, and the funds may well be among the best in their field (ask to see performance statistics from an independent measurer such as Standard & Poor's Micropal and Fund Research, for example).

However, as a general rule, you are more likely to achieve better returns if your stockbroker is free to choose from the whole range of funds available.

More than one stockbroker?

Some investors like to retain a good financial planner, who will keep the whole of the family's finances in order, and to use a stockbroker for the direct equity selection.

> Some investors like to retain a good financial planner, who will keep the whole of the family's finances in order, and to use a stockbroker for the direct equity selection.

This approach makes a lot of sense, but you should think carefully before you decide to split your assets and appoint two or more stockbrokers. While it can be reassuring to know that you have limited the damage if one stockbroker underperforms, there are additional costs involved, in terms of both annual fees and dealing costs. Also you could end up with duplication if the brokers decide to use some of the same shares and funds.

How to pay for your advice

Independent advisers may work on a commission or on a fee basis. Many will accept both. In some cases commission payments represent a fair exchange for the work undertaken. In others, particularly where you want to invest a large sum, the commission will be out of proportion to the work. Moreover, purists argue that what you should pay is a fee for the advice, not a commission for the purchase of a financial product.

Professional firms usually do not accept sales commissions and where these are paid – for example by a unit trust company – the commission is offset against your fees.

Stockbroker charges fall into two categories. First there are the commissions which are charged on the purchase or sale of securities. Usually this is a percentage of the money invested. Alternatively the firm may charge a fee once or twice a year for a continuing investment management service. Some firms use a combination of both fee and dealing commissions.

Finally, you may be able to negotiate performance-related fees. If you wish to do so, first read Chapter 18 which discusses this topic.

Investor protection

Under the Financial Services Act there is an investors' compensation scheme which pays out if you lose money through an adviser's fraud or negligence. However, it won't pay out if your selected shares and funds do not perform well.

One problem with the scheme is that the maximum payout is £48,000. For many investors this is too low and therefore it is important to check that your adviser has appropriate professional indemnity (PI) insurance. Typically, the firm's PI insurance should be able to pay up to £1m per valid claim.

Summary

■ The two main factors that affect your return are performance and the cost of your investment, including the advice.

■ You can learn a great deal from other investors if you join an investment club.

- Unless you are sure of your ability to research the market thoroughly, seek independent advice.
- Consider which type of firm is suitable – for example, do you need a stockbroker to advise on direct equity investment or would you be happy with one of the firms of advisers that specialize in collective investments such as unit and investment trust plans?
- Check in particular the level of qualifications held by the staff and the firm's research resources.
- Ideally pay for your advice by fees rather than commission as this removes any potential bias in the firm's recommendations.
- Check the firm's level of professional indemnity insurance.

chapter four

Risk and your investments

- ■ Inflation risk

- ■ Capital risk

- ■ The importance of spreading risk

- ■ Your risk assessment kit

- ■ Tax efficiency

AT A GLANCE

This chapter explains how to identify your short-term and longer-term investment goals. Crucial to this process is a clear understanding of your attitude to that four-letter word 'risk'.

The technical definition of risk, in financial terms, is 'the standard deviation of the (arithmetic) average return'. This is very handy for statisticians, but for most private investors its meaning is more simple: the biggest risk is the loss of your original capital.

There is no such thing as a 'safe' investment or saving scheme, but some are safer than others in terms of protecting your original capital. On the other hand, they may not protect you from inflation.

The two chief dangers for private investors, therefore, are *capital loss* and *inflation*.

We mentioned in Chapter 2 the equity risk premium – that is, the payoff you may receive for taking the risk of investing in equities. Clearly, then, when you take a risk you expect a commensurate reward.

The reward for investors is the *total return*, which is usually expressed as a percentage increase of the original investment. This may be a combination of income (or yield) plus capital growth (or rise in the market price).

In conclusion, risk is very subjective. Like beauty, it is in the eye of the beholder. To help you gauge your attitude to risk it is helpful to consider the twin evils, capital loss and inflation.

Inflation risk

Savings and investments that expose you to inflation risk usually fall into the 'safe' category. For example, we all tend to think of building society deposit accounts as risk free. But are they? If you are worried about the risk of losing your original capital, then provided you stick to the well-regulated UK building societies, you can put your money on *deposit* and your original capital will indeed be safe.

Your capital will not diminish; indeed, it will grow, assuming income is reinvested. However, the growth will be modest, and in real (that is, inflation-adjusted) terms, it may even be negative, depending on the rate of inflation.

This does not mean you should ignore deposit accounts. In practice they play a very important part in providing you with an easy-access home for emergency funds and for short-term savings where capital security is your primary goal (see Chapter 3). The point about access is important. You will find that in order to get a better rate of interest you may need to tie up your money for one, three or twelve months, for example, while the particular deposits may be run as postal accounts to minimize the borrower's overheads. Fortunately, instant and easy-access internet accounts have improved the saver's lot considerably in recent years.

As a general conclusion, over the medium to long term, deposit accounts may give rise to *capital erosion*.

Bonds, which are issued mainly by the government (gilts) and companies (corporate bonds – see Chapter 16), can offer the prospect of higher returns than a deposit account, but there is a risk that the borrower may dip into your capital in order to maintain the flow of income. Also, like deposits, conventional bonds do not offer any guaranteed protection against increases in inflation.

Capital risk

Historically, if you wanted to match or beat inflation over the long term you would have had to invest in *equities*. However, with equities, unless your fund offers a guarantee (and these can be costly – see page 166), your capital certainly is at risk. So, when you see the statutory wealth warning that your investment can go down as well as up, take it seriously.

> When you see the statutory wealth warning that your investment can go down as well as up, take it seriously.

The importance of spreading risk

Risk can be managed in different ways. You can concentrate it in a single investment or spread it over a wide range. For example, if you invest all your money in a single share and it does well, you will be in clover. If the company goes bust, you could lose the lot.

It is wise to spread risk by investing in a range of shares either directly or through collective funds such as unit and investment trusts. Note, however, that even with collective funds the risk rating varies considerably. At one end of the spectrum are the higher-risk specialist funds which tend to be small and managed on an aggressive basis. At the other, more comfortable end are the large UK or international equity funds which offer greater immunity to the capricious behaviour of stock markets. Bear in mind, though, that even the most broadly diversified funds will be hit when stock markets crash.

You can protect yourself further from risk if you diversify into different asset classes – for example, instead of just investing in different types of equities, you could include some bonds, gilts, deposits and, possibly, property in your portfolio. These behave in a different way from equities and therefore do not share the same vulnerabilities to certain economic cycles.

Your risk assessment kit

Before you consider the various investment options outlined in the following chapters, you need to get acquainted with a set of benchmarks which will help you judge the merits of an asset class, product or scheme and compare it with alternatives.

It doesn't matter if you are looking at deposit accounts, collective funds, direct equity and bond investments or high-risk investments such as enterprise investment schemes, which invest in the shares of unquoted trading companies. In each and every case the benchmarks will help you judge whether this is right for you.

The benchmarks will also help you to focus on the important fundamentals as opposed to the bells and whistles which are used so successfully in marketing literature to make products and services look more attractive, safer, tax-efficient or ethical than they really are.

These are the most important questions you should always ask:

■ *Aims:* what are the stated aims and benefits of the investment? Do these fit in with your own objectives?

■ *Returns:* compare the potential net returns of the investment with after-tax returns on very low-risk products such as 120-day-notice building society deposit accounts, short-term conventional gilts and National Savings. Is the potential outperformance of your chosen investment really worth the additional risk?

■ *Alternatives:* which other investments share similar characteristics? Are they simpler, cheaper, or less risky?

■ *Investment period:* for how long can you genuinely afford to invest your money? Compare this with the stated investment term and then check how the charges undermine returns in the early years. Also make sure you know about any exit penalties and remember that anything described as a 'loyalty bonus' usually acts as a penalty in disguise if you don't stick out the investment for the required period.

■ *Risk:* what is the risk that the investment will not achieve either its own stated aims or your private objectives? What is the most you can lose? Is your capital and/or income stream at risk? What is the likely effect of inflation? Find out how the investment is regulated and what happens if the firm/investment manager goes bust.

■ *Cost:* look at the establishment costs and ongoing charges. Watch out for high annual management charges on collective funds, particularly for long-term investments, as these will seriously undermine your return. With direct equity portfolios watch out for the high transaction charges and turnover costs associated with 'portfolio churning'.

■ *Tax:* the way the fund and you, the investor, are taxed is important because it will affect your ultimate return. Check for income tax and capital gains tax implications and consider how these might change over the investment period.

Tax efficiency

Tax is worth a further mention. Many investments covered in the next section are tax efficient for at least one, sometimes several, categories of investor. In some cases you benefit from income tax relief at your top rate. In others you may qualify for limited tax relief on income and capital gains.

But if there is one piece of advice central to successful investing, it is this: never invest purely for the sake of obtaining tax relief. Your investments must be suited to your circumstances and must be able to stand up with or without the tax breaks.

Summary

- Whatever the investment, check whether your money is at risk from capital loss or capital erosion due to inflation.
- The total return from capital growth and income is your reward for taking a risk.
- Diversification reduces risk.
- Always use the risk assessment benchmarks provided to assess a new investment opportunity and to compare it with alternatives.

Savings and investment products

.

Savings schemes and income-generating products

- Your investment aims

- Income earners

- Halfway houses

In a good financial plan there is always a place for simple deposits to house your emergency, instant-access funds. Many investors, particularly the retired, also need other income-generating investments which guarantee to protect their original capital.

The object of the exercise, therefore, is to identify the right products for the job and accept their shortcomings. As mentioned in the previous chapter, the main demon to bedevil this category of products is inflation.

If you are still not convinced about the risk from inflation, consider this. Since the Second World War annual inflation has averaged over 6 per cent. At this rate, in retirement if your annual investment income from deposits, gilts and bond funds is a level £10,000, its real purchasing power after just seven years will shrink to £6,450.

Your investment aims

This chapter, which is aimed primarily at those with short-term savings needs and investors looking for income, takes you through the various savings and investment opportunities where important guarantees are offered – but at a price. The trick is to recognize the guarantees for what they are and use them wisely, but avoid the trap of investing too much in products that are not designed to provide capital growth.

'Safe', like 'risk', means different things to different people. It might be 'safe' to shift your pension fund into long-dated gilts and deposits in the run-up to retirement, but it would be far from prudent to adopt the same investment strategy for a personal pension in your early thirties. The phrase 'reckless conservatism' aptly sums up the hidden risks in going for investments which appear to be safe but are in fact wholly inappropriate and therefore expose you to the risk that inflation will seriously damage your long-term returns.

Before you invest any money it is important to be sure it really is surplus. If you have checked you have the essential protection insurance for you and your family, then it is time to consider your slush fund.

Easy-access deposits for rainy days

All investors need an immediate-access emergency fund to pay for unforeseen events such as sudden repairs on the house and car. However, this is not a role for equity-based investments. If you have to pull out of an equity unit trust in a hurry you could lose money, particularly in the early years when your investment is 'working off' the effect of initial charges or when the investment manager may impose an exit charge. You also need to time sales of equities carefully owing to the volatility of markets.

The traditional home for cash is the building society. Stick with it, but avoid the common mistake of keeping too large a reserve when part of your money could be earning a potentially better return elsewhere.

The size of your emergency fund should be determined by your monthly expenditure, your liabilities

> The size of your emergency fund should be determined by your monthly expenditure, your liabilities and the level of padding you feel is appropriate for your lifestyle and peace of mind.

and the level of padding you feel is appropriate for your lifestyle and peace of mind. As a very rough guide it is worth keeping three times your monthly outgoings in an account that has one week's notice. Accounts offering a higher rate of interest with, say, three months' notice can be used for known future capital expenditure – for example a new car, a holiday or school fees. If you manage your cash flow carefully, you can feed money from your other investments to your high interest rate account well in advance of the dates these more substantial bills fall due. Keep a regular check on your longer-term deposits as rates change frequently. Postal and internet accounts tend to offer the best rates.

Probably the best source of up-to-date information on savings products is the monthly *Moneyfacts* guide to mortgage and savings rates, which covers everything including savings accounts, children's accounts, cheque accounts, credit cards, store cards, bonds, gilts, mortgages, National Savings, and loans. *Moneyfacts* also publishes a separate monthly guide to life assurance and pension products. Subscription details are provided at the end of this chapter.

You can also find useful information on the best rates for a variety of savings accounts in the personal finance pages of the weekend newspapers. Most papers publish useful summaries of best buys for different types of products and accounts (many of which are provided by *Moneyfacts*).

Safety at a price

Before you lock into a fixed-income product remember that if interest rates rise you will have committed yourself to a low rate of return. Of course if the reverse happens and you lock in before rates plummet you will congratulate yourself on having done the right thing. However, if the experts consistently make errors in their predictions of interest rate trends, the chances of your getting it right are slim.

For most people, some form of inflation-proofing is an essential element in their income-generating portfolio of investments. The purchasing power of £100 will be worth just £64 after 15 years of inflation at 3 per cent and £48 if the inflation rate is 5 per cent.

The hidden cost of income guarantees is a reduction in the real purchasing power of your capital. As a rule, guaranteed-income products limit, or exclude altogether, any prospect of capital growth. With some products part of your capital could be used to bolster income if returns are lower than expected. Exposure to this type of investment should be limited.

If investing for income *growth* is a better way of describing your requirements, you should include at least some equity investments within your portfolio. Clearly this introduces risk, but provided you aim for diversity and avoid the exotic your main concern will be fluctuations in income rather than the prospect of losing everything.

Tax status

This is a crucial factor in your choice of savings products. For example, the income from National Savings pensioners' bonds is paid gross but the income from insurance company guaranteed bonds in effect is paid net of basic rate tax and you cannot reclaim this. In theory this should make the NS bonds a clear winner for non-taxpayers, but the slightly higher income available on the insurance bonds can offset this tax advantage. Depending on rates at the time, non-taxpayers should consider both products.

In the following pages we outline some of the most popular savings and investment options for income seekers – and one or two unusual opportunities you may come across in your research.

Income earners

National Savings

National Savings offers a wide range of accounts and bonds designed for every age and tax status. **Income bonds**, for example, have a three-month notice period for withdrawals and the bonds must be held for a minimum period of one year. If you don't give the required notice you lose 90 days' interest.

NS Savings certificates can be either fixed rate or index linked and both run for five years. All returns are tax free even with early repayment, although if you don't go the full five years the interest rate drops. **NS pensioners' guaranteed income bonds** can be bought by anyone over the age of 60 and offer a monthly tax-free income guaranteed for five years. NS also offers two accounts with a pass book – the investment account, which requires one month's notice, and the ordinary account, which offers instant access at Post Office counters.

One of the attractions of NS products is that you can buy them through the Post Office and there are no charges. Bear in mind though that NS changes its interest rates less frequently than building societies so you should always compare rates before committing yourself.

For details of the complete range of NS products ask at your local Post Office or use the contact details provided at the end of this chapter. Remember, NS does not pay commission to advisers – which may explain why many commission-based advisers fail to recommend these products.

Tax-exempt special savings accounts (Tessas)

Tessas were withdrawn for new investment after April 5, 1999 but if you have an existing account that is coming up to maturity you can reinvest the capital in a special Tessa-only Isa. The amount transferred does not count towards your annual Isa allowance.

Tessas were not specifically designed to generate income but it is possible to make partial withdrawals of the interest and retain the tax-exempt status. Most Tessas pay a variable interest rate, although a few providers offered a fixed rate for either one year at a time or for the full five years.

If your first account has matured, provided you act within six months of the maturity date, you can transfer the capital (up to a maximum of £9,000) to the Tess/Isa and enjoy a further five years' tax-free growth.

Cash individual savings accounts (Isas)

Isas are discussed in more detail in Chapter 7. Part of your £7,000 annual subscription can be paid into a deposit account. This was £3,000 a year at the time of writing. You can hold this in a cash-only or mini Isa but if you take out one of these you can't invest the rest of your subscription in a separate equity Isa.

Despite the low maximum annual limit the cash Isa is a tax-efficient way to boost your savings and for many investors the tax break on the mini Isa is more valuable than that associated with the equity maxi Isa. This is because cash Isas give complete exemption from income tax on the interest, while investment Isas are still liable for some income tax on dividends, although they have complete exemption from capital gains tax and no income tax is paid on bonds or bond funds.

> Watch out for inflexible clauses that penalize you if you want to transfer your fund elsewhere.

Interest rates tend to be excellent on the top Isas (see *Moneyfacts* for the best rates), but keep an eye on providers that offer a special rate for just a few months in order to entice you in but then drop back to a much more mundane level of interest. If you are prepared to tie up your money you can get an even better rate on notice accounts.

Watch out for inflexible clauses that penalize you if you want to transfer your fund elsewhere, for example. If you stick to CAT-marked Isas then the accounts must offer you instant access, among other features. CAT stands for charges, access and terms.

Gilts and bonds

Gilt-edged stocks are bonds issued by the UK government via the UK Debt Management Office (DMO), an executive agency of the Treasury. If you buy gilts you are lending the government money in return for a tradable bond that promises to pay a fixed regular income for a specified period, at the end of which the government repays the original capital. Investors can buy and sell gilts throughout the lifetime of the issue.

Gilts play an important part in a defensive or income-producing portfolio, although investors might also look at corporate bonds to improve their yields. For more information on gilts and how to buy them, see Chapter 16.

Corporate bond funds and guaranteed-income bonds

Historically gilts have played an important part in the more defensive portfolio and particularly as a safe, interest-generating asset for the retired. However, given the low rates of interest currently on offer, many private investors are turning to corporate bonds for a better return.

There are risks, of course. Gilts are guaranteed by the government and are considered ultra-secure. Corporate debt is guaranteed by companies. Some of it may be secured on assets but generally speaking the security is much lower than for government stock. This is reflected in the company's credit rating. A very low credit stock – that is, less than BBB – can have a very high yield. However, the potential for capital loss is equally high.

Two quite different ways to invest in corporate bonds are through collective funds, such as **corporate bond unit trusts**, and through **guaranteed-income bonds** (GIBs). Corporate bond funds can be held in an individual savings account. GIBs are used as comparatively short-term investments, while corporate bond funds are medium to long-term investments. With a GIB your capital and income are guaranteed. Corporate bond funds offer potentially higher yields but neither the capital nor the income is guaranteed. Here it is vital to examine the underlying bonds held to achieve the yield and to check the charges.

A leading GIB provider such as AIG Life will invest in top-quality debt, including high quality corporate bonds, sterling eurobonds, sterling-denominated AAA government bonds, and World Bank AAA debt, among other instruments. Some of the bond funds that offer a higher yield achieve this by buying lower-quality debt instruments that can expose the investor to greater risk.

Advisers do not recommend corporate bond funds for the short-term investor owing to the buying and selling costs. They also suggest you should avoid bond funds that deduct the annual management charge from capital instead of income as this structure may be used to inflate the potential yield artificially.

Guaranteed-income bonds offer a fixed rate of interest over a specific term. Most investors go for three years or less. You can invest anything from £5,000 and at maturity you get back your original capital plus interest, unless you elect to have interest paid out during the term of the bond.

In addition to the one to five-year bonds, AIG Life and GE Life offer 'odd-term' or made-to-measure GIBs for wealthy investors who need to fix for a specific period. AIG Life also offers variable-rate accounts for those who need total flexibility of access, although obviously here the income is not guaranteed.

With such a variety of terms available, the made-to-measure bonds are considered ideal for two very different types of investor: risk-averse older people who need a regular income from savings, and wealthier individuals who want a first-class cash management system. The odd-term bonds are often used to hold cash set aside to pay large income and capital gains tax bills each year on January 31.

The taxation of life assurance funds is complicated, but according to AIG Life, if you are a higher-rate taxpayer, a deposit account rate of 5 per cent gross will actually yield £3 for every £100 invested, while the GIB will yield £3.28. Remember that GIB providers are forced to quote their rates net of basic-rate tax whereas the banks and building societies quote gross rates. To compare like with like, a higher-rate taxpayer will need to deduct 40 per cent from the building society rate and only 18 per cent from the GIB rate.

GIBs pay interest net of basic-rate tax and if you are a non-taxpayer you cannot reclaim this. For this reason GIBs are generally considered unsuitable for non-taxpayers. However, since these bonds generally pay slightly higher rates of income than the tax-free NS products, it pays to consider both options.

A higher-rate taxpayer who owns a GIB can defer any additional liability until the end of the investment term. Furthermore, once a bond matures, if you want to reinvest your capital you can defer the tax liability if the insurance company issues a formal offer to you to reinvest the entire proceeds in a new bond.

Given the fluctuating yields on the underlying assets, GIB rates change frequently, so seek advice on the timing of your investment. Most GIB providers will sell only through independent financial advisers. The rates usually assume a commission payment so where the adviser arranges for this to be reinvested, your income will be even higher.

Two other options that guarantee to return your original capital are **National Savings premium bonds** and **guaranteed equity bonds**. However, both are unsuitable for income seekers. In the case of premium bonds, no income is paid and you have to rely on the probabilities of winning to earn the equivalent of interest on your investment.

Guaranteed equity bonds use derivatives to guarantee a percentage of stock market growth or to guarantee the unit value of fully invested funds. A few of these funds offer to pay an income but only when the relevant index has achieved a specific return.

Halfway houses

Many investors, particularly pensioners, need to squeeze as much income as possible from their savings and are reluctant to take any risks with the capital. The trouble with this approach is that inflation eats into the real value of both capital and income. This is why most advisers recommend that income seekers should have at least a portion of equity-based investments in their portfolios.

But if you genuinely believe you cannot afford the risk of ordinary shares it is worth considering a halfway house – that is, investments which offer some capital protection plus a rising income. This category of investments includes **index-linked gilts** and the **stepped preference shares of split capital investment trusts**.

Index-linked gilts

These bonds are issued by the government and guarantee to increase both the six-monthly interest payments and the 'nominal' or original capital investment that is returned to you on the redemption date. The capital increases in line with the Retail Price Index (RPI).

Since the starting RPI figure used is eight months before the date of issue, the final value of the investment can be calculated precisely seven months before redemption (RPI figures are published a month in arrears). But, as we discussed on page 20, guarantees offered by government or corporate bonds apply only if you hold the bonds to maturity. Like conventional gilts (see page 54), the index-linked variety are traded actively, so the price and real value can fluctuate significantly between the issue and redemption dates.

> If you genuinely believe you cannot afford the risk of ordinary shares it is worth considering a halfway house – that is, investments which offer some capital protection plus a rising income.

Investors seeking absolute guarantees from their income-yielding portfolios may be tempted to put all their money in gilts. In this case you might be better off with a balance between conventional gilts, which offer a comparatively high fixed income but no index linking of the capital value, and index-linked gilts, which offer a low initial income but protect both the income and the capital from rising inflation.

Stepped preference shares of split capital trusts

'Stepped prefs' offer an income that is guaranteed to rise each year at a fixed rate, and a fixed redemption price for the shares when the trust is wound up. Each trust offers a different yield and annual increase, depending on the nature of the underlying assets.

The factors to consider are the risk profile, the current dividend yield, and the gross redemption yield – that is, the total return expressed as an annual percentage, assuming the share is bought at the present price and held to maturity.

The best source of information on all types of investment trust is the Association of Investment Trust Companies (AITC), which publishes useful fact sheets and a Monthly Information Service, which provides a breakdown of all the member trusts and performance statistics. (For contact details, see page 264.)

Purchased life annuities (PLAs)

Annuities, sold by insurance companies, guarantee to pay a regular income for life in return for your lump sum investment. The annuity 'rate' – or the level of regular income you secure in return for your lump sum – will depend on several important factors including your life expectancy and interest rates. Women tend to live longer than men so usually receive a lower income in return for the same level of investment. If you are in ill health you may be able to get a better rate if the insurance company thinks your life expectancy is less than the average for your age. This is known as an ill-health or impaired life annuity. The main point to remember with annuities is that unless you pay extra for a capital guarantee, once you hand over your money it is gone for good, even if you die the following day. Annuity rates are interest rate sensitive and fluctuate considerably, so seek expert advice over the timing of the purchase and the annuity company.

Summary

■ Remember that many 'safe' investments do not protect your capital from inflation.

■ Keep at least three times your monthly outgoings in an account that has one week's notice.

■ Most income seekers are actually looking for income and growth and therefore need an element of equity investment in their portfolio.

■ Make sure the taxation of the product is suitable for your tax status.

■ National Savings does not pay advisers sales commission.

Further information

Moneyfacts is available in larger libraries and by subscription. You can also buy a single copy by credit card – 01603 476476. Price at the time of writing was £5.95.

Visit the Debt Management Office website at *www.dmo.gov.uk*. The site includes an online version of the informative *Private Investors Guide*.

You can contact the Bank of England brokerage service on freephone 0800 818614 or go to the website at *www.bankofengland.co.uk*. A link appears on the DMO site.

For details of the complete range of National Savings products, call 08459 645000 or visit the website at *www.nationalsavings.co.uk*.

Collective funds for equity investment

- A daunting choice

- Unit trusts and open-ended investment companies (oeics)

- Investment trusts

- Insurance funds

- Alternative investments and hedge funds

- Offshore funds

As a very rough guide, investors with less than £100,000 to invest are usually advised to choose a range of collective funds rather than invest directly in equities. This is partly because you need a decent spread of equities to diversify and reduce risk, and partly because the cost of buying and selling would be uneconomic for a smaller portfolio.

In practice many investors hold individual shares because they belong to an employee share option scheme at work, or they received free shares when their building society or life assurance company demutualized.

Equally, investors with a large portfolio will often use collective funds to gain exposure to more specialist areas – for example smaller companies and overseas markets.

For most people, the biggest long-term investments are earmarked for some specific purpose – for example, to repay your mortgage, to pay school fees and to provide an income in retirement. However, it is important not to compartmentalize these investments but to include them in the overall portfolio planning.

This chapter looks at the main choices of collective funds.

A daunting choice

Ironically, one of the main problems you are likely to encounter with collective funds is the sheer number available. Some of these will qualify for certain tax-efficient wrappers such as pension plans and schemes and individual savings accounts, which replaced personal equity plans for new investment from April 1999.

Tax-efficient vehicles do not offer a magical solution to investment performance. What they do offer is a shelter from income tax, capital gains tax, or both. If you run your own pension plan or Isa then you can invest in most asset classes and the returns will be enhanced due to the tax breaks.

The important point here is to set your investment goals first and only then to decide which types of assets are best held in the different tax-efficient plans.

The internet

These days there is a wealth of information available on funds on the internet. Some of the most useful sites are mentioned in Chapter 21, which also gives details of several fund supermarkets. These sites allow you to mix and match different funds and managers all within a single Isa.

The selection process

When it comes to selecting a good fund, there is plenty of advice on what not to do and very little on positive selection criteria, so what follows is to some extent subjective. No doubt over the years you will develop your own pet theories.

The financial press and several firms of consultants produce annual surveys that highlight the best and worst in the various categories of funds. You must take great care when you examine past performance statistics because these can be misleading.

What the surveys do offer are some ideas on how to screen funds, so it is well worth checking out the methodology used in the most authoritative examples. Standard & Poor's Fund Research, for example, awards single, double and triple A status to collective funds it examines, and these ratings are worth looking out for. Fund objectives should be clearly defined and the objectives should be measurable, so that there are clear benchmarks against which performance can be judged. The investment processes – asset allocation and stock selection – should also be well defined.

Past performance statistics are a useful aid to gauge future performance, provided you bear in mind the following important caveats:

■ they must be coupled with a clear understanding of how past performance was achieved;

■ they must be combined with an assessment of the current investment style of the management team;

■ the individuals responsible for past performance must still be in place.

Your choice of collective funds

This chapter describes the four most popular types of collective funds in the UK. Although these funds share many features in common and offer a similar broad investment scope, there are differences in structure and taxation. Your choice will depend on the finer details.

Unit trusts and open-ended investment companies (oeics)

Although there are differences between the unit trust and oeic structure, as far as the private investor is concerned these two types of fund can be treated as identical. For the sake of simplicity, where we refer to a unit trust this covers both products.

> Although there are differences between the unit trust and oeic structure, as far as the private investor is concerned these two types of fund can be treated as identical.

A unit trust is a collective fund with a specific investment aim. The trust can invest in a range of assets which are suitable for the relevant investment criteria: for example, it can aim to produce an income through investing in higher-yielding UK equities, or to generate capital growth through investing in new or expanding industries or, more riskily, in emerging markets.

Unit trusts sold to the public are authorized by the chief financial services regulator, the Financial Services Authority (FSA). (You may hear about another type. 'Unauthorized' unit trusts are used as internal funds by financial institutions and are not marketed to the public.) Unit trusts are 'open ended', which means they may create or cancel units on a daily basis depending on demand.

Investors purchase units in the fund, the value of which fluctuates in line with the value of the underlying assets. In this respect a unit trust functions in a similar way to other collective funds – insurance funds for example – although the tax treatment for these two types of fund is quite different (see below).

Investment scope

Unit trusts can invest in 'transferable securities' (securities which can be bought and sold on the open market) listed on any market that meets the criteria set out in the European Union's Undertakings for Collective Investment in Transferable Securities (Ucits) directive. Basically, managers are free to decide which markets are suitable for their funds but they must ensure the markets operate regularly, are open to the public and offer the appropriate levels of liquidity.

Most funds invest mainly or wholly in equities, although the number of corporate bond funds, which invest in corporate bonds, preference shares and convertibles, among other assets, is growing rapidly.

Some Isas (and previously, Peps) based on unit trusts offer capital guarantees or guarantee to provide part of the rise in a stock market index and protect you from the falls. The guarantee is 'insured' through the use of derivatives – financial instruments which are used to protect a fund's exposure to market fluctuations.

For the more cautious investor these 'protected' unit trusts, as they are called, when held within an Isa could represent a tax-efficient method of gaining a high exposure to equities without the usual risks. However, it is important to remember that protection carries a cost – in this case the price of the derivatives – which will be passed on to the investor through increased management charges. Some advisers argue that you might be better off gaining full exposure to an index through one of the low-cost index tracking Isas now available and hedging your exposure to risk by investing part of your capital in gilts or National Savings, for example.

To date the guaranteed fund market has been dominated by insurance companies with their popular guaranteed bonds. Insurance bonds are pooled funds similar in concept to unit trusts, but there are important differences that are discussed below.

Investment trusts

An investment trust is not a trust as such but is a British company, listed on the UK Stock Exchange, which invests in the shares of other quoted and unquoted companies in the UK and overseas. As public companies, investment trusts are subject to company law and Stock Exchange regulation. The prices of most investment trusts are published daily in the *Financial Times*.

Investment trusts are controlled by boards of directors who are appointed by and answerable to their shareholders. The board presents annual accounts to its shareholders.

The difference between investment and unit trusts

Investment trusts are different from unit trusts in several important ways and offer the active investor additional opportunities. However, these opportunities also make investment trusts potentially more volatile than unit trusts.

Investment trust companies have a fixed number of shares, so unlike unit trusts 'units' cannot be created and cancelled to meet increased and reduced demand. As with any quoted company, the shares are available only when other investors are trying to sell. This means there are two factors that affect investment trust share prices. The first is the performance of the underlying assets in which the company invests. This factor also affects the price of units in a unit trust.

However, where unit trust prices directly reflect the net asset value of the fund, investment trust share prices may not. This leads to the second factor, which is that the market forces (supply and demand) to which investment trust shares are subject may make the shares worth more or less than the underlying value of the company's assets. If the share price is lower than the value of the underlying assets the difference is known as the discount. If it is higher the difference is known as the premium.

Investment trusts can borrow money to invest, an activity known as gearing. This adds extra flexibility and if the shares purchased with the borrowed money do well, the company and its shareholders will benefit. A poor return on the shares will reduce the profitability of the company.

'Split capital' investment trusts can have two types of share – one that has a right to all the income and one that has a right to the capital growth. There are several other types of share, each offering different features, for example stepped preference shares (see page 58), which offer dividends that rise at a predetermined rate and a fixed redemption value paid when the trust is wound up.

Taxation outside an Isa or Pep

In terms of taxation, the unit and investment trust routes are very similar. Where these investments are held outside an Isa (or a Pep), in both cases the capital gains tax liability falls on the investor who can offset any tax liability against the annual CGT exemption (£7,500).

There is no easy way to explain the taxation of dividends, so here's one we took from the *Financial Times*: dividends are taxed at 10 per cent up to the basic-rate limit and 32.5 per cent thereafter. However, each dividend also comes with a tax credit (up to April 5, 2004) valued at 10 per cent of the grossed-up amount. This means that a basic-rate taxpayer has no further tax to pay. Higher-rate taxpayers pay an additional 22.5 per cent. (See Chapter 7 for taxation within an Isa or Pep.)

Charges on investment trusts are generally lower than on unit trusts, with the exception of index tracker unit trust Isas/Peps. However, tracker funds available as Isas are confined to the UK stock market and therefore do not offer such broad diversification as the larger and older international investment trusts.

In conclusion, unit trusts, with the exception of the index trackers, are generally considered slightly more expensive than investment trusts but less sensitive to market movements.

Insurance funds

Like unit trusts, a lump sum premium in an insurance company bond buys units, which directly reflect the net asset value of the fund's underlying investments. The charges for the two types of collective funds are broadly similar, although insurance company bonds may have slightly lower annual charges but tend to pay advisers higher rates of commission than unit trusts.

However, the tax treatment is quite different. Insurance company bonds pay tax broadly equivalent to the basic rate on income and capital gains. The income tax cannot be reclaimed so, generally, these bonds are not considered suitable for non-taxpayers. Moreover, the capital gains tax paid by the fund cannot be offset against an individual's exemption. Experts tend to regard this feature as a serious drawback.

There are circumstances in which the unique features of bonds can be attractive to higher-rate taxpayers who may be able to defer or avoid altogether a proportion of the tax generated by the fund.

Despite the confusing array of investments offered by insurance companies to the public, most fall into one of three main categories:

- **Maximum investment plans (MIPs)** are regular monthly or annual premium investments and usually run for ten years. Once this term is complete you can either take the proceeds or leave the fund to continue to benefit from investment growth. You can also make tax-efficient annual withdrawals.

- **Insurance company investment bonds** are similar to MIPs but here you invest a single premium or lump sum.

- **Endowments** combine investment with a substantial element of life assurance.

With maximum investment plans and insurance company investment bonds your premiums are invested in a choice of funds, most of which are unit linked, similar in concept to unit trusts in that your premiums buy units in a collective fund and the value of those units rises and falls in line with the value of the underlying assets.

Although sold by life assurance companies, most of these regular and single-premium plans offer minimal life cover, as their main purpose is investment. If you die the company might pay out 101 per cent of your original investment or the value of the fund, whichever is greater.

The third category – the traditional endowment – is most commonly used as a repayment vehicle for a mortgage. The distinguishing feature of an endowment is that it combines a significant element of life assurance with your savings plan so that if you die during the term of the policy the combination of the value of your fund plus the life assurance is sufficient to repay the debt.

In addition to the unit-linked three investment options, you can also invest in 'with profits' funds. With profits and unitized with profits endowments invest in a mixture of equities, bonds and property and have a rather idiosyncratic method of distributing profits. This is discussed below.

Taxation of life assurance policies

At the end of the investment period, the proceeds of a life assurance policy will be treated as though the fund had already paid the equivalent of basic-rate tax. For lower and basic-rate payers that is the end of the story. But what happens next for higher-rate payers depends on whether the policy is classed by the Inland Revenue as 'qualifying' or 'non-qualifying'.

With a qualifying policy there is no further tax liability for higher-rate payers. However, to attract this special tax status the policy must abide by various conditions. First, it must be a regular premium plan where you pay a predetermined amount each month or each year. Second, it has to be a long-term plan – usually a minimum of ten years. Third, it has to provide a substantial amount of life cover.

> The important point to note about life assurance policies is that the income tax cannot be reclaimed, so generally these policies are not considered suitable for non-taxpayers.

This means that single-premium investment policies are non-qualifying but the regular-premium MIPs may be classed as qualifying depending on the term and level of life cover provided. Mortgage endowments, which tend to be long-term regular-premium plans, usually are qualifying owing to the substantial element of life cover.

The important point to note about life assurance policies is that the income tax cannot be reclaimed, so generally these policies are not considered suitable for non-taxpayers. Moreover, the capital gains tax paid by the fund cannot be offset against an individual's exemption, as is the case with unit and investment trusts. Financial advisers tend to regard this feature as a serious drawback.

Unique tax features of bonds

However, there are circumstances in which the unique features of investment bonds can be attractive to certain investors. With bonds there is no annual yield as such, since income and growth are rolled up within the fund. But up to 5 per cent of the original capital can be withdrawn each year for up to 20 years. The Inland Revenue treats these withdrawals as a return of capital and therefore at the time of payment they are free of tax, so the higher-rate tax liability is deferred until you cash in your policy. (Withdrawals above 5 per cent are treated by the Inland Revenue as though they are net of basic-rate tax, so the higher-rate liability must be paid, not deferred.)

'Top slicing relief'

Even if you invest in a non-qualifying life policy you may be able to reduce or avoid the deferred higher-rate tax bill via the effect of 'top slicing relief'. Top slicing relief averages the profit over the number of years the bond has been held and adds this profit slice to an investor's income in the year the bond matures. If part or all of this falls into the higher-rate bracket, it would be taxed. However, with careful tax planning investors can avoid this liability by encashing the bond when they become basic-rate taxpayers – in retirement for example.

Higher-rate taxpayers who have used their full CGT allowance may also find bonds and MIPs attractive because the 5 per cent withdrawals do not have to be declared for income tax purposes in the year of withdrawal.

One advantage of bonds over most unit trusts is that insurance companies generally offer a low-cost switching facility between a large range of funds. Otherwise the charges for the two types of funds are broadly similar, although the tax status of life offices usually allows them to operate with slightly lower annual charges and this can have a significant effect on your fund's growth over the long term.

Investment choice

The investment choice under life assurance policies is as follows.

Unit-linked plans offer a very wide choice, ranging from UK and international equities to UK and international fixed-interest securities, index-linked gilts, property, and commodity and energy shares. Your money buys units in the fund's assets and the unit price rises and falls directly in line with the performance of these assets.

Clearly it is possible to select different types of fund depending on your preferred asset allocation but for investors just starting out and for those with limited amounts to invest, a managed fund is ideal. Managed funds usually invest in a range of the company's core funds – for example a managed equity fund would invest in the company's main UK and international equity funds. Managed funds may also include different types of assets – for example equities and bonds – to provide a better balance of risk or to generate a higher income than could be achieved with a pure equity fund.

With profits funds are simply heavenly if you thrive on jargon and obscurity – which is a pity really because they can play an important role in a more cautious investor's portfolio. The with profits fund is the fund of the life office itself and invests mainly in a range of international and UK equities, bonds and property. The way the fund's profits are distributed resembles a cross between a building society deposit account and a unit-linked fund. Under the original structure for with profits – now known as 'conventional with profits' – you are guaranteed a 'basic sum assured' and to this sum is added an annual interest or 'bonus' (sometimes referred to as a 'reversionary' bonus). Once this has been added it cannot be taken away, although the rate for future years is not guaranteed. To avoid dramatic fluctuations insurance companies 'smooth' their bonus rates, holding back some of their profits in the good years to maintain a reasonable return in the bad years.

In addition to the annual bonus, you receive a final or 'terminal' bonus at the end of your investment period or when you die. The final bonus is discretionary (that is, voluntary on the part of the insurance company) and tends to reflect recent performance.

The more modern version – unitized with profits funds – invest in the same assets but do not offer a basic sum assured. Also, unitized with profits funds have a feature which allows the insurance company to reduce the value of your units if there is a run on funds – after a market crash, for example. Most companies rarely use this market value adjuster but its very existence means that your fund value is never totally guaranteed, as Equitable Life policyholders have discovered.

However, in favour of unitized funds is the ease with which you can switch to and from unit-linked funds, an exercise that can be difficult with conventional with profits.

In recent years bonus rates have fallen, partly owing to cuts in interest rates and partly to compensate for what many commentators regard as over-generous bonuses paid in the late 1980s. This does not mean that with profits policies represent poor value – some companies continue to achieve very good results over the medium to long term. However, it does mean that you cannot rely on bonus levels of the past continuing in future.

Distribution bonds, pioneered by Sun Life in 1979, are becoming an increasingly popular alternative to with profits owing to their 'safety first' approach to investment. Unlike a typical managed unit-linked fund, which would be primarily invested in equities, distribution bonds tend to have a much higher proportion of bonds, gilts, deposits and property. In this way they cope well with most market conditions. They also tend to offer a higher yield than managed funds and so can be particularly attractive for investors seeking a regular income.

Friendly society policies

Friendly societies are often snubbed as the small fry of the investment industry. However, in contrast to life assurance funds, which have to pay both income and capital gains tax, friendly society funds are tax free.

Unfortunately, there are several drawbacks that detract from this attractive feature. First, the amount you can invest is small – £270 a year (£300 if you pay your premiums on a more regular basis than just once a year) – and most plans run for ten years. There are societies that accept a lump sum investment to cover payments for the full ten years.

Second, the performance of some friendly society funds tends to be lacklustre, but several offer good investment management and in some cases a link to one of the big institutional groups.

The third disadvantage is charges, which tend to be high in relation to the amount invested. However, again there are exceptions and several societies offer charges that compare well with personal equity plans.

In conclusion, for small investments, perhaps for a child or grandchild, these plans can be worth considering. However, look carefully at past performance and charges and compare these with what is on offer from Isa managers and unit and investment trusts which offer low-contribution regular savings plans.

Early surrenders of life policies

Long-term life assurance investments tend to deduct the commission costs for the entire investment period during the first year or two. This is why so many people have got back so little from their policies if they have pulled out during this 'initial' period.

Your best bet is to avoid the commission structure altogether if you can by paying your adviser a fee and asking for the commission payments to be stripped out of the policy. Alternatively ask for a single-premium commission structure, where about 4–5 per cent is deducted from each premium throughout the entire term. This means that if you are forced to stop your policy during these early years your fund should still have a reasonable value.

> Beware of salespeople who try to persuade you to surrender an existing investment in order to start a new policy for the whole of the mortgage.

An endowment – or indeed any investment – is portable when it comes to mortgage repayment. If you buy another house and need a larger mortgage, keep the policy you have already got and top up with a repayment or interest-only mortgage backed by the savings plan of your choice. You do not need to take out another endowment – an Isa may be a more tax-efficient alternative if you are not already using up your annual allowance.

Beware of salespeople who try to persuade you to surrender an existing investment in order to start a new policy for the whole of the mortgage. This almost certainly would lead to penalties and is bad advice.

Alternatives to surrendering a policy

If you simply cannot continue a policy for some reason, don't just stop payments without first considering the alternatives. You could, for example, make the policy 'paid up', which means you no longer pay premiums but you do not withdraw your fund until the maturity date. You should still benefit from investment growth, but check the ongoing charges and what penalties apply before taking this step.

If you need the capital, you might be able to take a loan from the insurance company, based on the surrender value of your policy. Alternatively, you might get up to 30 per cent more than the surrender value if you sell your policy on the second-hand endowments market. In this case an investor buys it from you and takes over the commitment to continue the premiums in the hope that the final payout will be well in excess of the purchase price plus the cost of the outstanding premiums.

The two main options are to auction the policy or to sell it to a market maker who, naturally, will charge a fee or take a percentage of the profit. (The profit is the difference between what you would have got as a surrender value from your insurance company and the actual price achieved.)

Alternative investments and hedge funds

Investments are described as 'alternative' where the risk and returns of the fund or asset do not correlate with (or behave in a similar way to) more traditional investments such as equities and bonds. Hence they are described as having a 'low correlation' with traditional equity and bond markets.

The most common alternative investment you are likely to come across is the hedge fund. Hedge funds aim to produce 'absolute' returns – that is, a positive return in all market conditions – and to eliminate market risk. The way they achieve this varies and the fund strategies are complicated.

The classic hedge fund picks undervalued stocks, which the fund manager buys, and overvalued stocks, which the fund manager sells. The latter technique is known as 'short selling' and involves selling securities one doesn't own in order to buy them back at a lower price to return to the lender, while pocketing the profit. This basket of stocks that is sold short is the hedge or insurance against a fall in the markets. Not an easy concept.

While hedge funds may be an excellent idea in theory, in practice there are as many different styles as there are hedge fund managers. Some are indeed low risk but others are very risky, particularly where the fund borrows heavily (gearing). Advisers suggest that if you are interested in this type of investment approach you would be wise to start with a fund of hedge funds so that you spread risk across a range of managers. Several hedge funds can be held in an Isa.

Offshore funds

In certain cases for more wealthy, risk-tolerant investors it may be appropriate to consider offshore funds (but not before you have used up your annual Isa allowance). Whether an offshore fund would be suitable will depend on the tax jurisdiction of the fund, the way the fund itself is taxed and your own tax position as an investor.

Points to consider with offshore funds include the charges – which often can be very high compared with UK funds – and the regulation: for example, if it is outside the UK, what protection do you have if the company collapses or the fund manager runs off with your money?

As a general rule for a UK investor in UK securities, once you have used up your Isa allowance, unit and investment trusts are likely to prove more cost-effective and simpler than offshore funds. There are two main types of offshore insurance bond – distribution bonds, which pay a regular 'income', and non-distribution bonds, which roll up gross.

Investors who may gain by going offshore include UK and foreign expatriates who are non-resident for UK tax purposes and who can benefit from gross roll-up non-distribution bonds if they do not pay tax in the country where they live. Higher-rate taxpayers may also benefit from the gross roll-up but you have to pay tax when you bring the money back into the UK, although of course you may have switched to the basic rate tax bracket if you have retired by the time the non-distribution bond matures.

Summary

- The structure of investment trusts offers greater investment opportunities but at the same time greater potential risk than unit trusts.

- For most investors, particularly lower and basic-rate taxpayers, unit and investment trusts are more tax-efficient than insurance company funds. Some higher-rate taxpayers can benefit from the insurance funds.

- The insurance companies offer a wider range of lower-risk funds than unit trusts and allow for greater flexibility in switching.

- 'With profits' funds are less risky than unit-linked funds but are also transparent.

- Unitized 'with profits' funds offer a halfway house between the two products but remember that there are fewer guarantees compared with the conventional 'with profits' fund.

- Distribution bonds offer a careful mix of assets designed to help the fund withstand most market conditions and are therefore suitable for the more cautious investor, particularly income seekers.

- If you have an endowment and want to cancel, consider all your options – for example, you might do better if you sell it through the second-hand endowment market.

■ Hedge funds aim to provide absolute returns – that is, a positive return throughout all market conditions – but they are very complicated and in many cases very risky.

■ Unless there is a very good reason, don't go offshore.

Further information

If you are interested in buying or selling an endowment contact the Association of Policy Market Makers on 020 7739 3949. *www.money-world.co.uk/apmm*

Individual savings accounts and personal equity plans

■ Personal equity plans

■ Individual savings accounts

A T   A   G L A N C E

This chapter considers the most important tax-efficient investment apart from pensions – namely the individual savings account. We also consider how investors with the predecessor of Isas – Peps – can best maintain and monitor their Pep portfolio.

Personal equity plans

Over the 12 tax years – from January 1987 to April 1999 – that personal equity plans were available you could have invested a maximum of £85,000. After April 1999 you could no longer contribute to a Pep but any existing funds you had built up through your plan could remain in the tax-efficient wrapper and be managed as a separate portfolio.

Until April 5, 2001 there were two types of plan – general Peps and single company Peps – and these two plans had to be kept separate. In the general Pep, after several changes to the rules, you could save up to £6,000 per annum and hold a range of collective funds. You could also use this annual allowance for a self-select Pep that allowed you to hold individual equities and bonds as well as collective funds. The single-company Pep, introduced in 1992, could be used to invest a further £3,000 per annum in the ordinary shares of a UK or EU listed company. Only one company's shares per annum were allowed.

This distinction has now been abolished so there is only one type of Pep and you are allowed to merge your investments. The government also lifted the geographical restrictions so that those who wish to do so can change their asset allocation to create a more international spread of investments.

In practice, many investors who took advantage of the Pep rules from the beginning are coming up to retirement and therefore you may prefer to change the asset allocation to reflect an increased income requirement. Pep investors also have access to a wider range of corporate bonds and, for the first time, to gilts and other fixed-interest securities issued by European governments.

If you would like to make some changes to your Pep – including transfers to other managers – it is best to seek independent advice to make sure you fully understand the more flexible rules.

Individual savings accounts

Isas were introduced in April 1999 and offer similar advantages to Peps. Like Peps, Isas are not investments in themselves; they are simply Revenue-approved wrappers in which you can hold your investments. The range of investments is very flexible and includes a wide range of collective funds (see Chapter 6). You can also use a 'self-select' Isa to hold a portfolio of funds and individual shares and bonds. These are discussed below.

Clearly, if you have comparatively small amounts to invest it does not make sense to run your own portfolio because trading in small volumes is disproportionately expensive. For many investors, therefore, buying into collective funds through packaged Isas is cost effective.

Moreover, if you are happy to stick within a range of unit trusts and open-ended investment companies, you can split your £7,000 allowance between several managers if you buy through a fund supermarket. This enables you to get round the one-Isa-per-year rule.

The Isa rules

Currently you can invest £7,000 a year in an Isa if you are 18 or over and a UK resident. There is no tax relief on the contribution but gains and income in the Isa fund build up free of tax. You do not pay tax on dividend income or interest. It is the fund manager's job to claim back the tax you are 'deemed' to have paid on all UK company dividends. Currently the credit is 10 per cent on share income although this will be reduced to zero in 2004. You can get back 20 per cent on bond income. There is no capital gains tax liability for Isa investors (although this means you cannot offset a capital loss within an Isa against other gains).

> Clearly, if you have comparatively small amounts to invest it does not make sense to run your own portfolio because trading in small volumes is disproportionately expensive.

There are two types of Isa plan, known as the mini and the maxi. You cannot take out both in the same tax year. You can invest in three separate mini Isas run by different managers. The limit is £3,000 in a cash mini Isa, £3,000 in shares and £1,000 in life assurance funds.

Alternatively you can take out a single maxi Isa with one manager and still invest in shares, cash and life funds but you can, if you wish, put the whole £7,000 into shares. Fund supermarkets allow you to invest across a range of managers within the single maxi plan (see Chapter 21).

CAT-marked Isas   CAT stands for charges, access and terms. If you buy a CAT-marked product you are not guaranteed that it will be better than non-CAT-marked Isas but you can be sure the manager has agreed to certain conditions.

CAT-marked equity Isas
- Annual management maximum charge of 1 per cent.
- Minimum regular saving from £50 per month or a minimum lump sum of £500

CAT-marked cash Isas

■ Must not have charges except for additional services, for example if you ask for an extra statement.

■ Must allow savers to pay in or withdraw as little as £10 on no more than seven days' notice.

■ Must not impose other conditions such as how frequently you can make withdrawals.

■ If interest rates go up, the Isa rate must follow within a month.

CAT-marked insurance funds

■ Maximum annual management charge of 3 per cent.

■ Minimum premiums from £25 per month or £250 per year.

■ Must not apply a penalty if you cash in your account.

■ When you surrender your account (cash it in) you must get back at least all the premiums you paid three years or more before the date when you cash in.

Self-select Isas

However, if you want maximum flexibility, the facility to invest directly in equities and bonds, and access to the full range of unit trusts, oeics and investment trusts in your collective Isa funds, you need a self-select plan. Self-select Isas are offered by many firms of stockbrokers (the Association of Private Client Investment Managers' website is at *www.apcims.co.uk*) and a few independent financial advisers, for example certain members of the Association of Solicitor Investment Managers (*www.asim.org.uk*).

Apart from the wider investment choice, one of the immediate benefits of the self-select structure is that it enables you to make changes to your portfolio on the same day. With packaged Isas it can take weeks and sometimes even months to switch between managers. This can be frustrating and costly in a rising market. You can also hold cash within the self-select plan and earn interest on this while you are waiting to reinvest the money.

This cash facility is particularly attractive if you want to make use of your Isa allowance but are concerned about the jittery markets and would rather wait a few months before making your investment decision. Also, dividends can be reinvested in the investment of your choice within the Isa, whereas if you invest with just one unit or investment trust manager, for example, any dividends earned must be reinvested with that manager or taken as tax-free income.

The main perceived disadvantage of the self-select route is the cost. If you buy a single packaged Isa, the plan costs are included in the standard charge. The cost of the Isa wrapper for unit trusts and oeics purchased through a fund supermarket is paid for by the fund managers out of their annual management charge. With the self-select plan the charge is in addition to your investment costs.

However, charges on packaged Isas are not necessarily as low as they seem. Even where the initial charge is discounted you are likely to find that your adviser receives 'trailer' commission. This is an annual charge, typically 0.5 per cent, which is deducted from your fund from year two onwards.

The cost of your self-select plan will depend on the stockbroker or adviser's charges. This might be a flat annual administration charge, which could suit the larger portfolios, or the fee might be linked to the value of the fund (for example 0.5 per cent per annum plus VAT). Some will have no annual fees but will charge for dividend collection, which, on a large portfolio, could add up quickly. One thing to look out for is high dealing charges, especially on shares. What can appear cheap because of a low or zero annual management charge can prove costly if there is little or no discount on unit trust purchases and if sharedealing charges for buying and selling are in excess of 1 per cent.

Finally, don't forget that the self-select route can provide you with as much or as little advice as you want depending on whether you opt for a discretionary service, where your stockbroker makes all the investment decisions for you, an advisory service, where you and your stockbroker discuss your options before you make a decision, or execution only, where you make all the decisions yourself and your stockbroker simply carries out your instructions.

How to choose a self-select

It is important to shop around for your self-select plan to ensure you get the right type of service for your needs. For example, if you want to run your own portfolio and are happy to buy and sell on an execution-only basis, you might consider a plan offered by an internet broker. However, if you want a discretionary or advisory stockbroker you need a firm with a full range of services.

Most stockbrokers offer a self-select Isa to existing clients as part of their overall portfolio management service but very few are available on a stand-alone basis, so your choice of plan may be dictated by your choice of stock-broker.

An alternative to the stockbroker route is to invest a nominal sum in an investment trust that also offers a self-select plan. The best example of this arrangement is the Alliance Trust, which provides a free administration service through its subsidiary Alliance Trust Savings, and access to a wide range of equities, investment trusts, corporate bonds, gilts and other collective funds. The only requirement is to invest £50 with either Alliance Trust or the 2nd Alliance Trust. Dealing charges for the two trusts are just £1 plus stamp duty. Charges for other transactions vary and are not as swift as an execution-only service.

Summary

- UK residents aged 18 and over can invest £7,000 in an Isa.
- Any investments held in a personal equity plan will retain their tax-exempt status. There is no capital gains tax on investments held within an Isa or a Pep. There is a limited amount of tax relief on dividends.
- The Isa allowance cannot be carried over to the following tax year.
- There are two types of Isa plan, known as the mini and the maxi. You cannot take out both in the same tax year. You can invest in three separate mini Isas run by different managers. The limit is £3,000 in a cash mini Isa, £3,000 in shares and £1,000 in life assurance funds.
- Alternatively you can take out a single maxi Isa with one manager and still invest in shares, cash and life funds but you can, if you wish, put the whole £7,000 into shares.
- CAT-marked Isas must offer low charges, easy access and fair terms.
- Fund supermarkets allow you to invest across a range of managers within the single maxi plan.
- Self-select plans allow you to hold any combination of funds and individual bonds and equities.

Pension schemes and plans

- Company pension schemes

- Final salary schemes

- Money purchase company schemes

- Small company schemes

- Stakeholder schemes

- Personal pensions

- Self-invested personal pensions

- Your choice at retirement

AT A GLANCE

Like individual savings accounts, there is no magic associated with a pension scheme or plan. These are simply long-term investments that build up a fund, which is used to generate an income in retirement. Most schemes and plans are based on collective funds, but in some cases they can also be used to hold individual equities and bonds.

Company pension schemes

For most employees membership of the company pension scheme represents the most important and valuable benefit after the salary itself. But don't assume just because there *is* a company scheme that it is automatically going to see you right in retirement. Scheme benefits vary considerably and you may need to top up your pension if your employer is less than generous.

Company schemes are very tax-efficient. Your contributions are paid free of basic and higher-rate tax, the pension fund builds up virtually tax free and a significant chunk of the final benefits can be taken as tax-free cash at retirement. The pension, whether drawn from a company scheme or from a life office in the form of an annuity, is subject to your top rate of income tax.

There are two main types of occupational schemes: 'final salary', also known as 'defined benefit', and 'money purchase', also known as 'defined contribution'. With a final salary scheme the employer bears the investment risk and backs the pension guarantees. With a money purchase scheme the investment risk falls fairly and squarely on your shoulders as the scheme member and there are no guarantees.

If you earn less than £30,000 per annum you can be a member of a company scheme and at the same time pay into a personal pension plan including one of the new stakeholder schemes (see page 90).

Final salary schemes

Final salary or defined benefit (DB) schemes are still the most prevalent among employers in the UK and base the pension calculation on the number of years you are in the scheme and your salary at or near retirement. A typical scheme guarantees to provide a pension that builds up at the rate of 1/60 of your final salary for each year of service up to an Inland Revenue maximum of 40/60 – that is, two-thirds final salary at retirement (restricted for some higher earners – see below).

How much do you contribute?

Employees can contribute up to 15 per cent of gross pay to an occupational scheme, although the most common rate is about 5–6 per cent. 'Pay' in this context is defined as basic salary plus, in some cases, benefits such as overtime, bonuses, and the taxable value of fringe benefits. If overtime or sales commission form a significant proportion of your gross earnings and this is not taken into account in your pensionable pay, you could consider topping up your pension (see below).

Contributions and benefits for higher earners

Over the past few years the Revenue has restricted the pensions of certain high earners. In particular, some employees are subject to a cap of £95,400, for the 2001–2002 tax year, on which contributions and the final pension can be based. The cap applies to members of final salary schemes set up after the 1989 budget and members who joined any final salary scheme after June 1, 1989. For these employees the maximum contributions for the 2001–2002 tax year are limited to £14,310 (15 per cent of £95,400), while the maximum pension will be about £63,600 (two-thirds of the cap).

> Over the past few years the Revenue has restricted the pensions of certain high earners.

Unapproved schemes

There are unapproved retirement benefit schemes to cater for earnings above the cap. These are not as tax-efficient as mainstream schemes but nevertheless represent a valuable benefit. You might also be offered a mixture of additional salary and shares or some other perk if you are a higher earner and the company has no specific pension arrangement to cater for your earnings above the cap.

Topping up your company pension

By law every scheme, with a few minor exceptions, must provide an additional voluntary contribution (AVC) scheme, which allows members to top up their company pension. Since 1987, employees have also been able to contribute to individual top-up plans known as free-standing AVCs (FSAVCs), which are sold by insurance companies and other financial institutions. However, in most cases FSAVCs are more expensive than the in-house AVC scheme. AVC and FSAVC funds must be used at retirement to buy an annuity, which provides a taxable income.

If you earn less than £30,000 you can also use a personal pension, including a stakeholder scheme (see page 90), to top up your company pension. This is considered a more flexible arrangement as you can draw the benefits any time between the age of 50 and 75. Moreover you can take up to 25 per cent of the fund at retirement as tax-free cash. The rest must be used to buy an annuity.

Tax-free cash

The maximum tax-free cash you can take from your company pension scheme is one and a half times your final salary after 40 years' service. This is limited in the case of some higher earners. If you take the tax-free cash – and almost everyone does – your pension will be reduced. (The tax-free cash rules are slightly different in public-sector schemes.)

Money purchase company schemes

Money purchase or defined contribution (DC) schemes can be attractive because you have an identifiable pot of money that you should be able to take from job to job. Contributions are invested to build up a fund, which at retirement is used to buy an annuity from an insurance company. An annuity pays an income for life in return for a lump sum.

The most important point to bear in mind with money purchase is that the level of income your fund buys is not guaranteed but will depend on four factors:

- how much you and your employer contribute;
- the investment performance of the fund;
- the level of charges deducted from your fund by the pension company;
- annuity 'rates' – that is, the level of income your fund will buy at the time you retire.

You should be offered a choice of funds, but if you don't want to make the investment decisions your scheme should also offer a lifestyle investment strategy. This is a managed fund that provides you with the long-term growth potential of equities in the early years but protects your capital as you approach retirement by automatically switching from equities into cash and bonds over a period of years.

Contributions

Some money purchase schemes follow the same maximum contribution and benefit rules as final salary schemes. However, most new schemes are set up as group personal pensions (GPPs), in which case they follow the stakeholder/personal pension contribution limits. This means you can pay up to £3,600 per annum to any personal pension irrespective of earnings (and even if you have no paid employment).

For contributions over £3,600 per annum, personal pension contribution limits start at 17.5 per cent of 'net relevant earnings' (equivalent in this context to pensionable pay) for employees up to the age of 35, and rising in stages to 40 per cent for employees aged 61 and over. Employer contributions, if they are paid, must be included in these limits.

Small company schemes

Small self-administered schemes (SSASs) are suitable for up to 12 members. Membership is usually restricted to the directors of the company because the fund can be used to invest in the business – for example to buy new premises. All investments must be at arm's length – so, in the case of a property purchase, the company would have to pay the scheme a commercial rate of rent.

SSASs are complicated and require expert advice.

Stakeholder schemes

In April 2001 the new stakeholder pension schemes became available. Stakeholders are a type of personal pension that is strictly regulated by the government to ensure it offers fair terms, low costs and penalty-free entry and exit.

With stakeholders came a new tax regime that applies to all personal pension plans. The most important feature is that there is no link between earnings and pension contributions so that everyone under the age of 75 – including children and non-working adults – can belong to a scheme, provided of course that they have the money to pay contributions.

Stakeholders are intended to encourage people who have not had a private pension to save for retirement. From October 2001, most employers who do not already offer a company scheme and who have five or more employees must make a stakeholder scheme available and be prepared to deduct contributions through the payroll. You can also join a stakeholder scheme directly. Your employer may contribute to your stakeholder personal pension but is not obliged to do so.

With their low charges – the maximum annual charge for stakeholder personal pensions is 1 per cent – and their ability to accept low contributions (anything from £20 per month), these new pension plans are ideal for lower earners. However, the rules will also appeal to wealthier people who want to set aside money in a pension for their children and, perhaps, for a non-working spouse.

Stakeholder pension schemes are registered with the Occupational Pensions Regulatory Authority (Opra – *www.stakeholder.opra.gov.uk*).

It is important to bear in mind that some personal pensions that do not qualify for stakeholder status offer equally good value. It is also vital to consider the long-term performance prospects. For higher earners who intend to pay substantial contributions, the charges arguably are less important than performance.

> It is important to bear in mind that some personal pensions that do not qualify for stakeholder status offer equally good value.

How much can you contribute?

The contribution limit is £3,600 for 2001–2002 and anyone under the age of 75 can pay this into a personal pension, irrespective of whether they have any earned income. This figure includes tax relief at the basic rate. For example, if you made a contribution of £2,808 this would be increased to £3,600 by way of a refund of tax from the Inland Revenue (assuming a basic rate of tax of 22 per cent). The tax relief is credited even if you do not pay tax, which is why this is so attractive for non-earners.

If you have earnings that entitle you to pay more than this, you can do so provided you do not exceed the percentage of earnings shown on page 92, which starts at 17.5 per cent for those aged up to 35 and rises to 40 per cent for those over 61.

Personal pensions

If you want a particularly wide investment choice or want to invest more than £3,600 per annum, you may prefer a personal pension rather than a stakeholder. Like company pension schemes, personal plans are a very tax-efficient way of saving for retirement:

- contributions qualify for full tax relief;
- the pension fund grows virtually free of tax;
- up to 25 per cent of the pension fund at retirement can be taken as tax-free cash.

The rest of the fund must be used to purchase an annuity.

Contribution limits

The annual contribution limits are as follows:

Age	% net relevant earnings*
Up to 35	17.5 per cent
36–45	20 per cent
46–50	25 per cent
51–55	30 per cent
56–60	35 per cent
61–74	40 per cent

*All personal pension contributions (but not the emerging pension itself) are subject to the earnings cap, which limits the amount of salary that can be used for pension purposes to £95,400 for the 2001–2002 tax year.

How to get best value

With the help of a good independent financial adviser you should be able to narrow down your choice of pension companies by considering the following:

- the financial strength of the provider (it is important to be confident your pension company can survive; this very competitive market is in the throes of merger mania);
- the performance track record, with the emphasis on consistency over the long term and stability of staff;
- the level of charges deducted throughout the investment period (this is a maximum of 1 per cent with a stakeholder scheme);
- the flexibility of the contract – for example, there should be no penalties for reducing and stopping contributions, transferring the fund and early retirement (this is guaranteed with a stakeholder scheme).

Fund choice

Your primary aim is to ensure you are in the most appropriate asset class for your age and circumstances (see Chapters 2 and 10). The range of funds on offer will vary but there should be at least one fund for each major asset class, plus a 'lifestyle' option that makes the asset allocation decisions for you (see below). Ideally you should seek independent advice to make sure the pension funds you choose dovetail with other investments.

There is no right fund for the entire time you are in the pension scheme or plan. Your first consideration is asset allocation. It may look safe to invest contributions in cash and gilts but for a younger employee this is likely to produce poor results over the long term. At this stage the main objective is to beat inflation and to maximize returns. You should not be too worried about volatility and day-to-day fluctuations.

Advisers usually recommend scheme members to opt for 100 per cent in equities until they are 5–10 years off retirement in order to generate maximum capital growth. Try to diversify within your equity holding. You might choose a global equity fund or split the contributions so that 60 per cent goes into the UK equity fund and 40 per cent into the overseas equity fund.

As you get closer to retirement you need to switch gradually into safer assets such as bonds and gilts. By the time you retire and want to buy your annuity, a good benchmark is to aim to be 75 per cent in an 'annuity matching' fund, which would consist of gilts and bonds, and 25 per cent in cash. This enables you to calculate with some accuracy the value of your cash and annuity at retirement. It also avoids any unpleasant surprises at the eleventh hour. If you stay in equities your fund could fall sharply just before retirement and you will not have time to make good your losses.

A good stakeholder or group personal pension scheme will recognize that some employees don't have the time or inclination to make asset allocation decisions. This is why they offer a 'lifestyle' programme, which keeps you in equities until a few years before retirement and then gradually switches you into gilts, bonds and cash.

Experts agree that the lifestyle structure is the best default programme for investors who do not want to make their own decisions or who might otherwise put too much into cash and bonds at an early age. However, it does have its drawbacks. For example, you may feel that to start switching out of real assets (that is, assets that grow in value with the economy) ten years before retirement is too soon. Arguably the effect of compound interest on regular contribution plans is at its greatest during this last decade of investment. For this reason some schemes delay the switch out of equities until five years before your retirement date.

Moreover, standard lifestyle programmes do not cope well with those who retire early, who may find themselves 100 per cent in equities at the wrong time. In contrast, members who intend to transfer to an 'income drawdown' plan at retirement, which allows you to keep your fund fully invested while drawing a regular income, need to maintain a high equity exposure and should not switch to gilts.

Summary of pension investment choice

A good stakeholder scheme or personal plan will offer at least the following basic funds. These should be run by a competitive asset manager and should allow you to switch when you need to change your asset allocation.

■ Equities – possibly a global equity fund or a choice between UK and overseas equities. There may also be a passive UK equity fund which offers a lower risk profile than a more aggressive actively managed fund, assuming the FTSE All-Share is your benchmark.

■ Bonds and gilts – to enable you to match the assets that back annuities as you draw closer to retirement. This might be called a pension or annuity-matching fund.

■ Cash – to enable you to allocate part of your fund to generate the tax-free cash lump sum (typically 25 per cent of your total fund).

■ Lifestyle – which selects the asset mix right for you, typically starting with 100 per cent in equities until you are 5–10 years away from retirement, when you gradually switch into cash and gilts/bonds.

Self-invested personal pensions

Self-invested personal pensions (Sipps) follow the same basic rules as standard personal pensions but in addition allow you to exercise much greater control over your investments. Like self-select individual savings accounts, a Sipp is a tax-efficient wrapper in which to shelter your assets. The administration is usually carried out by a specialist life office and you either tackle the investment yourself or appoint an investment manager (a stockbroker, for example) to construct and run the portfolio for you.

Sipps can also be used by partnerships. These taxpayers are excluded from the company-sponsored small self-administered schemes, but they can use a Sipp with virtually the same effect and, if they pool their contributions and funds, they can achieve beneficial economies of scale.

There is a wide choice of investments which includes the following:

■ stocks and shares (e.g. equities, gilts, debentures) quoted on the UK Stock Exchange and including securities on the Alternative Investment Market;

■ stocks and shares traded on a recognized overseas exchange;

■ unit trusts and investment trusts;

■ insurance company-managed funds and unit-linked funds;

- deposit accounts;
- commercial property.

A Sipp fund cannot purchase a firm's existing business premises from the partnership but it can buy new offices into which the partnership can move, provided the property is leased back on a commercial basis. You can also use your Sipp fund to borrow on the strength of its assets to help with property purchase. However, the Sipp cannot lend part of the pension fund back to you, the investor.

Your choice at retirement

If you have a money purchase pension you have four broad options at retirement:

- You can buy a conventional annuity from an insurance company. This provides a guaranteed income for life which can be fixed or rise annually. The conventional annuity effectively locks you into current gilt yields.
- If you have other sources of income, you can leave your pension fund in the pension plan until you are 75 at the latest. Your fund will continue to grow virtually tax free but you will not be able to take your tax-free cash or draw an income. At 75 you must buy an annuity.
- You can buy an investment-linked annuity and hope to improve the level of your annuity income through good investment returns.
- You can transfer to a drawdown plan, which offers full exposure to the stock markets as well as inheritance tax (IHT) planning opportunities. You can draw an income from the fund.

If you are moving into semi-retirement or you have a source of income – for example from investments or a family business – you may decide to leave your pension fund where it is for the time being. The most flexible home for a substantial fund is a self-invested personal pension which allows you to invest directly in equities and bonds as well as in a wide choice of funds. You can stay in a Sipp or standard personal pension until the age of 75, when you have to convert the fund to an annuity. If you die while the fund is in the personal plan, the fund forms part of your estate and can be passed on to your dependants, so this is attractive from the inheritance tax perspective.

Assuming that you need to draw an income, you will have to 'vest' part or all of your pension plan. This means you can take the tax-free cash –

usually about 25 per cent of the fund – and use the remainder to generate an income through an annuity or drawdown arrangement. It is important to remember you do not have to put all your eggs in one basket. It is possible to combine one or more of these options. For example, you may decide to use half your fund to lock into the safety of a conventional annuity and with the other half buy an investment-linked annuity.

To find out more about your options, consult, an independent adviser with pensions, tax and investment expertise.

Summary

- In most cases it is in your interests to join the company pension scheme to take advantage of the employer's contributions.
- Higher earners may find the salary on which benefits and contributions are based is capped.
- If necessary, top up your scheme benefits with additional voluntary contributions or through a stakeholder scheme.
- Make sure your money purchase pension does not impose penalties if you stop or reduce contributions.

Further information

The Department of Social Security provides guidance about state pensions, stakeholder schemes, company schemes and personal pensions. Visit *www.dss.gov.uk*.

Employee share ownership

- ■ The different options

- ■ ShareSave (Save As You Earn)

- ■ Company share option plans (executive plans)

- ■ Unapproved schemes

- ■ Profit-sharing schemes

A T   A   G L A N C E

Employee share ownership can bring excellent rewards and, with the general schemes, at little or no risk until you decide whether to buy. Buying shares through a company scheme is also tax-efficient if you make a capital gain above the annual exemption, as these shares are classed as business assets and the rate of CGT can be as low as 10 per cent (see page 256).

There are more than 5,000 companies in the UK with approved employee share schemes, with about 3.5 million participating employees enjoying the tax benefits.

The different options

The best source of information on the range of company share schemes is ProShare. Contact details are provided at the end of this chapter and most of the material that follows was drawn from its publications.

Currently, there are three Inland Revenue-approved share schemes.

- ShareSave is the most popular, with over 1.75 million participants and more than 1,200 schemes in place.

- Profit-sharing schemes have around 1.25 million participants and 900 schemes in place.

Both of these schemes are all-employee share schemes, which means that all employees must be offered the opportunity to participate.

- Company share option plans (CSOPs), have 450,000 participants in over 3,750 schemes. This scheme has discretionary eligibility, which means that companies may choose which employees they would like to participate.

The government has introduced two additional share schemes:

- The New All-Employee Share Option Plan (AESOP).
- The Enterprise Management Incentives Plan (EMI).

In addition to the approved schemes above, companies may also offer 'unapproved' share schemes. Although these do not offer the tax relief available under the approved schemes, they do offer more flexibility in design, which means that companies can create a bespoke scheme to meet their needs.

In this chapter we focus on the most popular arrangement, ShareSave.

ShareSave (Save As You Earn)

The ShareSave scheme is also known as the Save As You Earn (SAYE) or Savings-Related Share Option Scheme, and was introduced under the 1980 Finance Act. There are currently over 1,200 approved ShareSave schemes in operation according to the Inland Revenue, with 1.75 million participants.

The ShareSave scheme is the most popular of the all-employee share schemes.

General features

Under a ShareSave scheme employees have the right (known as an 'option') to buy shares at a future date at a price fixed shortly before the options are granted. The company can discount the price of the shares by up to 20 per cent off the market value.

Shares can only be purchased with the proceeds of savings made under a special SAYE savings contract, set up with a bank or building society for a period of three or five years. The length of the option can be three, five or seven years. For the seven-year option savings are made for five years only, but the money remains in the account for a further two years. Savings are made by payroll deduction from employees' net salary.

> Shares can only be purchased with the proceeds of savings made under a special SAYE savings contract, set up with a bank or building society for a period of three or five years.

The benefits

While you are saving you are in a 'no lose' situation. If the share price falls to below the option price, there is no requirement to exercise the options. Instead you can simply take the proceeds of your savings contract plus the tax-free bonus at maturity (see below).

Who is eligible?

The scheme has to be open to all eligible employees of the company. A qualifying period of employment can be set but this must be no greater than five years. The majority of companies operating a ShareSave scheme have a much shorter eligibility period.

You can save between £5 and £250 per month. At maturity (the three, five or seven-year anniversary from the contract start date if no payments have been missed), a tax-free bonus is paid. However, you lose the option to purchase shares if you close the savings account and withdraw your money before the end of the period of the contract. In this case the payments would attract interest at a rate of 3 per cent as long as the account was open for more than one year.

Also, if you miss more than six of the monthly contributions, the savings contract is effectively closed and the money returned to you. In this case the option to purchase shares would also lapse.

Buying the shares

At the maturity of the option, you have six months in which to exercise your right to buy. However, there is no obligation to purchase the shares. Your choices are as follows:

- close the account and take the savings plus the tax-free bonus; or
- close the account and use all of the proceeds to take up the option to purchase shares; or
- close the account and take up the option in part (funds not used for the purchase of shares would be returned to the employee).

If you have missed any monthly payments (up to a maximum of six), the maturity date will be extended by the corresponding number of missed payments.

Income tax

There is normally no tax liability when you buy the shares. However, in the event of an early exercise of options (for example if the company you work for is taken over or sold) within three years from the date of granting the option, you may have to pay income tax on any gain.

Capital gains tax

When you buy the shares, if you then sell them there may be a liability to CGT on the gain between the sale price and the exercise price. (See page 255 for more details about CGT.) If you have been unlucky enough to make a loss on the shares, you can also offset this loss against any other gains you have made in that tax year.

Transfers to individual savings accounts

From April 6, 1999, shares released from the scheme can be transferred into an Isa. The value of the shares transferred will depend upon the year you want to make the transfer and the type of provider. For example, you could go to one Isa provider for the whole plan (a maxi Isa) or to separate providers for each component (mini Isa). For more details about Isas see Chapter 7.

What happens if you leave the company?

If you change jobs and leave your current employer, you can no longer exercise the options. You can either carry on saving and take the cash and bonus at the end of the savings period, or close the account and take the payments made together with any interest, which is paid at 3 per cent per annum. However, employees have considerable discretion with these arrangements, so check the rules for your particular scheme.

If you leave due to special circumstances – for example redundancy, injury or disability – you have six months in which to exercise the option to buy from the date of leaving, using the amount saved plus any interest. If an employee dies, the option may be exercised by the personal representatives. In these circumstances, the option must be exercised in the 12 months following the death of the employee, or the maturity date, whichever is earlier. If the personal representatives do not exercise the option, the employee's savings, plus any bonus or interest due, will be paid to the estate.

Company share option plans (executive plans)

The main alternative to SAYE is a company share option plan, which in 1995 replaced the discretionary share option scheme. These were, and still are, commonly referred to as executive share option schemes because they are often open only to executives and directors. The plans are not linked to a savings contract, so you have to use spare capital to purchase.

Under the plan you do not pay income tax on the grant of an option or on any increase in market value of the shares in the period before you exercise the option. You can purchase the shares between three and ten years after the option was granted. Once you have made a purchase you have to wait another three years before you can exercise a further option to buy. Given the long period in which you have to choose, you might wish to take advice on when the experts consider the price is right.

The new schemes are not as attractive as the old executive schemes where the shares could be offered at a discount of up to 15 per cent and the maximum value of options per employee was the greater of £100,000 or four times salary. With the new plan the shares cannot be offered at a discount and there is a limit of £30,000 on the value of all the shares on option held by an employee.

Unapproved schemes

Some companies run 'unapproved' executive share option schemes. These do not offer the tax advantages of company share option plans, but in theory there is no limit to the size of the option. However, options granted from November 27, 1996 will, on exercise, be subject to income tax under the Pay As You Earn (PAYE) system. This leads to difficulties if the employee's income tax charge is so large that it exceeds his salary and the company is unable to deduct it from monthly pay.

Profit-sharing schemes

You might also come across a profit-sharing scheme. Until April 2001 employers could set up a trust to give you an immediate gift of tax-free shares equivalent to a proportion of profit. The shares remain in the name of the trustees.

The maximum limit in value per employee is the greater of £3,000 a year or 10 per cent of annual salary, subject to a ceiling of £8,000. Provided you do not sell the shares before the end of the third year after allocation, there is no income tax to pay, although there may be a capital gains tax liability.

Summary

■ Company share schemes offer you the opportunity to buy shares in your employer at a discount and in a tax-efficient manner.

■ There are over 1,200 ShareSave schemes in operation. This is the most popular and common scheme.

■ Shares are usually purchased with the proceeds of a regular savings scheme that runs for three, five or seven years.

■ If the share price falls below the option price, you can take the proceeds of your saving scheme and, if you complete the full term, a bonus is paid at maturity.

■ Senior employees may be offered a different type of scheme that requires them to buy shares out of capital.

■ Some executives are offered shares as a long-term incentive. This type of scheme may link the option to the company's performance.

Further information

Your employer should provide clear details of the various ways you can buy shares in the company. You can also contact your local Inland Revenue office for leaflets on the subject. These may be available in bank and building society branches.

A useful guide to employee share ownership is published by ProShare. Contact ProShare, Library Chambers, 13–14 Basinghall Street, London EC2V 5BQ. The website, at *www.proshare.org*, covers all the main arrangements.

How to select and buy individual equities and bonds

The importance of asset allocation

- What is your starting point?

- Reweighting your portfolio

- Collective funds for overseas exposure

- Achieving the right asset allocation

- Model portfolios for the FTSE/Apcims private investor indices

- Market cycles

- Stockbroker model portfolios

This chapter explains how to reduce risk through diversification using direct equity investment, bonds and gilts, and a range of collective funds.

Your starting point is an asset allocation plan. The large institutional pension funds refer to this important exercise as an asset/liability study. This is a helpful description because it focuses on your liabilities first.

In the case of a pension fund the liabilities are the income it requires to pay the pensions and the capital it needs in fairly liquid form to draw on to pay the expected tax-free lump sums of members on retirement and also the unexpected death benefits when a member dies.

For a private investor the 'liabilities' can cover a wide range of objectives. For example, your children's school fees fall due each term and represent a known cost which must be paid on specific dates in the future.

Another liability is the mortgage repayment. If you have an interest-only loan, typically you might need to save over a 25-year term at which point you need a large lump sum to repay the outstanding debt.

The same is true of pension plans, which usually build up a fund to buy an annuity in retirement. In return for your lump sum payment, the life assurance company guarantees to pay you a regular income for life.

Alternatively, if you decide to keep your fund fully invested in retirement (see page 95 for details on income drawdown) your objective is to provide a regular stream of monthly income, while keeping most of your fund invested in the stock markets.

In addition to these obvious liabilities you may have several other aims which require different periods of investment – for example, an expensive holiday abroad, a new car, or a temporary income while you or your spouse stops work in order to raise a family.

You can see from these examples that while your overall objective may be capital growth, you also need to manage the liquidity of your capital in order to pay off the big debts on time, and the cash flow in order to meet more regular income needs, where relevant. If this exercise is particularly complicated in your circumstances then a good financial planner or stockbroker should be able to help you draw up a plan and review it on a regular basis.

This chapter is largely devoted to asset allocation, which means deciding on the right type of investments before actually selecting individual shares, bonds and funds.

In the following chapters we take a closer look at share picking and how market cycles affect market sectors and individual companies.

What is your starting point?

Your portfolio should reflect your current financial position (and that of your family), your current and future investment objectives, and your tax status. It may also reflect your ethical views, which might prevent you from investing in a range of companies with whose business goals or methods you disagree (see Chapter 13).

> **T I P**
>
> Make sure you have a clear perception of your tolerance to risk. Whether you use an adviser or deal direct, this is critical.

Don't settle for a vague sentiment, but consider each investment in turn in the context of your overall asset allocation, and use the risk analysis guide on page 44 to determine which investments are appropriate for you and which ones you should avoid.

Dealing with risk

The problem with risk is that usually there is a wide grey margin between the worst that could possibly happen and the likelihood of this actually taking place. For example, in theory, if you invest in equities you could lose the lot if the company goes bust. As a shareholder you are last in the line of creditors, so it is quite likely that you would get little or nothing back if there are insufficient assets to go round.

> To what extent are you prepared to trade off higher risk against higher potential expectations – and conversely, higher potential losses?

So, how likely is it that a company will go bust? Clearly this depends to some extent on the companies you select and the state of the economy. But in practice the risk is a lot more tangible than you might think. In a stockbroker's survey, 45 per cent of the private investor participants had seen one of their equity investments go into receivership.

Your task, then, is to quantify the level of risk and decide whether you feel comfortable with it. In other words, to what extent are you prepared to trade off higher risk against higher potential expectations – and conversely, higher potential losses?

This does not alter the case for equities; it just means you have to choose with care and spread risk.

Despite the low-inflation environment of recent years, it is probably not safe to build investment policy on the assumption that inflation has been beaten for good. Noting that even an inflation rate of 3 per cent halves the value of money in just over 20 years, it seems advisable to continue to place the emphasis on equities. The gap between gilt and equity returns is likely to be much narrower than in the past but should still favour equities by a significant margin.

At the same time the private investor will generally find it advisable to maintain a higher weighting in defensive assets than the institutional investor.

For a cautious investor a suggested weighting in defensive assets is 30 per cent of the portfolio in fixed-interest, index-linked gilts, foreign bonds and cash. A further 50 per cent is held in UK equities and 20 per cent in overseas equities.

However, do bear in mind that any model portfolio is aimed at the mythical average investor. Clearly, each individual needs a private benchmark which reflects their own requirements, over both the short term and the longer term. For example, some investors may avoid foreign bonds owing to the currency risk, while others will regard them as an important diversification into overseas markets.

Diversification is not such a big issue within the conventional gilt market because all gilts are issued by the same source, namely the government. This does not mean that gilts are free from volatility. The nominal coupon and redemption date are known but the real value or price during a gilt's lifecycle is not known.

If you are interested in corporate bonds because they pay a slightly higher income than gilts, it is important to diversify in a similar way to an equity portfolio. It is rare for a company to fail to the extent of its equity capital but not its loan capital. Therefore in practice the prior charge of a loan stock provides little protection and a loan stock is best viewed as equity risk.

Reweighting your portfolio

If you take your existing portfolio to a stockbroker, be prepared to allow your broker to sell some of your existing shares if they believe they are inappropriate for your investment aims or that they represent too large a proportion of your portfolio and therefore create a concentration of risk.

Consider, for example, the type of portfolio you may have if you responded to privatization offers, received free 'windfall' shares from a building society or life assurance company and applied for cheap shares through your employer's share option scheme.

Your portfolio may have done very well in the past, but it will not have a good spread of shares in the main All-Share sectors. Instead it is likely to consist of privatization issues (utilities), windfalls (financials) and whatever category your employer happens to fall into. In this case your portfolio could lack representation in important sectors such as foods, pharmaceuticals and retailers, among others.

It is also important to remember that if you intend to invest a large sum – for example an inheritance, or the proceeds from a pension or endowment plan – there is no need to complete the process in a matter of days. This could be a very unwise approach.

Timing is critical to successful investments and in practice it could take 6–12 months to construct or rebalance your portfolio. During this period, keep any uninvested capital in an easy-access account and be sure to shop around for the best rates.

Your stockbroker will also have to consider your tax position, particularly the capital gains tax implications of selling large chunks of shares. If you have not been making use of your annual capital gains tax exemption (£7,500 for the 2001–2002 tax year), then your larger holdings could well carry a hefty CGT liability. This could be reduced through indexation and taper relief (see Chapter 20).

Tax may become more complicated if you are retired or close to retirement. In addition to your income tax and CGT concerns, you should give careful thought to inheritance tax planning.

Collective funds for overseas exposure

Don't be surprised if you end up with a large chunk of your money invested in collective funds, even if you have a substantial sum to play with. It makes sense to adopt this route if you want to gain exposure to certain markets – smaller UK companies and overseas markets, for example. It can be risky or impractical to invest in one or two smaller companies (there are more than 400 in the SmallCap index) – unless, of course, you really are convinced of a company's merits.

> Don't be surprised if you end up with a large chunk of your money invested in collective funds

Overseas markets can be more expensive to enter and individual share prices too large. In this respect the UK is quite unusual in having a relatively low price per individual share (this characteristic is maintained by companies that split shares when they become unwieldy).

Swiss companies, for example, commonly have a share price of £5,000 each, so if you have £100,000 to invest overseas it is not sensible to have, say, two shares in one Swiss company. Rather, you should have £10,000 in units in a collective Swiss blue chip fund if you are keen on Switzerland, or possibly £20,000 in a European blue chip fund, which would invest in a selection of leading European companies.

In Chapter 6 we discussed the important issues to consider when you choose a collective fund. One point to bear in mind if you use a stockbroker is that some firms offer only their own funds, while others select from the entire range. This is a tricky one and there are no hard-and-fast rules. In theory, if your stockbroker has a good reputation for fund management, and in particular where it has a large institutional manager as its parent company, the firm's funds should be among the better performers. However, few managers can boast a top-quartile (top 25 per cent) performance for all their funds, so in general you might expect a better return if the choice of funds is not restricted.

Achieving the right asset allocation

To give you an idea of how the experts approach the task of asset allocation for private investors, it is helpful to look at three very different sources. First, the private investor indices constructed by FTSE International in conjunction with Apcims. The indices are also discussed in Chapter 18, which offers some tips on monitoring the performance of your portfolio.

Second, we consider how a firm of stockbrokers constructs its model portfolios.

Third, we recap on the income from equities *v.* gilts issue.

Model portfolios for the FTSE/Apcims private investor indices

Although each investor's objectives will be different, for the sake of simplicity the three models we consider here are for income, growth and balanced portfolios.

In 1997, FTSE International, which manages and develops worldwide equity and bond indices, formed a joint venture with Apcims, the private client stockbroker organization, to launch three indices which allow investment managers and individuals to monitor their portfolios more accurately. The asset allocation of each model portfolio is based on research from a wide range of private client fund managers and stock-brokers.

The weightings are amended on a regular basis, so the figures in Table 10.1 will not necessarily be up to date, but nevertheless they serve to highlight the different strategies used to achieve the three most common investment goals.

As you can see from the table, the difference in the UK equity weighting is not as great as you might expect, but the individual shares would be selected with different priorities in mind. Growth would be achieved by taking a slightly more aggressive approach, and while you would expect a fair number of blue chips, there would also be some small and medium-sized companies to boost growth prospects.

The income seeker

By contrast, for the income seeker the income portfolio would focus on higher-yielding shares. Some investors might have a preference for the larger companies (for example the FTSE 100 companies), which tend to have a more steady track record on dividend payments than some smaller companies.

The point to bear in mind here is that size and risk do not go hand in hand, but represent two different decisions for income seekers. Some smaller, higher-risk companies can provide a high yield but might not be appropriate for a retired income seeker.

However, many retired investors are looking not just for short-term income but for income over 10–20 years. Over this period the bond and cash element would provide a stable guaranteed income but equities would be needed to provide an element of capital growth to maintain the real value of the portfolio.

Don't assume, though, that just because you are growing older you should switch part of your portfolio out of equities and into gilts, bonds and cash. Many investors who retire early cannot or do not want to draw their pension immediately – either because it will not be paid until the

Table 10.1 Private Investor Indices' asset allocation

Asset class	Growth %	Balanced %	Income %
UK equities	60	55	50
International equities	25	20	5
Bonds	10	20	40
Cash	5	5	5

Source: FTSE International/Apcims published in the 'Weekend Money' section of Saturday's FT.

employer's official pension age of 65 or because the pension would be substantially reduced. In this case you might be looking for an immediate and high income from your portfolio rather than long-term income and growth.

International equities

International equities play an important part in the growth portfolio. This would provide exposure to foreign markets with good growth prospects. Of course, the level of risk would depend on where you invested. There is a big difference between, say, the European Union or North American countries and the Japan/Pacific region or the emerging markets of South America, Africa, and Central and Eastern Europe.

Bear in mind that foreign investment also exposes you to currency fluctuations and, in some countries, exchange control problems. Political instability and hyper-inflation may also be features of emerging economies.

Bonds and cash

Finally, the weighting of bonds and cash is probably the clearest indication of the portfolio's aim. In this case the income portfolio has almost half its assets in this class, while the growth portfolio has only 10 per cent. A younger investor with a robust attitude to risk might not even bother with this amount but might go wholly for UK and foreign equities.

UK equities

For most investors, whether looking for income, growth or a balance of the two, at least half of the portfolio will be invested in UK shares. Although there is a tendency to regard the FTSE 100 companies as somehow 'safer' than medium and small companies, it is not true to say that big is synonymous with secure.

A common strategy is to invest directly in FTSE 100 companies because these are well diversified and often have overseas interests. Exposure to the FTSE 250 (the 250 largest companies by market capitalization after the top 100) and in particular to the SmallCap (the remaining 470 or so shares in the All-Share) can be achieved through collective funds, or directly, depending on your attitude to risk and confidence in your ability to research less well-known companies adequately.

The FTSE All-Share, which covers about 98 per cent of the UK stock market total capitalization, has 39 industrial sectors. Some include a large number of companies representing a broad spectrum of industry – engineering and retailers, for example. Others are designed to categorize just a few important companies in a very specific market. Gas distribution, for example, has only three companies but this includes the enormous British Gas plc.

Overseas equities

Since 1979, when UK exchange controls were abolished, the average pension fund has increased its weighting from 5 per cent to 25 per cent in overseas equities. Private investors have also demonstrated a keen interest in overseas stocks and have been rewarded with generally good returns.

As mentioned above, in practice, for many investors, the need for diversification argues against direct overseas equity investment except where the portfolio is very large. Specialist unit and investment trusts represent a cheaper entry and a good way to gain exposure to these important markets without undue risk of over-specialization.

Having said that, if you are interested in certain sectors – say, car manufacturing – the choice of UK shares is very limited and you may wish to buy US shares, for example, to obtain the level of exposure you desire.

Investment managers believe that investing overseas is very important from the point of view of diversification. In other words, the benefits lie with reducing risk rather than increasing return. However, with the increasing globalisation of UK companies the degree of diversification overseas need not be as high as in the past.

> Since 1979, when UK exchange controls were abolished, the average pension fund has increased its weighting from 5 per cent to 25 per cent in overseas equities.

Market cycles

As a general rule the companies in a sector share certain characteristics which make them respond in a certain way to changes in the market cycles. This is why it is important, although not essential, to build a portfolio which spans all the major sectors. This helps to spread risk and avoids your portfolio's crashing in a nasty way as the economy enters or emerges from a recession. (Economic cycles, including some help with bear markets, are discussed in Chapter 14.)

Remember, though, that many of the blue chip companies which form the FTSE 100 index have considerable exposure overseas and so are not affected only by economic cycles in the UK. As mentioned above, this is generally seen as a plus point for investors keen to spread risk.

Stockbroker model portfolios

Some private client stockbrokers maintain model portfolios and it is worth asking to see examples in order to gain a view of the manager's approach. In addition, a good independent guide can be found in *Investors Chronicle*.

Understandably, brokers may be unwilling to publish details of the specific stocks they recommend at a given time. This is partly because they guard their stock selection process from the eyes of competitors but, probably more to the point, a recommended selection of shares quickly becomes out of date as company information and economic reports flood in.

So, without revealing the names of specific stocks, the following information from Henderson Global Investors gives you an idea of how the process works.

In its 'Select Portfolio Management Services', for clients with more than £100,000 to invest, Henderson runs three model portfolios, again aiming for growth, a balance of growth and income, and income. (A tailored service is offered for those with around £300,000 minimum to invest.)

So, for example, if you want to pay your children's school fees out of your portfolio, initially, assuming the children are still very young, you would be aiming for growth. Later, part of your portfolio would be adjusted so it can generate the cash required to pay the fees on the dates they fall due, without forcing you to sell your shares at the wrong time.

Where individual equities are mentioned in these model portfolios, they are selected from the FTSE 100 index and equal weighting is given to each stock. Exposure to small and medium-sized companies for this size portfolio would usually be achieved through investment trusts. Exposure to overseas markets would be achieved through a combination of equity-based unit and investment trusts.

Growth portfolio

Gross income yield: 1.63% (March 2001).

Suitable for: those who can afford to leave their money invested for some years.

Objective: to achieve capital appreciation over the medium to long term.

Method: actively managing investments in UK listed equities and in investment and unit trusts covering major global markets.

Asset allocation

Cash 2.3%

Fixed interest (one fund) 8%

UK equities (18 individual shares) 49.7%

UK equities Small/Mid Cap (four unit/investment trusts) 12.5%

Overseas 27.5% as follows:
- Europe (two funds) 12%
- North America (one fund) 6.5%
- Far East (one fund) 2.5%
- Japan (one fund) 5%
- International (one emerging markets fund) 1.5%

Balanced portfolio

Gross income yield: 2.71% (March 2001).

Suitable for: investors seeking a balance between growth and income.

Objective: to provide an income marginally in excess of the FTSE All-Share index, with the prospect of long-term capital appreciation.

Method: investing predominantly in income-generating equities listed on the London Stock Exchange, as well as gilts and bonds when appropriate. Again, overseas investments are made through equity-based unit and investment trusts.

Asset allocation

Cash 2.5%

Fixed interest (two gilts) 15%

UK equities (18 individual shares) 52.5%

UK equities Small/Mid Cap (three funds) 10%

Overseas 20% as follows:
- Europe (two funds) 10%
- North America (one fund) 4.5%
- Far East (one fund) 1.5%
- Japan (one fund) 3%
- International (one emerging markets fund) 1%

High income

Gross income yield: 4.48% (March 2001).

Suitable for: investors seeking an immediate income.

Objective: to generate a high level of income significantly in excess of the

FTSE All-Share index, with the prospect of a degree of capital growth.

Method: to construct a portfolio weighted towards UK gilts and bonds, with the remainder invested in high-yielding UK listed equities, unit trusts and investment trusts, selected for their longer-term income and capital growth prospects. Overseas exposure is likely to be small.

Asset allocation

Cash 5%

Fixed interest (four gilts) 45%

UK equities (12 individual shares from the FTSE 100) 35%

UK equities Small/Mid Cap (two funds) 7%

Overseas 8% as follows:
- Europe (one fund) 3%
- North America (one fund) 2%
- Japan/Far East (one fund) 3%

Summary

- Before you can decide which asset classes you should hold, you need to refer to your objectives. Then you can match assets with liabilities/goals. Institutional funds call this an asset/liability study or model.

- Your portfolio should reflect your current and expected future financial position, your tax status, any ethical views, and your tolerance to risk.

- It is not wise to build a portfolio based on the assumption that inflation has been beaten for good.

- Building a new portfolio or reweighting your existing collection of shares may take up to a year. Keep any spare cash in a deposit account during this period.

- Collective funds are commonly used to achieve exposure to overseas markets and smaller companies.

- Even an income portfolio may invest up to 50 per cent of its assets in equities.

- International equities may be held to reduce risk rather than improve returns.

Further information

Details about the FTSE International/Apcims private investor indices can be found at the FTSE International website at *www.ftse.com*, where a service called On Target will allow you to analyze the performance of the portfolios free of charge. Alternatively, the indices are reported in the 'Weekend Money' section of the *Financial Times*, in other financial newspapers and publications, and on a number of data vendor terminals.

Henderson Global Investors is at 4 Broadgate, London EC2M 2PA. *www.henderson.com*.

Chiswell Associates is at 4 Chiswell Street, Finsbury Square, London EC1Y 4UP. *www.chiswell.co.uk*.

How to select your shares

- Your starting point

- Investment aims

- How shares are categorized

- The FTSE International indices

- Classification by sector

- Shareholder perks

- New issues

- When to sell

Stock picking, we are frequently told, is an art, not a science. You can try to make it a science if you like, but most professionals have given up on this one, at least in the active management market.

Passive management (index tracking) is a different kettle of fish and aims to eliminate the risk of individual stock selection. So, if your portfolio or collective fund holds a sample of different stocks or actually replicates every stock in an index (the FTSE 100 usually, but sometimes the 250 or the All-Share) over the long term, you can't lose provided your benchmark is the index itself.

Of course this does not mean your portfolio is guaranteed to rise. If the index takes a tumble, your portfolio will follow. Nevertheless, low-cost index-tracking unit trusts are very popular and worth considering.

The fact that stock picking is an art does not mean you should abandon the pursuit of knowledge and select your shares by sticking a pin in the 'Companies and Markets' section of the *Financial Times*. What it does mean is that you are never guaranteed success (unless you indulge in a spot of skull-duggery). Nor is your stockbroker. This is why investing in shares can be very risky, particularly over the short term when the volatility of markets can temporarily depress the share price of even the best of companies.

The difference between the art of stock picking and the pin-sticking exercise is information and strategy. Pin sticking is all about pure luck; stock picking is all about making informed decisions in the light of your investment aims.

Most of the discussion on equities so far has focused on their importance as an asset class. This chapter looks at the share selection process, while Chapter 14 shows the importance of timing and the influence on share prices of market cycles. Page 265 recommends some reading material. A good book on investment is *The Motley Fool UK Investment Guide* by David Berger with David and Tom Gardner, published by Boxtree. The website is at *www.fool.co.uk*.

Your starting point

If you have more than £100,000 to invest (some stockbrokers put the figure much higher), you could consider including direct equity investments in your portfolio. The optimal minimum number of shares depends on what you are trying to achieve.

Opinions vary greatly on this point, but as an absolute minimum you should aim to hold ten different shares. Twenty or thirty would be even better since this would help spread risk, provided each holding was a sensible minimum size. Again, opinions also vary, but as a very rough guide you could consider a minimum holding as anything between £1,000 and £5,000, depending on the costs involved.

> If you have more than £100,000 to invest you could consider including direct equity investments in your portfolio.

To avoid over-exposure to the risks inherent in smaller companies, some advisers recommend you put at least half of your capital destined for equities in FTSE 100 companies. An alternative is to achieve your exposure to the FTSE 100 companies through index-tracking unit trusts. On top of this you can buy a handful of carefully selected individual equities to boost your portfolio's potential growth.

Investment aims

Whatever your starting point, it is important to have an objective and to stick to it. The more disciplined you are in this respect, the more likely you are to achieve your aims and not get sidetracked by events.

There are two important risks to consider here. First, there is the subjective risk that you might get it wrong. Second, there is a risk that you might not achieve your private goals.

A very simplistic approach is to determine whether you are looking for growth, income or a mixture of the two. These portfolio types were discussed in Chapter 10, where models for asset allocation were examined.

You also need to devise a sensible selection process. If you ask the right questions before you buy, while there is no guarantee of success (always remembering that this is art not science), you will avoid the fads (such as the technology boom in the late 1990s) and, what may be more difficult, the shares that look genuinely attractive but are entirely inappropriate for your portfolio aims and investment timescale.

The following explanations and tips may prove useful in your search. If you already have an appropriate portfolio up and running, pay particular attention to the section on selling. It's no good selecting your shares with care if you do not have a strategy for weeding out the losers at the right time. Also see Chapter 18 for advice on how to maintain the portfolio and monitor performance.

Avoid frequency of trading

> **TIP**
>
> Before you start, it is worth pointing out one of the most obvious pitfalls for private investors, namely that the cost of frequent dealing can quickly outweigh minor gains.

The mechanics of dealing are considered in more detail in Chapter 15, but as a very rough guide you will find that the price of shares you buy will need to rise by about 4–5 per cent before you work off the sale or purchase costs.

So, a simple but nevertheless worthy tip for the largely risk-averse investors and those with comparatively small portfolios is to trade as infrequently as possible. Of course, this does not mean you should hang on to bad shares.

Moreover, even if you buy for the medium to long term and do all your homework before investing, you need to keep an eye on your shares to make sure they still offer the same package of attractions as when you bought them. You also need to keep an eye on new offers to see if any might usurp the old favourites in your affections. Loyalty is a misplaced emotion in the private investor.

This might seem a rather mundane and pedantic way to manage your portfolio, but unless you deliberately set out to be a frequent trader, it beats other systems which might rely on a percentage price drop, for example, to trigger a sell signal.

How shares are categorized

Shares fall into all sorts of different categories and each label tells you something important about the investment prospects. Size and type of business are the two most obvious categories.

Does size count?

The simple answer is yes, and this is as good a starting point as any.

The London Stock Exchange has more than 2,000 listed companies and is the main securities market in the UK. It acts as a *primary market* for new issues and also as a *secondary market*. (Gilts and bonds are also listed on the Stock Exchange. See Chapter 16.)

In theory, large companies that are well diversified should be more stable than smaller companies, partly because of their sheer size and deep pockets but also because, through diversification of product and service range in the UK and overseas, they should be less vulnerable to market cycles and economic factors such as a rise or fall in interest rates or a recession.

If one part of the company is affected by a fall in retail sales, for example, other parts of the group might still be thriving. In this way an investment in a blue chip company carries an inherent spread of risk, whereas a small, specialized company is much more vulnerable to economic conditions and market sentiment.

Clearly, the reverse is also true. If you pick a small, growing company which doubles its turnover in one year then your shares could boom. Larger companies are less likely to experience sharp rises as well as the sharp downturns, although there are always exceptions to this rule.

In practice, of course, a large company can get into serious trouble or even go bust unexpectedly. It is always a nasty shock to discover in retrospect just how well the directors can hide what should have been clear signs of impending doom.

Finally, income seekers need to decide what risks they are prepared to take. A high-income-generating portfolio can also be highly speculative – it does not have to be confined to larger companies.

The FTSE International indices

The quickest way to assess the size of a company is by looking at the FTSE International indices, published each day in the *Financial Times*. The indices and how to read them are discussed in more detail in Chapter 18, but it is helpful here to consider the chief characteristics of the main equity indices, which are likely to contain your most popular shares.

> The quickest way to assess the size of a company is by looking at the FTSE International Indices.

Bear in mind though that these are theoretical characteristics. In practice markets may move in a totally unpredictable fashion, so it is important to look at actual trends, not just the theory.

The FTSE Actuaries indices were developed by the *Financial Times*, the Stock Exchange and the Institute and Faculty of Actuaries. Since November 1995 the indices have been managed by a joint company, the FTSE International (*www.ftse.com*).

These indices are arithmetically weighted by market capitalization so that the larger the company the greater the effect its share price movement will have on the index. 'Market capitalization' is the stock market valuation of the company, which is calculated by multiplying the number of shares in issue by their market price.

The FTSE All-Share

This is the most comprehensive UK index and consists of about 770 companies with a total market capitalization of above around £1,720bn. The All-Share is regarded as the professional investor's yardstick for the level of the UK equity market as a whole and represents about 98 per cent of UK stock market capitalization. Within the All-Share, companies are allocated to 39 different categories of shares according to industrial sector. There are also sub-indices, including the FTSE 100 and Mid-250.

The FTSE 100

This index consists of the 100 largest UK companies by market capitalization and is the standard reference point for defining Britain's 'blue chip' companies (a blue chip being the highest-value chip in a game of poker). The FTSE 100 companies together represent about 78 per cent of the UK stock market capitalization.

Place in your portfolio: These are large companies, many of which are multinationals with substantial overseas exposure. Companies in this index tend to do better in a recession than smaller companies and their size and diversification tend to make them fairly stable investments.

Advisers usually recommend that once you have your portfolio of collective funds, this is the best place to start with direct equity investments. To further enhance your spread of risk, make sure you choose your shares from a wide range of sectors.

If you are more adventurous and want to spend your time hunting down value for money among the smaller companies in the All-Share, you could always buy units in a UK tracker fund which replicates the FTSE 100 and gain your blue chips this way, leaving you free to spend time researching smaller companies.

The FTSE 250

This index consists of the next 250 companies below the FTSE 100 and can include or exclude investment trusts. The Mid-250s are companies capitalized at between £350m and £3bn. Together, these companies represent about 13 per cent of the UK stock market capitalization (including investment trusts).

Place in your portfolio: These companies may have less exposure to manufacturing in overseas markets although they may rely heavily on exports. During an economic recovery companies in this index tend to experience higher returns than the FTSE 100 but still manage to avoid exposure to the volatility experienced by some of the smaller companies in the All-Share index. A good bet, therefore, after you have built up your collection of blue chips – but make sure you research the individual companies well before taking the plunge.

The FTSE SmallCap

This index does not have a fixed number of constituent companies but instead it comprises all the remaining companies in the All-Share which are too small to qualify for the top 350 (about 420). Together they account for about 4.4 per cent of the total UK capitalization.

Place in your portfolio: Clearly, All-Share companies which fall outside the FTSE 350 (the FTSE 100 and Mid-250 combined) are potentially more risky and volatile than the larger companies. However, this is an area in which private investors traditionally have done well. These companies are less sought after by the professionals because very large funds cannot trade in these shares easily, since the size of the deal might in itself push up or depress the share price. As a result, these companies usually are less well researched than the FTSE 350.

Certainly, if you have local knowledge of a company and you believe it has a good management team and is in an up-and-coming market, you could do very well. However, beginners and the risk-averse should not commit too much money to any one company because this would concentrate the risk in your portfolio.

The Fledgling index

The Fledgling market covers all the companies which are too small at present to be in the All-Share index but otherwise are eligible to join the Exchange – about 680 companies. Together the SmallCap and Fledgling indices are known as the All-Small index.

Place in your portfolio: Once you get down to this level you really have to be careful. Whatever their business, the share price of small companies can be extremely volatile. A company that specializes in one or two products is very vulnerable to price competition and a sudden reduction in demand.

Moreover, a signal from a tip sheet to buy a small company's shares could be enough to send the price through the roof, while a panic to sell on the part of very few investors can be enough to force the share price down into the doldrums.

In conclusion, intensive research and a strict ceiling on the amount you invest in any one company are essential. Also, these shares may not be very liquid, so buying and, in particular selling, can be a problem. If you plan to use a stockbroker, find one that specializes in smaller companies to save you some legwork.

The Alternative Investment Market (AIM)

AIM replaced the Unlisted Securities Market (USM) in 1995 and lists about 500 companies. It allows small and relatively new companies which are growing quickly to go public without having to go through the expensive and time-consuming full listing procedures required for a Stock Exchange main listing. Private investors should also note that AIM companies are not regulated as strictly as fully listed companies. In due course a successful AIM company may move into the All-Share.

Place in your portfolio: These are risky companies. As with the smaller company shares listed on the Exchange but outside the All-Share, you must be sure you have done your research well before parting with your cash. Again you should watch out for lack of liquidity with AIM companies.

Companies ineligible for the All-Share

Some companies are not eligible to join the All-Share or the Fledgling market. This is not usually a question of size but of some other characteristic. For example, the following are ineligible:

■ foreign companies (which would also be listed on their home country stock market), e.g. Americans, Canadians and South Africans, which are listed after the AIM countries in the *FT* 'Companies and Markets' section;

■ subsidiaries of companies already in the All-Share;

- companies with less than 25 per cent of shares in 'free float' (i.e. over 75 per cent is held by the family or directors);
- companies whose shares were not traded for a minimum number of days in the previous year;
- split capital investment trusts.

Classification by sector

The sectors used by the FTSE International categorize the All-Share group companies according to what they do. In theory this helps because the companies in a sector are likely to be affected by a similar range of economic factors. For example, if we are in a dire recession people still need to eat, so companies in the 'Retailers, food' sector might be a good place to find some defensive stocks, while 'Breweries, pubs and restaurants' and 'Leisure and hotels' might feel the pinch as consumers cut back on non-essential items.

However, stock picking purely by sector is not necessarily a good technique. Some sectors represent a very concentrated market whereas others – transport, for example – represent a diversified range of companies. The point to remember here is that you must consider the profile of the sector and the company itself. Just because one company is experiencing good growth does not mean that you can pick any company in the sector and be guaranteed a winner.

> **Stock picking purely by sector is not necessarily a good technique.**

Where the sector classifications can help is in determining your investment position relative to the 'market'. If your aim is to beat the All-Share index, for example, you need to have a clear idea of how the index is constructed and deviate where you feel a sector is likely to perform well under the current market conditions.

Shareholder perks

Some shares offer certain perks, for example a discount at the company's stores or free tickets to certain events. In most cases these are no more than the free gift in the cereal box, but for some sport, entertainment or other enthusiasts the perks may well swing it. Do check, however, whether you will qualify for the perks, particularly if you use a *nominee account* (see page 178).

New issues

Over the past decade or so new issues have been dominated by the government's privatization of previously public-sector companies. Many new investors have done very well out of these companies, which have fallen mainly into the utilities sector. British Gas, for example, was sold off the back of the famous 'Sid' campaign.

More recently several major building societies and life assurance institutions have converted from 'mutual' status, where they are owned by their members, to public limited companies owned by shareholders. Most demutualizations have been characterized by the huge *windfall* share payments, where free shares in the new company are given to existing savers and borrowers.

Both of these categories of shares have done fairly well, but there are many other reasons why a company comes to the stock market, some of which are dealt with in Chapter 2, which explains why and how companies can raise finance to expand. For example, private owners may want to realize their capital and use it for other purposes.

When a company first comes to the market it must be accompanied by a prospectus, which provides information similar to that contained in the annual report and accounts, although usually there is more detail.

The company may go public in one of four ways:

- *Offer for sale:* where a set number of shares is offered for sale at a set price. Privatizations have generally used this route. On several occasions the price has been attractively low so that investors who secured an allocation of shares did very well. With this type of issue you can consider becoming a 'stag' – that is, an investor who seeks an allocation, only to sell immediately for a quick profit.

- *A tender offer:* where the company's advisers set a minimum price but do not set the final price until all the offers are in. This makes stagging virtually impossible, and the fact that you do not know the actual purchase price at the time you seek an allocation of shares often puts off private investors.

- *Placings:* when a company offers its shares directly to financial institutions, rather than to the general public. Placings can be combined with 'intermediary offers', where up to 50 per cent of an issue placed with financial institutions can be clawed back if there are enough offers from private investors through stockbrokers.

- *Introductions:* where a company already has a number of shareholders and applies to the Stock Exchange to introduce its shares to the market.

■ *Demergers:* where a company decides to hive off part of its operation into a separate company, often by offering free shares to existing shareholders. These shares are then listed separately on the Stock Exchange.

When to sell

Deciding when to sell a share can be every bit as tricky as deciding when to buy. Again, there are no fixed rules but stockbrokers recommend that you lay down some guidelines at the outset to avoid panic reactions.

Price alone is not a good guide. It is always tempting to sell when a share price starts to fall, on the assumption that gravity is at work and what goes down must keep on going down.

What you want to avoid is either holding a share so long that it has outgrown its usefulness, or selling a share at the drop of a hat before you have fully investigated the information. Good shares can, over time, either turn into mediocre shares or grow so much that they knock your portfolio out of balance.

> Deciding when to sell a share can be every bit as tricky as deciding when to buy.

There are those who argue that if you research a company thoroughly and buy for the long term there is no need to change your selection on a regular basis. While this is a very sensible approach for the private investor, clearly it is important to review your shares regularly and to ensure that your original assumptions still apply and that your choice of shares meets your specific requirements, particularly when your financial circumstances have changed.

Summary

■ Information and an investment strategy are important.

■ As an absolute minimum you should aim to hold ten shares. Twenty or thirty would be even better.

■ To avoid overexposure to smaller company risks, some stockbrokers advise a 50 per cent allocation to blue chips in the equity portfolio.

■ The cost of frequent trading can outweigh any modest benefits in share prices.

■ Each method of categorization tells us something about a share.

■ Size is important in terms of risk and diversification of business interests.

■ The FTSE All-Share is the professional investor's yardstick for the UK equity market.

■ SmallCap, Fledgling and AIM shares should be selected with great care as these may be under-researched and the market may not be very liquid, particularly if you want to sell.

■ Classification by sector helps define a share's characteristics in terms of market cycles but stock picking by this method alone is not recommended.

■ Knowing when to sell is as important as knowing when to buy.

chapter twelve

How to assess a share's value

- Important information from the company

- The selection process

- How to value shares

- Key indicators in practice

- Making comparisons

This is where you need to know your companies inside out. Each one may have particular characteristics which could make it a good addition to your portfolio or a non-starter, no matter how attractive it might be in general terms.

This chapter provides an introduction to some of the most important considerations in stock picking. Real enthusiasts can find out a lot more by consulting specialist publications. *A Guide to Stockpicking* by Gillian O'Connor is lucid, entertaining and highly recommended.

Important information from the company

By law a company listed on the Stock Exchange must produce a considerable amount of documentation for its shareholders (and, of course, the regulators and accountants, among others).

Typically, this will include two sets of profit figures at six-monthly intervals. The first set in the company's financial year is known as the interim results while the second set, the final results, is produced at the company's financial year end.

These figures provide a detailed analysis of the company's trading year and its profits or losses. Chapter 17 takes a closer look at the annual report and accounts, which are available to existing and prospective shareholders.

The *FT* London Share Service

A very useful source of information is the *Financial Times*' London Share Service. In the 'Companies and Markets' section you may see a symbol after the company name. A club symbol indicates you can obtain the current annual or interim report free of charge. All you have to do is phone a 24-hour number quoting the reference number provided in that edition of the *Financial Times*.

> A very useful source of information is the *Financial Times*' London Share Service.

The selection process

Every investor has their favoured selection process, so the following tips are intended as a guide only.

Once you have made your asset allocation decisions, your first step might be to decide which types of companies are suitable for your portfolio. This involves asking yourself some specific questions.

Do you have ethical or environmental views?

This topic is covered more fully in Chapter 13, but briefly, if you have strong views about the ethical or environmental habits of the companies in which you invest, you need to formulate a clear policy and screen out those companies which do not meet your standards.

A good source of information on this subject is the Ethical Investment Research Service. EIRIS maintains a database which you can use to filter an existing portfolio of directly held shares and collective funds. The service allows you to pick and choose the particular issues which concern you and to build your own screening process (full details in Chapter 13).

Be warned though. A fairly comprehensive ethical and environmental screening will eliminate over half of the FTSE 100 companies. This tends to weight ethical portfolios towards smaller companies which can provide exciting growth prospects but can also introduce extra risks.

What are your income needs?

> If a company's shares generate a high income, this does not mean the company is large or 'safe'.

Remember the earlier point about income and risk. If a company's shares generate a high income, this does not mean the company is large or 'safe'. Decide whether you are looking for value (that is, inherent value which in your analysis is not represented in the share price) or potential growth. Then consider the key indicators, for example yield, the price/earnings ratio and, where appropriate (for example with investment trusts), the discount to net asset value. These factors are discussed later in this chapter.

Are you cautious or can you afford to take risks?

This will depend partly on your attitude to risk and partly on your investment timeframe. Short-term investors should avoid risky companies because if the share price takes a tumble there will not be sufficient time to recoup your losses before you need the capital back. Longer-term investors can take more risks if they wish.

As a general rule of thumb, if you are very cautious and cannot afford to take big losses, stockbrokers recommend you stick to the well-researched FTSE 100 shares unless you happen to know a great deal about a smaller company. If you want some exposure to smaller companies, consider a collective fund.

Remember, however, that stockbrokers and the big investment managers all have their UK equity teams which tend to focus on the FTSE 100 companies. These shares are popular because they can be bought and sold easily and in large quantities. The large institutions simply cannot afford to own a substantial chunk of a smaller company because this would make selling very difficult. So, the point is, you are unlikely to spot anything of interest in blue chip companies that has not already been noticed by professional analysts.

Some brokers and managers also specialize in smaller companies but generally you stand a better chance pitting your wits against the experts in this market, particularly when you have a thorough knowledge of a company.

Are you a very active investor or do you invest for the long term?

If, nevertheless, you are an active investor you can take advantage of sudden changes to a company's prospects or ratings, which make a share attractive for a short period.

Clearly, frequent traders should avoid churning their portfolios as the costs of frequent purchases and sales will probably outweigh the advantages offered by a comparatively cheap share price. Equally, the less active trader should review the portfolio on a regular basis to make sure it is still achieving its targets and does not hold any duds.

Use your eyes

Not all research into companies has to involve complicated ratios. It is also possible – and in some cases makes a lot of sense – to use your experience to back up your selection process. This is not as difficult as it sounds. You can attend the annual general meeting, for example (see Chapter 19), or wander into as many branches of a retail company as possible. Boots, Dixons, Marks & Spencer, Safeway, Sainsbury and Tesco are all within easy reach.

Are they expanding, and if so are they attracting crowds of new shoppers as a result? Are both the quality and the price of products competitive or is the checkout queue full of grumbling shoppers planning to go elsewhere in future?

First-hand knowledge of a company can be combined with information from the annual report and accounts (see Chapter 17) to build up a more accurate and detailed picture which reflects a company's prospects.

Directors' dealings

One way to gain knowledge is to examine the number and value of shares in a company bought and sold by the directors. By law directors have to report any transactions in their own company shares to the Stock Exchange within five days. This information in turn is published by newspapers, including the *Financial Times*, and other specialist sources.

If the directors are buying in any significant quantity, in theory this indicates confidence in the

One way to gain knowledge is to examine the number and value of shares in a company bought and sold by the directors.

company's prospects. Of course, in practice it is not so simple, and you should be careful how you interpret the signals.

Sales are considered to be less indicative than purchases because they could just mean that the director needs some cash. However, purchases could also be used by directors as a smoke screen to give an aura of confidence when in fact behind the scenes all is not shipshape.

In conclusion, for the private investor, directors' share dealings can be of interest but they are not a reliable basis for an investment decision. Use the information as just one useful piece of the jigsaw.

Balance sheets

As mentioned, the annual report and accounts provide some very detailed information about the company and its prospects. Chapter 17 shows you how to read these documents and highlights the most important information to look for.

Is the company fashionable?

If something looks like a fad you may be better off avoiding it, even if the share price of certain companies or of a whole sector is rising. By the time the broker research and newspapers have identified a trend, you can bet your bottom dollar that the best bargains will have gone.

It is a sad but true fact that most trends are over by the time the private investors start piling in. Such is the certainty of this behavioural pattern that some professionals interpret private investor enthusiasm as a signal to get out!

Do you need a defensive position?

Some companies continue to plod along whether the rest of the market is dipping or soaring, while within each sector there will be companies which tend to do well at different phases in the market cycle. Whether you need to boost your holdings in companies that demonstrate certain characteristics at different stages in the economic cycle will depend on your view of the economy and on the long-awaited bear market.

If this is your concern you might also consider investing in asset classes other than equities. Gilts, bonds and cash might also be appropriate defensive weapons, particularly for older investors and income seekers, while in certain cases the use of derivatives can protect you from a sudden fall in prices. (See Chapter 14 on defensive measures.)

How to value shares

Once you have identified the shares which appeal to you and seem to fit well in your portfolio, it is time to take a closer look at the mathematics. (Alternatively, if ratios leave you cold then this is one of the best reasons for appointing a stockbroking firm which employs its own analysts!)

There are two basic exercises here. First, you need to make a general assessment of how well or otherwise the company is doing compared with the market as a whole, and of how well it is doing compared with its peers within the appropriate sector.

Check the company's recent history. There are several online sources of information (see page 174), while the *Financial Times'* London Share Service (see page 135) provides recent news stories about the company, profit forecasts and a five-year financial and share price performance review, among other details. Follow up this information with a thorough reading of the annual report and accounts, but remember that this document will be out of date and should be supplemented with any recent news.

The second exercise is to consider how the market views the share price. This is a more precise activity and requires an understanding of how professionals make their calculations.

There are several important yardsticks, some of which are discussed in Chapter 17. Here we consider the *dividend yield* and the *price/earnings ratio* (or earnings multiple), which are two common yardsticks when assessing a share's value.

We also explain various other ratios employed by analysts. For some companies it is necessary to look at the *net asset value* (investment trusts and property companies, for example – see Chapter 14). *Gearing* – or the amount the company has borrowed compared with what it actually owns – is also an indicator of the company's security and an investor's sensitivity to company performance. (Gearing is known as leverage in the US.)

The following guide explains the general principles behind the ratios. Ratios or yardsticks are best employed when making comparisons between companies in the same sector.

The dividend yield

This is a method of examining the income from an investment based on historic information. It is the annual gross dividend as a percentage of the market price. This shows the rate of gross income a shareholder would receive on an investment at that particular share price – rather like the way you might describe the before-tax interest paid on a deposit account. As with an ordinary deposit account, there is no guarantee that the dividend yield will be maintained.

The Barclays study (see Chapter 2) explains that a low dividend yield is associated with a high valuation for the stock market because it tends to be followed by low returns, whereas high dividend yields tend to be followed by high real returns, especially over the following 12 months.

The trouble is that we cannot assume that the past is a guide to the future. Much will depend on the economic environment. The Barclays' study explains:

> *A prolonged period of low inflation and sustained economic growth could maintain the stock market at levels that might appear high by past standards … The lesson of history is that the benchmarks for valuation can and do change.*
>
> *Investment is therefore more about gauging the direction of markets and hence appreciating the new valuation norms than relying on past guidelines. Changes in the economic environment are the main determinant of changes in valuation standards. In particular, changes in the inflation rate are a major influence on the markets.*

Key indicators in practice

Clearly, there are no hard-and-fast rules with dividends because they reflect the current state of the business. If the company is prone to follow the dips and peaks of market cycles (see Chapter 14), this will be reflected in the dividend payments.

That said, the larger companies, particularly the FTSE 100, tend to maintain fairly consistent dividend payments, partly because of their size and level of profits but also because they are expected to do so and it upsets professionals and amateurs alike if they chop and change. (The pension funds, for example, rely on a stream of income to pay the pensions and other benefits guaranteed to scheme members.) This does not mean that a FTSE 100 company will never slash its dividend – it's just not common.

As mentioned above, analysts tend to assume that a higher dividend indicates that the shares are likely to produce above-average total returns over the long term, while some very successful investors invest only in high-yielding shares.

However, a comparatively high dividend is always worth checking out to make sure there is nothing untoward going on behind the scenes. Look at

---

T I P

It is also important to look at the total return – that is, dividends reinvested plus capital growth. Reinvested dividends account for a substantial proportion of the total return.

---

the company's gearing (debt) to see if it is borrowing to shore up its dividend commitment. Very high dividends can be a sign that the company is in trouble.

You might also come across the term *dividend cover*. This is a stock market ratio which quantifies the amount of cash in a company's coffers. If the dividend cover is high this means the company could afford to pay out the dividend several times over from earnings per share. This indicates that profits are being retained for the business. When the cover is low it means the company had to struggle to scrape together the dividend announced and may even have subsidized it from reserves.

The price/earnings (p/e) ratio

This is the market price of a share divided by the company's earnings (profits) per share in its latest 12-month trading period. As a very rough guide, a high ratio means the market considers that a company is likely to produce above-average growth, while a low p/e ratio means the opposite.

P/e ratios are a handy benchmark to use when comparing shares of similar companies within a sector – two supermarket chains, for example. You also need to check the ratio against the average for other sectors because it could be that at a particular point in the market cycle, all shares in the sector in which you are interested might be marked down if they move in line with economic trends.

> P/e ratios are a handy benchmark to use when comparing shares of similar companies within a sector – two supermarket chains, for example.

Both the dividend yield and the p/e ratio are shown in the *Financial Times* share price pages (see Chapter 18) and in the *Investors Chronicle*'s company tables.

Net asset value

This is an important feature for certain types of company, particularly property companies and investment companies. Take investment trusts, for example. These are UK companies which invest in the shares of other companies. Investment trusts have a fixed number of shares which are subject to the usual market forces, so the share price does not necessarily reflect the total value of the shares the trust owns.

If the share price is lower than the value per share of the underlying assets, the difference is known as the *discount*. If the share price is higher, the difference is known as the *premium*. As a general rule, an investment trust share trading at a discount may represent good value.

Financial gearing

This is the ratio between the company's borrowings and its capitalization – in other words, a ratio between what it owes and what it owns. As a general rule you should find out why a company is highly geared before you invest, particularly if interest rates are high, because servicing the debts could cause a considerable strain on its business and profits.

However, consider the gearing in the context of the company's business plans. If interest rates are low, a highly geared company which is well run can make good use of its debts – for example to expand into a new and profitable market.

Another way of looking at gearing is to consider how the profits compare with the interest payments made to service the company's debt. The number of times profits can cover the interest payments is known as *interest cover*. Company analysts suggest that in very broad terms, a ratio of four times profits to interest owed is healthy. A ratio of 1:1 is definitely not.

The acid test

Analysts also refer to something called the *acid test*, which is a ratio of the company's current assets (excluding stock) to its current liabilities. The reason stock is excluded is that if a company is in serious trouble its stock may not be worth the full market value. Sales and auctions following a liquidation usually sell at knock-down prices.

Analysts reckon that the ratio ought to be about 1:1, so that if the company did get into trouble it could meet all its liabilities (including payments to bond holders and shareholders) without having to rely on whatever the liquidator could raise by selling off its stock cheaply.

Asset backing

This is another way of looking at what the company would be worth if all else failed and it went bust. In practice this test is a common exercise in the analysis of a takeover bid. The aggressor and the shareholders need to know the real value of assets per share in order to calculate an attractive price for the bidding process. Clearly, the acquiring company needs to persuade the shareholders either to transfer their loyalty to the new prospective management team or simply to grab the money and run.

The pre-tax profit margin

This is the trading profit – before the deduction of depreciation, interest payments and tax – as a percentage of turnover. The pre-tax profit margin is considered a useful guide to the company's general performance and the management team's competence because it reveals the profits earned per pound of sales.

The return on capital

This is the profits before tax, divided by the shareholders' funds, and indicates the return the company is making on all the capital tied up in the business.

Making comparisons

All these ratios and measures must be considered in the context of a full financial picture of the company. Obviously if you rely on just one or two, you may miss something very important or get an unbalanced view of the company.

Don't fall into the trap of thinking that just because the figures indicate that a company will pay out high dividends in future or will experience capital growth this will automatically follow. There are no guarantees. All you can achieve is an informed prediction.

> All these ratios and measures must be considered in the context of a full financial picture of the company.

Also, remember that the real point about ratios is to spot where the market ratings are inappropriate to the company's actual prospects. Clearly, to identify this situation you would require a good deal of knowledge about the company itself and to understand why the market has got it wrong.

In conclusion, for most investors it is important to use as many sources as possible for information about markets, inflation, the economy and individual companies. However, some successful enthusiasts adopt a very specific style. Chartists and fundamental analysts, among others, were discussed briefly in Chapter 2.

Summary

- Examine the profit figures, both interim and final.
- Read the annual report and accounts to assess the company's trading year and profits or losses.
- The *FT* London Share Service provides a wealth of useful data for very little outlay.
- Consider your ethical and environmental views before you buy.
- Consider your income needs but remember that a high income does not go hand in hand with security.
- Directors' dealings can shed light on a company's prospects but can also be used as a smokescreen.
- There are many important yardsticks to consider, including the dividend yield and price/earnings ratio.
- As an investor you will be interested in the total return – that is, dividends reinvested plus capital growth.
- Financial gearing is important, but consider the figures in conjunction with the purpose to which the company puts its borrowings.
- The acid test is a good indicator of whether the company could afford to pay bond holders and shareholders if it went bust tomorrow.

Ethical investment

- What is 'ethical'?

- Define your views clearly

- Performance

- Smaller companies

- The ethical stockmarket index

- Alternative investments

AT A GLANCE

In the last chapter we discussed the importance of maintaining a rational selection process when you build your portfolio of shares and collective funds. In this chapter we consider how to put your ethical and environmental views into practice as an investor.

This is not necessarily easy. If you ask ten people what they think is ethical you will get ten different answers. Ethical views, by their very nature, are subjective.

What is 'ethical'?

Ethical investment is where the investor's personal views dictate the type of shares actively selected and the type of shares screened out. Environmental funds can also be regarded as ethical. Here the choice of shares will depend on a company's environmental policy in terms of pollution, ozone depletion, deforestation and waste management, among other criteria.

Whether you make your own selections or you wish to set guidelines for your stockbroker, it is essential to be able to translate your views into a clear mandate.

Bear in mind that some stockbrokers are much more sympathetic than others when it comes to ethical investment. A stockbroker who takes the matter seriously will have considerable research at their disposal. A cynic will probably try to dissuade you, pointing out the significant constraints on the choice of shares and how this can undermine performance.

Don't dismiss the apparently cynical approach. Remember, any strong ethical views you may have are likely to go against your stockbroker's natural instinct to make as much money as possible for you. (After all, the firm's fees are usually linked to the size of your portfolio.) If you proceed with an ethical portfolio, make sure you set an appropriate performance benchmark and do not expect it to reflect the market movements as a whole.

The advent of the ethical stockmarket indices (FTSE4Good – see page 152) will make it much easier for your investment manager to assess a company's approach to the environment or social issues like exploitative wages, for example.

Define your views clearly

The first problem you must face is where to draw the line. You may, for example, feel convinced about the exclusion of tobacco and/or alcohol companies. But what about the supermarkets that sell their products? If you are opposed to gambling, do you include all the outlets that sell tickets for the National Lottery?

Some investors operate a positive screening process because they are keen on the groundbreaking research of the pharmaceutical companies in their wars against cancer and AIDS, for example. Others might exclude the same companies on the grounds that they carry out experiments on animals.

In an extreme case, even apparently innocuous products like National Savings and gilts can cause problems because they are effectively 'sold' by the government. The same government is responsible for the massive expenditure on armaments (and animal experiments), via public and private-sector agencies and universities. You must decide whether these factors outweigh the benefits of expenditure on education, health and social security.

Negative or positive ethical stance?

Ethical investment can be tackled as a positive or negative process. Some of the ethical unit trusts, for example, work in a negative way by excluding certain categories of investment. The major evils tend to be arms, alcohol, tobacco, gambling, animal testing, environmental damage and the payment of exploitative wages in developing countries. But the list could extend almost indefinitely.

Some ethical investors take a more proactive approach and want to encourage companies which are working towards some desirable goal – 'green' companies involved in recycling or environmentally friendly waste disposal, for example. Beware of 'green' labels – it's the next best selling aid to 'tax-free'.

Clearly, ethical investment is a complicated subject and is not helped by the difficulty and cost of obtaining sufficient data upon which to form a view about the business of ethical companies.

EIRIS

A good source of information on this subject is the Ethical Investment Research Service. EIRIS maintains a database which you employ to filter an existing portfolio or to build one from scratch, using your own selection of a wide range of criteria.

EIRIS was set up in 1983 by a number of organizations including Quakers, Methodists, Oxfam and the Rowntree Trust. It monitors the screening and performance of ethical and environmental unit trusts, so if you are interested in collective funds, this is the best place to start.

It also offers a screening process for direct equity investors. The simplest way to use EIRIS research is to request an 'acceptable list' – a list of companies which meet your ethical or environmental criteria. A 'portfolio screen' enables you to find out more about the shares you hold, while for the real enthusiast, EIRIS factsheets provide all the information in the database on the companies in question.

EIRIS researches over 1,000 companies. The screening options from which you can choose include:

- alcohol;
- animals (meat production and sale, leather/fur manufacture and sale);
- arms and sales to military purchasers;
- community involvement;
- corporate governance;
- directors' pay;
- environmental issues;
- equal opportunities;
- gambling;
- greenhouse gases;
- health and safety convictions;
- human rights;
- intensive farming;
- military contracts;
- newspaper production and television;
- nuclear power (fuel, components and construction of plants);
- overseas interests (wage exploitation in emerging economies, deriving profits from countries with poor human rights records);
- ozone-depleting chemicals;
- pesticides;
- political contributions;
- pornography;
- Third World involvement;
- tropical hardwood;
- tobacco;
- waste disposal;
- water pollution.

A broad-brush approach

In practice many investors settle for a broad-brush approach that eliminates the obvious villains but does not go into too much detail. Using the analogy above, this would exclude the tobacco companies but not the supermarkets which sell cigarettes.

This approach would also screen out the companies whose primary business is armaments but could leave you with companies with a minority interest in arms.

Probably some element of compromise is called for, but you have to decide how far you are prepared to go to identify the ethical stars and whether you are prepared to accept the resulting restriction in investment choice.

> You also need to decide whether to limit your ethical investment views to your private portfolio of shares and funds or whether to take it further.

You also need to decide whether to limit your ethical investment views to your private portfolio of shares and funds or whether to take it further. For example, if you are in a company pension scheme, what influence, if any, can you have over the investment aims of the pension fund?

The chances are, this would be limited to your freedom to express your views to the trustees. Ultimately, you could decide to leave the scheme and set up your own ethical personal pension plan, but this could be a very high price to pay because the company scheme is a valuable benefit for you and your dependants.

Performance

> **TIP**
>
> Critics of ethical investment say that performance suffers as a result of the exclusion of many major FTSE 100 companies.

Exclusion of many major FTSE 100 companies could result in overexposure to certain risks and you might not be in a position to reap the rewards of a boom in certain sectors – chemicals, engineering or pharmaceuticals, for example.

Table 13.1 lists the main companies identified by Chiswell Associates that could be excluded in this broad-brush approach and notes the proportion of the stock market as a whole which these companies represent.

Even this very basic approach excludes about 7 per cent of the stock market by value and the figure grows if you add animal testing, nuclear power, environmental damage and so on. For example, Chiswell points out, the pharmaceutical sector accounts for about 11 per cent of the stock market and the oil sector for a further 11 per cent.

Smaller companies

In practice, if you want an ethical portfolio you will find it ends up weighted heavily towards medium-sized and smaller companies, which are easier to assess and less likely to fall foul of ethical criteria than a widely diversified blue chip company.

Table 13.1 Large companies commonly avoided by ethical investors

Company	Stock market weighting %	Arms	Alcohol	Tobacco	Gambling
Allied Domecq	0.27		X		
Bass	0.37		X		
BAT	0.64			X	
BAe Systems	0.66	X			
Cobham	0.06	X			
Diageo	1.48		X		
Gallaher	0.15			X	
GKN	0.29	X			
Greene King	0.02		X		
Hilton	0.18				X
Imperial Tobacco	0.21			X	
Marconi	1.15	X			
Rank	0.05				X
Rolls Royce	0.18	X			
Scottish & Newcastle	0.18		X		
Smiths Industries	0.26	X			
Spirent	0.32	X			
Tomkins	0.07	X			
Wetherspoon	0.04		X		
Whitbread	0.16		X		
Wolverhampton & Dudley	0.02		X		
Total	**6.76**				

Source: Chiswell Associates

The full EIRIS screening disqualifies up to 60 per cent of the FTSE 100 companies. So how does the weighting towards smaller companies affect performance? Smaller companies have the ability to outperform their larger counterparts but they are inclined to be more volatile and must be selected with great care. When the FTSE SmallCap (the smallest 420 or so in the All-Share) does well it is often due to the stunning outperformance of a handful of companies rather than to outperformance achieved equally by all.

On a year-by-year basis smaller companies can look very volatile. In 1997, for example, most general ethical funds underperformed the market as a whole because they had limited exposure to the sectors that did well – in particular, banks (excluded because most lend money indiscriminately to non-ethical companies and countries with poor human rights records), integrated oils (environmental damage) and pharmaceuticals (animal testing and, occasionally, exploitation in tests on humans in emerging countries).

However, performance figures suggest that the long-term performance of the average ethical unit trust has been very similar to the average UK equity unit trust, albeit with a wider range of year-on-year returns.

Ethical indices

In 2001 FTSE launched a new series of indices under the FTSE4Good banner. These will make it easier for analysts and fund managers to identify companies that are responding to calls for social and environmental performance.

Alternative investments

EIRIS provides details of investments which it believes offer a distinct social value but which are not listed on the Stock Exchange. Examples include investment in a company that imports tropical hardwood from sustainable sources, or one involved in fair trade with developing economies.

The attraction here is that by investing in these companies you help them to grow. However, the downside is that the shares may not pay dividends and can be difficult to sell. Moreover, all the usual warnings about small companies outlined in the previous chapter apply with a vengeance.

Summary

- Ethical views are very subjective so it is essential that you give your stockbroker a clear mandate on exclusions.
- Decide if you want to screen in a positive manner or simply to eliminate the main culprits.
- Use the EIRIS screening service to draw up your list of acceptable companies.
- Be aware that an ethical portfolio will usually consist mainly of small to medium-sized companies.

Further information

Ethical investment: *Chiswell Compendium of Stockmarket Investment*, (Chiswell Associates, 4 Chiswell Street, Finsbury Square, London EC1Y 4UP. Tel: 020 7614 8000. *www.chiswell.co.uk*).

EIRIS Money & Ethics, a guide to collective funds, is available from EIRIS. Also available free from EIRIS are a guide to financial advisers who offer advice on ethical investments and a guide to fund managers and stock-brokers who manage portfolios with ethical constraints. Tel: 020 7840 5700 or visit *ethics@eiris.win-uk.net*.

To order the financial adviser and list of services for the private investor, phone 0845 606 0324. *Life and Pensions Moneyfacts* lists ethical and environmental life assurance and pension funds plus unit trusts. Contact Moneyfacts, Moneyfacts House, 66–70 Thorpe Road, Norwich NR1 1BJ. Tel: 01603 476100 to buy a copy.

chapter fourteen

Market cycles and how to beat the bears

■ How bubbles burst and markets crash

■ Your survival kit

■ How to read economic information

■ The market cycles

■ How to deal with bears

One of the most worrying aspects of stock market investment is the tendency of professional and private investors alike to behave like lemmings under certain economic conditions. Mass hysteria can trigger a dramatic fall in equity prices and even a full-scale crash.

In fact crashes are few and far between. Of more concern – and a much more likely contingency – is a slow slide into a long bear market. At the risk of over-simplification, a bear market is where share prices are falling, while a bull market is where shares are rising. If you are feeling bearish you believe share prices are due to take a tumble, while if you are bullish you believe the opposite.

Given the volatility of markets in recent years and the negative returns experienced by many private and institutional investors alike, this chapter concentrates more on the bearish aspects.

How bubbles burst and markets crash

To understand the lemming-like activity associated with a market crash (or 'burst bubble', as in South Sea and Mississippi) it is useful to consider the period leading up to these events to spot the common denominators. This is not a technical exercise. The most obvious features of the pre-crash market mentality are those well-known human characteristics greed and fear.

In a wise little volume called *Bluff Your Way in Economics* (Ravette Publishing, 1996), Stuart Trow describes the bubble mentality and what happened when the Mississippi bubble burst:

A speculative bubble occurs when people become obsessed with a particular investment. Fear plays a large part in the bubble's build-up, with investors desperate not to miss the boat and willing to buy at any price, completely disregarding logic.

History provides some examples which are both illuminating and, with the passage of time, quaintly amusing. Take the Mississippi Bubble. In the early 18th century, the Mississippi Company held a monopoly on all French territories in North America. The King of France and the French government were enthralled by the prospect of untold riches promised from the New World to the extent that they allowed the Royal Bank to issue bank notes backed not by gold or silver as was common at the time, but by shares in the Mississippi company.

> The most obvious features of the pre-crash market mentality are those well-known human characteristics greed and fear.

Trow explains: 'When the company crashed in 1720, the entire French monetary system was wiped out. Even people who had not invested in the company lost out as the bank notes became worthless.'

Britain escaped a similar fate, but nevertheless thousands of investors suffered terribly when the South Sea Bubble burst after the collapse of the extraordinarily speculative South Sea Company in the 18th century. This followed a period of extreme stock market activity so the sudden loss of confidence in one company appeared to trigger a loss of confidence in the entire market.

So we can see that market crashes are devastatingly indiscriminate. For tumbling along with the bubble company's shares go the share prices of some of the most respected companies in the economy.

Nor do markets always recover quickly – hence the need to take a long-term view with equities. The Wall Street Crash of 1929, for example, saw US stocks lose almost 90 per cent of their value. They did not regain their pre-crash levels until the mid-1950s.

Turning to more recent history, in October 1987 the UK stock market crashed. Although pundits still argue about the precise cause, the essential point is that once again greed and an unbridled speculative frenzy had overtaken logic. Investors continued to buy shares because they failed to see that the prices could not go on rising indefinitely.

The bubble mentality does not apply just to shares. Other assets are equally vulnerable. A similar frenzy was characteristic of the UK housing boom in the late 1980s when people paid silly prices only to find themselves in the negative equity trap once the housing bubble had burst.

We are just as vulnerable today as we were in 1987. Some would argue more so, owing to the increased number of leveraged investors, where people take out a loan in order to invest in the stock market. In fact, leveraged investors are more common than you might think. It sounds highly risky, yet this is precisely what an increasing number of home owners do when they arrange an interest-only mortgage backed by an endowment, Isa or pension plan. For this arrangement to succeed you need to achieve sufficient rates of return to service the loan and make a profit.

Your survival kit

To survive, and indeed thrive, during bull and bear market cycles you need a clear strategy. Fortunately, this is one time when private investors can score over the professionals because there are no clients waiting for their next quarterly figures and there is no pressure on you to follow the market trend.

Think first why you are in the market at all. If you are typical of most private investors, you will purchase shares for the long-term income and gains and will recognize that it is inefficient, time-consuming and costly to change or churn your portfolio on a regular basis.

> **T I P**
>
> So, in theory at least, if you invest in the right type of shares – even if it is at the wrong time – your portfolio should be able to ride market cycles. If, after careful research, you thought a company was worth investing in two weeks ago, its shares will still be worth holding today.

It will still pay out dividends, even if there has been a sudden switch from a bull to a bear market and capital growth has temporarily followed a few investment analysts out of the window. Provided you chose wisely in the first place, unlike the analysts, capital growth will return.

This logic is particularly sound when applied to blue chips because these businesses are themselves well diversified and represent a spread of risk across markets (and often continents too) within just one shareholding.

However, the logic does not necessarily extend to smaller, more speculative companies. In the run-up to October 1987, for example, some companies which came to the stock market were very speculative and considerably overpriced. They did not recover. In this case you would have got the worst of all worlds. You paid dearly for your shares in the first place, their price fell and they never recovered capital value. Moreover, you did not even benefit from a decent run of dividends.

Remember also that certain market sectors are cyclical. Shares in engineering or construction companies, for example, usually do well when the general economy is flourishing, while shares in consumer goods companies and retailers will do well while consumer spending is expected to rise.

So, while the following explanation attempts to demystify some of the economic jargon, bear in mind that these are generalizations only and that if you bought a tinpot company in the first place, no amount of economic alchemy is going to turn it into a crock of gold.

Tables 14.1 and 14.2 show the recent history of bull and bear markets in the UK.

How to read economic information

This is a *very* brief lesson in economic cycles and how they affect your shares. If it sounds theoretical, that's because it is. No sooner do we spot a clear trend for certain companies (categorized by size, sector, or some other characteristic) to behave in a certain way during a certain stage in the economic cycle than we are proved wrong. This is when we have to remember yet again that investment is an art, not a science. So, while it is useful to know the theory, never expect reality to mirror it.

First, let's get to grips with some handy vocabulary. The economic reports in newspapers rely on just a few key phrases and with these manage to mystify most of the people most of the time. Regard the jargon as no more than a form of shorthand and remember that it is one thing to understand the theory, but entirely another to interpret economic events correctly. Economics is a very imprecise science and the experts usually get it wrong, but nevertheless are paid a great deal for their views.

Table 14.1 A recent history of UK bull markets

	Months	Change %
9th November 1966 – 31st January 1969	27	106
27th May 1970 – 1st May 1972	23	100
13th December 1974 – 30th January 1976	13	179
27th October 1976 – 4th May 1979	30	145
15th November 1979 – 17th August 1981	22	55
28th September 1981 – 16th July 1987	69	365
10th November 1987 – 3rd January 1990	26	56
24th September 1990 – 11th May 1992	19	38
25th August 1992 – 2nd February 1994	17	70
24th June 1994 – 20th July 1998	49	99
5th October 1998 – 30th December 1999	15	47
Average	**28**	**115**

Source: UBS. Published in *The Chiswell Compendium of Stock Market Investments.*

Table 14.2 A recent history of UK bear markets

	Months	Change %
31st January 1969 – 27th May 1970	16	–37
1st May 1972 – 13th December 1974	32	–73
30th January 1976 – 27th October 1976	9	–33
4th May 1979 – 15th November 1979	6	–23
17th August 1981 – 28th September 1981	1	–22
16th July 1987 – 19th November 1987	4	–37
3rd January 1990 – 24th September 1990	9	–22
14th May 1992 – 25th August 1992	3	–22
2nd February 1994 – 24th June 1994	5	–18
20th July 1998 – 5th October 1998	2	–25
Average	**9**	**–31**

Source: UBS. Published in *The Chiswell Compendium of Stock Market Investments.*

The essential jargon

Before you start you need to understand what is meant by 'the economy'. Think of it in terms of old-fashioned home economics, which was all about making the housekeeping last for the entire week and boiling the Sunday roast bones for soup on Thursdays. Nowadays of course we all have credit cards so we don't have to make income meet expenditure – or at least not very often.

The economy is the financial state of the nation. The state of the economy tells us how much housekeeping is coming in and whether we are being prudent and boiling bones for soup, or borrowing in order to spend what we do not have.

Certain statistics, known as economic indicators, show the state of the economy at a particular time.

The most important economic indicators to remember are interest rates and inflation because whatever happens to the UK economy or the world as a whole, it usually ends up affecting one or both of these rates and this in turn has an effect on government lending policy and companies' performance, which in turn affect your investments.

Interest rates

Interest rates are important because they may directly affect the amount a company is charged for borrowing, although the extent will depend on the structure of the debt.

The Bank of England is responsible for setting short-term interest rates and uses them to curb or encourage spending. If we are all spending far too much ('we' being both individuals and companies), the Bank will increase interest rates to stop us borrowing to spend.

Likewise, if we are saving too much and not spending enough, the Bank might lower interest rates to encourage more borrowing and spending.

The Retail Price Index

The RPI is published by the Office for National Statistics every month and is the most common measure for inflation. It is calculated by constructing a so-called 'basket' of goods and services used by the typical household (based on a sample survey of about 7,000 households throughout the country).

The basket includes housing and household expenditure, personal expenditure, travel and leisure, food and catering, alcohol and tobacco.

You may come across other types of inflation. For example, underlying inflation is the unofficial term given to the inflation rate in an economy measured by RPI minus mortgage interest payments. Headline inflation is the full RPI including mortgage interest costs.

The impact on companies and their share prices

So how does all this come to affect your investments? Well, rising interest rates increase the cost of borrowing for the companies in which you invest. The profits of a company that is highly geared (that is, it has a high ratio of borrowing to assets) naturally will suffer if the cost of servicing its debts increases. This cost will be passed on to shareholders because it will lower the profits out of which it pays the dividends.

> The profits of a company that is highly geared (that is, it has a high ratio of borrowing to assets) naturally will suffer if the cost of servicing its debts increases.

At the same time the dividends available from equities will start to look uncompetitive to income investors, who will find better sources elsewhere if interest rates are high. High rates of interest on deposits are very appealing no matter what the rate of inflation is.

Moreover, high interest rates may damage a company's growth prospects because they will encourage a company to keep its spare cash in deposits rather than to take a risk and invest it in expanding the business.

Low interest rates have the opposite effect and can be good for companies because the cost of borrowing comes down, and the share value rises. So, although a fall in interest rates sounds gloomy because it follows news of high unemployment or a slowdown in the economic growth (usually expressed as the gross domestic product or GDP), for equity investors it can be good news.

Gilts react to fluctuations in inflation. A rise in inflation usually forces gilt prices down and therefore yields go up. This is because there is less demand for fixed-interest securities at these times. An improvement in gilt yields in turn can have a detrimental effect on the stock market because gilts become more attractive relative to equities.

The *public-sector borrowing requirement* (PSBR) also has an impact on the gilt market. The PSBR is the public-sector deficit – the amount by which government spending (including local authorities and nationalized industries) exceeds the income from taxation, rates and other revenues. One of the main methods the government uses to finance this debt is to sell gilts. If the PSBR is higher than expected, the price of gilts may fall, as there will be a greater supply.

The budget deficit is similar to the PSBR but includes income from occasional 'extraordinary revenue' – for example from privatizations of public-sector companies. So, a cut in the budget deficit or PSBR will be good news for gilts because supply is more limited and so prices rise. However, if the government has achieved the cut by increasing corporate taxation, this will be generally bad news for shares.

Other factors include the health or otherwise of retail sales, which obviously largely affects the retail stores and supermarkets, and housing starts (the number of new homes being built), which are generally viewed as a leading indicator of a future pick-up in the economy.

The market cycles

Everyone knows that the timing of investment decisions is critical. Getting it right is not easy though, even for the experts. As Mark Twain once said: 'October is one of the peculiarly dangerous months to speculate in stocks. The others are July, January, September, April, November, May …'

What follows is again a very brief overview of the main features of market cycles and their impact on share prices. Please remember, this is the *theory* and should not unduly influence your decisions.

If you have a large lump sum to invest then almost certainly you would be wise to drip-feed it into the market over a period of, say, six months to a year (see Chapters 11 and 12). In this case you would want to check how the economy is behaving at the particular times you invest in order to determine the effect on companies and sectors. But to switch from one sector to another in the hope of cashing in on the market's weakness or, even more risky, to keep one step ahead, is almost certain to fail all but the most dedicated full-time investor. Moreover, it will prove very costly.

Bear in mind also that all the institutional investors will interpret economic trends and anticipated changes in market cycles ahead of you, so share prices will reflect both the current and expected future trends. Trying to spot the change in cycle well before the professional analysts is not a game for the novice or indeed for anyone who values their capital. Some regard this activity as very scientific; others reckon it has nothing to do with informed investment decisions and everything to do with gambling.

Finally, remember that when it comes to shorter-term investment decisions all things are relative. Shares are worth the additional risk only if they offer returns well above what you can get from gilts, bonds and deposits, taking into account tax and the dealing costs. Always refer to the common-sense checklist on pages 44–5 before investing your money.

Phase 1: early stage of a recovery

At this point interest rates are high and economic activity is at a low ebb. Inflation is falling and interest rates also begin to fall – perhaps anticipated by rises in the bond markets. Blue chip companies begin to improve but interest in smaller companies is non-existent.

The first shares to benefit are interest-rate-sensitive shares such as banks, property, building and construction companies, some of which previously may have been very depressed. However, analysts view this as a dangerous phase because banks may regard their problem clients as more valuable if they go into liquidation. More companies go bust in the early stages of a recovery than in the depths of a recession.

Which shares may do well? Banks and well-financed property companies.

Phase 2: well into recovery

This is when the recovery gathers pace and short-term interest rates continue to fall. As a rule, at this point the recovery ought to begin to feed through into consumer spending. Share prices rise.

Which shares may do well? Retailers, car dealers, and manufacturers of durable goods, such as furniture, should begin to improve.

Phase 3: recovery

Interest rates have now reached the bottom and investors fear they may rise. At this point the market may see a major 'correction' to its generally upward trend.

Which shares may do well? Capital goods, engineering and other heavy industry.

Phase 4: heading for recession

The flow of money into the markets is rather like an oil tanker – it keeps going for quite a while after the signal to stop. So, the market makes sharp gains on heavy volume (in other words, there is a lot of money coming into the markets) despite rising interest rates. Smaller companies prove popular. Conglomerates, 'people' businesses and 'concept stocks' are all the rage. Commodity prices are booming and stoking up inflation for the future. (Commodities are raw materials and foodstuffs, among other items.)

Which shares may do well? While there will be money to be made in the stock market at this phase of the market cycle, it is important to recognize that this period is the one which generally will precede a fall. You might consider taking steps to anticipate a fall by gradually but steadily shifting some of your assets out of shares and into cash or other more defensive investments. Avoid trendy companies like the plague.

Phase 5: into recession

The stock market falls, possibly in response to an external event but in any event interest in shares dries up. Commodity shares might do well at this point because the underlying economy still has to turn down.

Which shares may do well? Defensive shares such as food, manufacturers and brewers will tend to do better than the market as a whole but may still drop in price.

Achieving a balance of sectors

No combination of investments will be absolutely suited to a particular phase of the market and even if you plan ahead you will find that each successive market cycle displays different characteristics. Nevertheless, a diversified portfolio is more likely to hold its value or at least limit the blows, compared with a portfolio that is weighted towards just one or two sectors.

How to deal with bears

If you are confident that your portfolio contains good-quality shares and are prepared to hold for the long term, you are probably as well placed as any to sit out a bear market. Even so, it is worth watching for opportunities to buy into quality companies at depressed levels.

If you want to take further action to prepare your portfolio for a bear market, there are certain steps you might consider. At all times keep in mind the aims of your portfolio.

Change your asset allocation

Gilts and bonds may be more appealing if you are concerned about the equity markets. If you are already looking for income then you might consider moving more of your portfolio into conventional gilts. Gilts and bonds are discussed in Chapter 16.

There are alternatives. You can try to spread risk by including more overseas equities in your portfolio. In addition you could build in a 'protection' by using more predictable investments (not all of which will be low risk), such as zero-dividend preference shares, National Savings Certificates and gilt and corporate bond funds. Remember though, if you invest directly, gilts and bonds are predictable only if you hold them to maturity. If you need to sell before this date you will find that these instruments can be almost as volatile as equities.

Derivatives

For a short-term bear market, derivatives can prove effective, if rather expensive.

There are three main methods. First, you can shield yourself from a fall in the market by buying a protected or guaranteed fund. Second, if you are a very active and confident investor you could consider using a bear fund to hedge your portfolio. Third, if you hold a large portfolio, you can buy derivatives direct.

> For a short-term bear market, derivatives can prove effective, if rather expensive.

The important point to note about these techniques is that the first is a comparatively safe, if expensive, bet for the medium to long term, provided you choose your fund carefully. The second and third methods – the bear fund and the directly purchased derivatives contracts – are tactical instruments which you can use to make short-term gains or to hedge your portfolio against a short, sharp drop in the market.

Protected funds

These are collective funds which limit the downside of an index and so protect your capital from severe loss.

It is important not to regard the guarantee as the investment goal. Provided the guarantor is financially sound these products will protect your capital in the event of a stock market crash.

So, the main attraction of these funds should be their potential for capital growth. In particular you should check whether your exposure to a rise in the market is limited to a certain percentage and whether the cost of the guarantee is likely to act as a significant drag on performance. Maximum growth is essential because these funds are mainly held in cash and so, unlike a true equity fund, the guaranteed fund does not benefit from reinvested dividends which, as mentioned before, on the FTSE 100 index typically account for half of the total return over ten years.

Moreover, many funds, particularly those offered by insurance companies, tie up your capital for five years. A better alternative is the type of protected unit trust fund which either has no specific term or has a quarterly lock-in.

The cost of the options purchased to protect your money is significant. Outside the protected/guaranteed market you can find a unit trust tracker fund with no initial charge and an annual management charge of 0.5 per cent. Compare this with the popular guaranteed Isas which charge an additional 1.5 per cent plus VAT per annum for the guarantee in addition to the 1 per cent unit trust annual management charge. Instead of a higher annual charge, some plans have an extra initial charge, typically of about 4 per cent.

Hedge funds

One way to try to achieve positive returns through a bear market is to invest in a hedge fund. These use different techniques to hedge against a falling market – in particular they borrow money to buy equities, sell and repurchase at the lower price. This technique is known as 'short' selling. Hedge funds are complex and risky vehicles – see page 73.

Bear funds

As mentioned at the outset, while protected funds can be a good idea for some investors provided the cost is not too high, very few private investors should consider dabbling in bear funds (authorized option unit trusts). The choice is very limited, so clearly managers do not see this as a boom business.

So how do these work? Essentially these funds operate like an index tracker in reverse. If the market goes up, the value of the bear fund falls, whereas if the market falls, the value of the bear fund rises.

The fund itself would be largely held in cash with a small proportion, say 5–10 per cent, used to purchase the derivatives that are sold when the market falls in order to make a profit. It is rather an oversimplification but basically, if the market falls by 10 per cent you can expect your bear fund to rise by 10 per cent. Since derivatives usually are far more liquid than the underlying conventional securities, this makes buying and selling easier.

These are highly specialized funds aimed at investors or managers who think they can make a profit from a short-term fall in the market. In this case you would be using the fund for tactical rather than strategic purposes. Your aim is to make a quick profit and then return to a portfolio of direct equities or collective funds based on active management principles.

Other investors might use them to hedge part of their portfolio. For example, if you have a significant holding in US equities and you fear a US bear market, you could buy a US bear fund so that when the value of your equities falls this will be offset by the rise in the value of the bear fund. This may be cheaper than selling your US shares and repurchasing them when the market looks set to rise again – and it avoids any potential capital gains tax implications.

Buying options direct

An alternative for the active and wealthy investor is to buy equity 'put' options which can be used either to profit from a fall in share prices or to protect the value of your equity portfolio against share price falls.

Put options give you the right to sell shares at a fixed price. So, if you buy a three-month individual put option at today's share price and in three months the underlying share price has fallen significantly, you stand to make a tidy profit. (There are also 'call' options which give you the right to buy shares at a predetermined price on a predetermined date in the future.)

If you want to hedge your portfolio, you can buy traded put options to match your individual equity holdings (options are available for about 70 leading UK companies) or, if you have a broad spread of blue chips, you can buy a FTSE 100 index put option. Again, if the shares plummet, or the index as a whole plummets, you can sell at the original higher price and make good your losses on your underlying shares.

The problem with buying equity options direct is that they are traded in whole contracts, which would normally represent 1,000 shares of the underlying security. This can cost several hundred pounds per holding, while to cover against a fall in the entire FTSE 100 index might cost several thousand pounds.

In conclusion, a put option can represent good value if the share price or the whole index goes down but it could prove to be a pricey insurance policy if your predictions of a market fall do not materialize.

Lower risk strategies

Alternatives to derivative backed strategies include with profits funds (see page 70) and, for pension investors, lifestyle strategies (see page 93). Both use asset allocation to protect your exposure to volatility, although this is achieved with varying degrees of success.

Summary

- Many private investors select shares for the long term and so, provided you choose well, you should be able to sit out market cycles.

- When share prices are depressed this might be a good time to pick up quality shares at bargain prices.

- Understanding the economic theory and indicators is very helpful but always remember that what happens in practice may be very different.

- Rising interest rates affect a company's ability to borrow and increase the cost of servicing the debt. This is likely to reduce profits and hence dividends.

- Gilts react to fluctuations in inflation. If inflation rises, gilt prices go down and so their yields go up.

- Be wary of investing directly in derivatives or derivative-based funds. This can be a useful tactic against a short-term market fall but can prove to be an expensive insurance policy.

Further information

ProShare's *The Private Investor's Guide to the Stockmarket* was the main source for the guide to economic cycles (*www.proshare.org*).

If you want to buy put options, contact your stockbroker or, for more information, contact the London International Financial Futures and Options Exchange (LIFFE) at *www.liffe.com*.

Buying and selling

- Administration

- Internet services

- Shares

- The mechanics of buying your shares

- New issues, privatizations and company share schemes

- Rolling settlement and nominee accounts

- Stock Exchange Electronic Trading Service

- Collective funds

- Fund charges

- Investments held within a Pep or Isa

- Information and dealing services on the internet

AT A GLANCE

This chapter covers the mechanics of buying and selling some of the most popular types of investments ranging from direct equities and bonds to collective funds.

Experienced investors are keen to arrange the best deals available and negotiation often pays off. For most people, however, it is important to keep a sense of perspective. Long-term investors may deal only a dozen times or fewer in any year, so the choice of shares is far more important than the saving of a few pence on transaction charges.

Administration

For those DIY investors who have not yet devised a sensible computer- or paper-based administration system, it is worth starting off with ProShare's 'Portfolio Management System', which will help you keep track of your transactions and calculate your profits and losses.

The ProShare system, for example, helps you to:

- record acquisitions and disposals of shares and fixed-interest stocks through the transaction log and profit/loss calculation record pages;
- account accurately to the Inland Revenue for the dividends and interest received;
- account to the Revenue for capital gains tax on disposals;
- keep track of your investments using charts provided.

Internet services

This section does not set out to provide a complete guide to internet services and trading but merely offers some tips on where to start. One of the best guides to online services is *E-cash* by Marianne Curphey (£10, published by Prentice Hall). This includes a run-down on the main online trading and information services. Marianne runs The Guardian Unlimited Money site at *www.guardian.co.uk*.

Also invaluable to the dedicated online trader is *The UK Guide to Online Brokers* by Michael Scott (Scott IT, 2000). There is an online version of the book at *www.investment-gateway.com*.

Many websites have share price charts and details of volume – that is, how many people are trading a specific share at the time – and a portfolio tool that allows you to see how your shares are performing. There will be a time delay for most information, although this is usually just a matter of 15 minutes. Real-time prices for shares usually hold for 30 seconds while you decide whether or not to buy.

Once you have registered, have opened an account and have a password, you can get access to the secure part of the site. The services are broadly similar but sites do try to differentiate themselves from the competition by including special features, so it is worth visiting a few to see which suits you best.

If you are after an online stockbroker, go to the Apcims website, which will help you search the register of members for this type of service. Apcims is at *www.apcims.co.uk*. Several other services list online brokers, and these include:

- Interactive Investor *www.iii.co.uk*
- Investors Chronicle *www.investorschronicle.co.uk*
- Financial Times *www.ftyourmoney.com*

Information sites

The following information sites (some of which also offer dealing services) might be of interest but are not in any way intended as a recommendation:

- BBC finance *www.bbc.co.uk/finance*
- DLJdirect *www.dljdirect.co.uk*
- E*Trade *www.etrade.co.uk*
- Market Eye *www.marketeye.co.uk*
- Hemmington Scott *www.hemscott.net*
- Charles Schwab *www.schwab-worldwide.com*
- UK Invest *www.ukinvest.co.uk*

Stock market news

- Bloomberg *www.bloomberg.co.uk*
- Financial Times *www.ft.com*
- Yahoo! Finance *www.yahoo.co.uk/finance*

Portfolio construction

Useful information sites, which in certain cases provide information on how to construct a portfolio, include:

- Motley Fool UK *www.fool.co.uk*
- Interactive Investor *www.iii.co.uk*
- UK Invest *www.ukinvest.co.uk*
- Investors Chronicle *www.investorschronicle.co.uk*

Fund prices and information

For collective funds *www.iii.co.uk* lists total expense ratios (TERs) which add up all the charges, fees and costs incurred by managers to give you a more complete picture of the total cost than you will find in marketing literature. For information about funds and their performance try:

- Trustnet *www.trustnet.co.uk*
- Micropal *www.micropal.com*
- Standard and Poor's *www.funds-sp.com*

A useful site for collective funds that includes details on the movement of star fund managers is *www.bestinvest.co.uk*.

Fund supermarkets

These are largely designed for individual savings accounts as they allow you to mix and match funds from different managers within a single Isa. Some offer a limited selection of funds. Bear in mind that investment trusts are not well represented on these sites. Isas are discussed in Chapter 7.

- Fundnetwork *www.fidelity.co.uk*
- Egg *www.egg.com*
- Fundsdirect *www.fundsdirect.co.uk*
- Interactive Investor *www.iii.co.uk*
- Tqonline www.tqonline.co.uk

Shares

How you buy your shares (this includes investment trust shares) will depend on the nature of the agreement you have with your stockbroker. If you have a discretionary or advisory stockbroker, the firm will act on your behalf once you have completed a terms-of-business agreement and paid a cash and/or stock deposit. The firm will automatically provide a tariff of charges.

The choice of stockbroker services was discussed in Chapter 3. You may prefer, and need, a traditional discretionary or advisory service from a stockbroker, but if you are looking for convenience and low cost and you have the expertise to make your own share selection, an execution-only firm will be adequate provided it offers a good combination of price and service.

> How you buy your shares will depend on the nature of the agreement you have with your stockbroker.

Typical costs if you buy through a stockbroker are 1.5–1.75 per cent per deal, with charges reducing proportionately as the value of the deal increases. Some execution-only services have a fixed charge for certain deals – for example for FTSE 100 companies.

On top of this you will pay stamp duty at 0.5 per cent. This is collected by the stockbroker and passed on to the Treasury. Where applicable you must also pay for the advice. This may be calculated on a time basis, or it may be an annual fee for unlimited advice or for a certain amount of advice, above which you would pay extra on an hourly basis. You may pay this advice fee separately or it may be included in the broker's commission charges.

The mechanics of buying your shares

To get an idea of the current price of the shares you wish to purchase you can refer to the *Financial Times* 'Companies and Markets' pages (or the financial pages of your preferred newspaper) to find yesterday's closing price. Online services will show more up-to-date information. This will be the mid-market price – that is, halfway between the bid and offer prices.

To remind you, the *bid price* is the price at which the market maker buys back from you shares or units in a collective fund. This is lower than the *offer price*, which is the price at which the market maker sells shares to you. The spread between the bid and offer price represents the market maker's fee or mark-up on the actual cost.

When reading the financial pages, remember the significance of the terms 'cum' (with) and 'ex-' (without). In most cases the shares will be *cum dividend* or occasionally *cum rights*. This means that you have the right as a shareholder to certain features such as the interim or final dividend payments, or the rights issue currently on offer.

Usually, if you have full rights the published details will not include the term 'cum'. If, however, the dividend or rights issue has been declared, for example, then as a prospective purchaser you will buy the shares *ex-dividend* or *ex-rights* – that is, without the entitlement to the dividends or rights issue, which instead will go to the previous owner.

The price of the shares will always reflect the status. (Chapter 18 explains how to read the financial pages, while Chapter 19 sets out your rights as a shareholder.)

To buy is quite simply a matter of logging on to your online dealer or picking up the phone and placing your order with your stockbroker. You must also state the price you wish to pay if you have a limit (this is usually a good idea for the smaller, more volatile shares) or you may ask the broker to buy 'at best', in which case they will obtain the best possible price at that time. Remember that if you opt for a postal service you have less control over the price.

When the shares are purchased you will receive a *settlement* note with the details of the number of shares and price paid per share. The total or 'consideration' is the former multiplied by the latter. The note should also tell you the time the deal was struck, so that you can check that the price was fair and accurate.

By the time you have taken into account the stockbroker's commission and stamp duty, plus the difference between the bid and offer price, your grand total is likely to be around 4–5 per cent more than the actual value of the shares purchased.

The stock market works on what is known as a five-day settlement basis, which means your broker must pay for your shares five days after the purchase date, and as an investor you have to make sure your money is there to meet the bill on time.

Many brokers now hold cash and shares on behalf of clients so they can settle claims rapidly. If not, check how your broker prefers to be paid. For example, will a credit or debit card be acceptable?

> Many brokers now hold cash and shares on behalf of clients so they can settle claims rapidly.

New issues, privatizations and company share schemes

As explained in Chapter 11, a new issue is when a company sells its shares on the stock market for the first time. These days very few new issues are sold directly to the public and where they are you will probably see large advertisements in the press which provide all the information you need to make your application.

Several stockbrokers have developed a special service which attempts to secure allocations for their clients. For details, request the ProShare guide *Brokers' New Issue Services* (see page 264).

Windfalls, as the name suggests, just drop into your lap. These are free shares from building societies and life offices which convert from mutual status – where they are owned by their members (the savers and borrowers) – to a public limited company. If you qualify for a windfall allocation when your building society or life assurance company joins the stock market, you will be informed directly by the company of your allocation and the date you can expect to receive it.

You should also be told how to buy more shares, if you wish, and how to sell if you do not want direct shares in your portfolio of investments. To help with the latter process the converting institution usually makes available a cheap and easy share disposal service for its customers.

Privatization issues are also relatively easy to understand. Usually, all you have to do is fill out a form and send off a cheque.

Company share option schemes are fairly straightforward and do not involve transactions in the secondary market. Once you have signed up for the scheme (see Chapter 9), the shares are automatically offered to you on a predetermined date. In most cases it is worthwhile buying even if you sell again immediately to make a profit.

Most of the FTSE 100 companies offer cheap dealing facilities to employees, usually through one of the major stockbrokers or banks.

The above cases are the exception rather than the rule. Most of the time you will be buying and selling in the secondary market and you will need a stockbroker's services to do so.

Rolling settlement and nominee accounts

In the past all deals completed over a two-week period had to be settled on just one day. The modern system, known as Crest (not an acronym), provides an electronic share dealing settlement and registration system which gives investors the choice to settle with or without the use of share certificates.

Crest works on a rolling settlement basis, whereby a transaction must be settled a certain number of days after dealing. This means that settlement is taking place every day.

Under five-day rolling settlement your stockbroker must pay for the shares you buy, or deliver the shares you sell five business days after the transaction was made. As an investor you must make sure that you supply your adviser with money or share certificates and signed transfers in good time to meet the deadline.

Nominee accounts

To help meet the deadlines you may be asked to use a *nominee account*. Under a nominee account you are still the *beneficial owner* of the shares but the share certificates are kept by the nominee company which is the registered shareholder.

This means that the nominee company's name appears on the share register for the companies in which you invest. The nominee company, which is legally separate from your stockbroker, can offer a range of services including administration and banking.

> To help meet the deadlines you may be asked to use a nominee account.

Nominee companies do not have to be authorized by one of the financial service regulators, so if you use a nominee account do check that your investment adviser accepts responsibility for any losses and has professional indemnity insurance to cover any claims of negligence.

If you would like to use a nominee account, ProShare suggests you ask your broker the following questions:

- What are the charges?
- Will I continue to get all information and other shareholder rights in those companies in which I hold shares?
- How often are dividends sent to me? Will they be sent immediately?
- If there are certain dates for dividend payments, will I receive interest on the money while it is held in the nominee account?
- Do you offer alternative ways of dealing in shares other than through the nominee?
- What is the limit on the insurance used to guard against fraud and other contingencies, including assets held in nominees?
- What compensation arrangements are available if the service goes bust? (Don't just rely on the Investors' Compensation Scheme – this only covers you up to £48,000 and is a last resort. The firm should have its own professional indemnity insurance, preferably of up to £1m per claim.)

You might also ask what happens to any perks offered by the companies in which you invest. Share perks are rarely a good enough reason on their own for investing, but some are nice to have – for example substantial discounts on retailers' goods. If your shares are held in a nominee account, you may not be entitled to the perks. This may not be the fault of the nominee. Some companies will exclude investors who hold their shares in a nominee account from perks and other shareholder rights. So check whether there are any additional charges for the basic shareholder information such as the annual report and accounts, and attending the AGM.

Finally, if you have windfall shares think carefully before you accept the converting company's nominee arrangements. In some cases the nominee account may allow you to hold only that one parcel of shares, so you would need a second nominee account to hold the rest of your portfolio of shares, which could make life unnecessarily complicated from the administration point of view.

The ProShare Nominee Code

To help investors who choose to hold their shares through a nominee account, ProShare has drawn up a code of practice for nominee operators to try to ensure that investors are clearly informed of the costs involved, the safety of their assets and the information they should receive from the companies in which they invest. (Not all stockbrokers subscribe to the code. If yours does not, ask why.)

The code requires nominee operators to:

■ disclose fully the charges involved, including withdrawals of holdings from the nominee account;

■ provide a clear statement of how your investments are protected while they are in the nominee account;

■ make arrangements, if requested, for investors to receive copies of the annual reports and accounts of the relevant companies in which they invest.

The code is voluntary but those firms which adhere to it are allowed to use the symbol. ProShare maintains and publishes a list of companies which subscribe to the code (for details about ProShare, see page 187).

Stock Exchange Electronic Trading Service

SETS was introduced in October 1997 and offers automated buying and selling of the top 100 UK companies (i.e. the FTSE 100, including those that have been in since October 1997 but subsequently have been demoted). Until the introduction of SETS all share transactions took place under a quote-driven service. SETS makes this market order-driven.

The quote-driven trading system uses market makers as middle men to quote prices at which they will buy and sell shares. This information is displayed on screens around the City. Brokers and market makers then speak to each other by telephone and agree trades.

The order-driven market is fundamentally different. Buyers and sellers enter their orders for shares and these are displayed to other market partic-ipants and executed against matching sales. This technology makes the intermediary role of the market maker redundant.

The traditional quote-driven system still applies to non-FTSE 100 companies, although gradually the FTSE 250 (the next largest 250 companies in the All-Share) will be added to SETS. Deals of under 1,000 shares (or 500 if the share price is over £5) are excluded from SETS.

Cost savings of SETS

In theory, for the FTSE 100 companies SETS should result in better prices for investors because the middle man is cut out. As a rough estimate, the average spread between the buying and selling price should drop from 0.6 per cent to 0.2 per cent, representing a saving of £100 on a £25,000 deal.

There should be other savings in future as the new electronic system helps brokers to cut down their paperwork and therefore reduce their costs. With luck these savings will be passed on to the customer through cheaper dealing commissions.

SETS has had its teething problems, particularly for execution-only stock-brokers, who have not always been able to secure a good price because they trade right at the very beginning or end of the trading day.

These teething problems should be overcome quickly, but in the meantime you should ask your stockbroker how they cope with the system and secure the best possible prices for your deals.

Collective funds

Buying unit trusts and insurance company funds is quite straightforward. All you have to do is contact your stockbroker or financial adviser or the financial institution directly and ask for an application form. If you feel confident enough to buy online, we list some useful websites on page 175. In most cases you have to register to get the most out of the service. This is usually free but there may be a charge for specialist information on some of the online share dealing sites.

Most major investment trust houses have their own share dealing service, set up by the management company to help its shareholders buy and sell. Effectively this is just an intermediary service between share-holders and the market makers. Nominee companies may also be used.

If you have some shares already you might consider a share exchange scheme, whereby you swap your direct holdings in return for the same or different shares, or a collective fund held within an individual savings account. This can be attractive if you have a few small holdings of shares – for example in the company where you work or from privatization issues. It could be cheaper to swap these rather than to sell them at private investor rates.

If your shares have recently come from an Inland Revenue-approved all-employee savings-related share option or profit-sharing scheme, from a privatization issue or from a preferential offer, you should not need to sell them if you wish to retain the same holdings within your Isa.

Fund charges

Most investment managers would argue, quite rightly, that good performance more than outweighs a high initial or annual management charge. However, since it is impossible to predict future performance it makes sense to ensure that returns are not undermined by excessive costs.

Unit trust and unit-linked charges

The 'initial' charge is deducted immediately from the original capital invested. It is calculated as a percentage of the lump sum – typically 5 per cent on a UK unit trust. The charge may include your adviser's sales commission, if applicable, which is likely to account for about 3 per cent. Many discount brokers cut the initial charge or eliminate it altogether. An increasing number of the low-cost index-tracking funds keep their charges to a minimum by eliminating the middle man and selling direct to the public. In this case there may not be an initial charge at all (but see 'The annual management charge' below).

> The 'spread' includes stamp duty, among other items, and as such represents the true purchase cost of the investment.

The initial charge does not reveal the full upfront costs, which instead are shown in the *bid/offer spread*. This is likely to be 0.5–1 per cent higher than the initial charge and in some cases the increase may be as much as 3 per cent. The 'spread' includes *stamp duty*, among other items, and as such represents the true purchase cost of the investment.

The annual management charge

This represents the cost of the investment management and administration and is deducted as an annual percentage of the fund, so its value grows along with your investment. The annual charge also includes the cost of any 'renewal' or 'trailer' commission paid to financial advisers – that is, the annual commission that is paid from year 2 onwards – typically 0.5 per cent of your fund value. Although included in the annual charge, your key features document will separate out the cost of the advice – that is, the commission paid – if applicable.

Most managers deduct the annual charge from income but some deduct from capital. The latter practice has the effect of artificially inflating the yield and has proved contentious in the context of corporate bond funds where it is likely to lead to capital erosion.

Although the initial charge often appears the most significant deduction, advisers warn that it is the compound effect of high annual charges that most damages your prospects of a good return over the long term. For this reason you should watch out for unit trust companies that have lowered or abolished their initial charges (often compensated by equally high 'exit' charges if you pull out early) and raised their annual charge. A typical exit penalty might be 4.5 per cent of your fund in year 1, 4 per cent in year 2, 3 per cent in year 3, 2 per cent in year 4 and 1 per cent in year 5.

Isa charges

Unit trust managers may add an extra layer of cost on top of the charges for the underlying unit trust to cover Isa administration. In practice, however, most managers charge the same whether or not the client invests through an Isa wrapper, and several companies reduce the initial unit trust charge to encourage Isa investment. The effect of any additional costs or discounts for the Isa wrapper must be shown in the key features document.

How to get the best deal

Unless you are an experienced investor, you should probably seek help from an independent financial adviser and accept that you will have to pay for the advice. However, there are opportunities for investors who know what they want and are looking for the cheapest way to buy.

Several companies offer a discount by cutting the initial charge when they sell direct or if the adviser has given up some or all of the commission.

Assuming you are satisfied that the timing is appropriate, it is easy and quick to sell units in unit trusts and unit-linked insurance funds. You can sell either your total holding or just some of your units, provided you leave sufficient to meet the manager's minimum investment requirements.

The documents you receive when you make your investment and the regular manager's reports should include an explanation of how to sell units. This may involve completing a special withdrawal form on the back of your unit trust certificate or it may be sufficient to send a written instruction. Alternatively you could ask your adviser to arrange a withdrawal for you.

Once the manager receives your instruction you should get your cheque, accompanied by a 'sell' contract note, within a week.

Income payments

If you elect to receive income you will do so on fixed dates each year or half year, or at whatever frequency you have agreed. Income is usually paid directly into your bank account unless you ask for it to be reinvested.

Investments held within a Pep or Isa

Selling investments held within a Pep or buying and selling within an Isa is quite different from the usual practice for shares and collective funds held outside the plan.

You can buy direct from the Isa manager or through your financial adviser. The adviser will handle all the paperwork for you and help you with any questions you may have. Some advisers are authorized to handle client money but many are not, in which case you must make out all cheques to the investment manager not the adviser's firm.

An increasing number of Isas and other collective funds are sold through advertisements in the press. Here the regulators insist that the company provide a considerable amount of detail so that you can make an informed decision. If you decide to go ahead you will deal directly with the investment manager. Once again, the idea is to eliminate the middle man and so to cut costs.

With an Isa, although the investor is the 'beneficial' owner, generally it is the Isa manager who is the title owner and who deals with all the paperwork. As an Isa investor you would not usually receive a copy of the reports and accounts of the companies in which you invest. You may not even receive the Isa manager's report unless you specifically request it. Some management groups make an additional charge for this information.

Information and dealing services on the internet

There are many guides to the internet itself and to the rapidly growing number of financial services available. Investors keen to explore these information sources should equip themselves with Stephen Eckett's *Investing Online*, which takes you on a conducted tour of the most important websites and includes a directory of the financial services on disk. As mentioned above, an excellent basic guide to internet services is *E-cash* by Marianne Curphey. (See page 187 for these books.)

If information is essential to successful investing then the internet is investors' heaven. As a method of communication, the internet does not have an equal.

Today, most large companies, financial institutions, stock exchanges, government departments, regulators and financial trade organizations have their own websites, so you can read all the latest news and trawl through the offers in the comfort of your own home.

Whether you want to investigate a company's trading history or buy shares and collective funds at bargain rates, the internet can help.

Wealth warning

What you must remember, though, is that the internet is like a high street. Indeed it has even been referred to as a galactic car boot sale, a description which conveys very well the potential dangers for the unsuspecting investor.

Bear in mind that although many of the companies that sell services or goods are regulated, the internet itself is not. Like the car boot sale, all the vendors display their wares in the most attractive way possible, but you are given no advice to help you spot the genuine bargains and pukka information. The websites are totally indiscriminate. The financial companies that offer value-for-money, well-regulated services jostle for space with the rip-off merchants and plain fraudsters.

So, use the internet with caution and check out any service very thoroughly before using it. Before you buy anything check the company's address and its regulatory status. The *Financial Services Authority* has a register of all firms authorized by the Financial Services Act in the UK (see page 262). If a firm is not authorized in the UK and you lose your money, there is virtually no hope of getting it back, and if the company goes bust, you won't get a penny from the UK's Investors' Compensation Scheme.

> The internet is like a high street. Indeed it has even been referred to as a galactic car boot sale.

Watch out in particular for the 'copycat' sites which fraudulent companies set up and then incorporate legitimate companies' web pages. The FSA urges internet users to take a close look at the website address. It may be very similar to one used by a well-known company but, for example, it might have an unusual overseas location or contain additional, misleading letters.

The internet makes it easy to buy goods and services from organizations in other countries without knowing that they are based abroad. A website with an address which includes .co.uk or just .uk doesn't necessarily mean it is based in the UK.

If in doubt the FSA recommends that you look up the firm's number in the phone book and call to double-check its site address. Don't rely on any phone number given on the site – the chances are that this will be false too.

The Consumers' Association also recommends that you print out relevant web pages, including terms and conditions, so that you have a permanent record in case of disputes.

What's available?

Bloomberg, Dow Jones Telerate, the *Financial Times* and Reuters all offer news services, market reports and price quotations to customer screens in financial institutions.

For the private investor, Stephen Eckett's *Investing Online* lists some of the highlights worth examining. Investors with an ordinary PC and local telephone call can:

■ view closing market prices for most markets in the world;

■ for many markets, view real-time stock prices and chart price histories;

■ in the UK and US markets, give orders via the computer;

■ monitor news stories on CNN and Bloomberg;

■ read online the daily financial papers, for example the *Financial Times* and *The Wall Street Journal*, and most other major newspapers worldwide;

■ monitor a portfolio's value and receive customized news stories relevant to the portfolio;

■ view real-time currency movements, with charts and technical analysis;

■ monitor the value and relative performance of collective funds;

■ read investment newsletters, which specialise in specific sectors;

■ consult online investment glossaries, read about futures and options, experiment with simulated trading programmes and receive buy/sell signals from online trading systems;

■ analyze company financial information and view corporate filings as quickly as the professional investors;

■ download economic data from government and bank databases and read regular economic reports and forecasts;

■ discuss all this with other investors online, and monitor what the market is talking about.

Many of these services are free.

Summary

■ How you buy shares will depend on the nature of the agreement with your stockbroker.

■ With the exception of shares from new issues, privatizations, windfalls and employee share option schemes, you will make your purchases in the secondary market.

■ Be prompt when your adviser asks for the money/shares and other paperwork necessary to settle a deal.

- Under Crest your stockbroker must pay for shares five days after the purchase date.

- Nominee accounts can help speed up settlement, but do check that your adviser accepts responsibility for any losses made by the nominee company.

- With collective funds, the annual charge is the one to watch on medium to long-term investments.

- Under rules which came into force in 1997, your adviser or plan manager must disclose the full cost of your funds in a pre-sale 'key features' document.

- For Isa investments, find out exactly what information you will receive – for example, if you want to see the company's or trust's annual report and accounts, do you have to pay extra?

- The internet provides a vast source of information, but before you use a service, particularly a dealing service, check that the firm is authorized with the Financial Services Authority (see page 262 for details of the FSA Central Register of authorized financial firms).

Further information

The Stock Exchange publishes useful leaflets on buying and selling shares and on rolling settlement and nominee accounts. For copies telephone 020 7797 1000 or write to The Stock Exchange, London EC2N 1HP. The Exchange's website is at *www.londonstockexchange.com*.

For a copy of ProShare's guide *Brokers' New Issue Services*, send an A4 SAE with a 39p stamp to ProShare New Issues Guide, Library Chambers, 13 & 14 Basinghall Street, London EC2V 5BQ. Also available from ProShare is the Portfolio Management System. Website: *www.proshare.org*.

The internet: Stephen Eckett's *Investing Online* is published by Pearson Education (including a financial internet directory).

E-cash by Marianne Curphey is published by Prentice Hall.

Selecting gilts and bonds

- Your guide to gilts

- How to assess the income from conventional gilts and bonds

- The safety of your investment

- Price fluctuations

- Index-linked gilts

- Corporate bonds

Gilts, corporate bonds and, to a much lesser extent, sterling foreign government bonds are popular with investors seeking income. In each case in return for the loan of your money the borrower, be it a company or a government, promises to repay the loan in full at a fixed date in the future.

With conventional gilts and bonds the borrower pays interest, known as the *coupon*, twice a year at a fixed rate. As a general rule, the longer the term, the higher the income – but also the greater the drop in the real value of your capital at the maturity or *redemption* date.

Both gilts and qualifying bonds (not convertibles and preference shares) are free of capital gains tax on any profits because the 'return' is classed as income. However, this is not a win-win situation since you cannot offset a loss against capital gains in excess of the exemption.

The merits of gilts and bonds were discussed in some detail in Chapters 2 and 10. Here we take a closer look at how to assess the income and the place these products have in your portfolio.

Gilt-edged stocks are bonds issued by the UK government via the UK Debt Management Office (DMO), an executive agency of the Treasury. If you buy gilts you are lending the government money in return for a tradable bond that promises to pay a fixed regular income for a specified period, at the end of which the government repays the original capital. Investors can buy and sell gilts throughout the lifetime of the issue.

Gilts play an important part in a defensive or income-producing portfolio although you might also look at corporate bonds to improve yields (see pages 55 and 198).

The DMO website (see 'Further information' at the end of this chapter) is an excellent source of information for private investors and maintains an up-to-date list of all the gilts in issue and sets out the relevant dividend payment and redemption dates for your gilts.

The most common category is the conventional gilt, which behaves like a conventional bond and pays interest twice a year. Index-linked gilts pay a dividend that rises each year in line with the Retail Price Index. The third category listed by the DMO – rump gilts – refers to issues where there are very few gilts in circulation (see 'Gilt jargon' below).

Private investors can buy gilts in several ways. You can purchase through a bank or stockbroker that is a member of the Gilt Edged Market Makers Association. If you buy and sell in this way, the bank or stockbroker will charge a commission for the transaction. Another route is through the Bank of England brokerage service direct (see 'Further information'), or via the Post Office.

Information on gilt prices and yields is published in the second section of the *Financial Times* on weekdays and in the first section on Saturdays.

Your guide to gilts

The DMO website provides a list of available gilts, an example of which is shown overleaf. The terms are explained as follows:

Name of gilt: The title of the gilt tells you the gross percentage of interest payable per £100 'nominal' of a conventional stock. The nominal value is the original purchase and redemption price. As gilts are traded between purchase and redemption, the actual price might be very different from the nominal value. The names of the gilts – for example 'Treasury' and 'Exchequer' – are of no particular significance but simply refer to the name of the government department that issued the gilt.

Redemption date: This is the date on which the government will repay the nominal value of the gilt. You are still entitled to a dividend on the redemption date.

Table 16.1 Stock in issue at April 5, 2001 (£m nominal). Total amount outstanding (including inflation uplift for index-linked gilts) = £281.80bn

Conventional gilts	ISIN codes	Redemption date	Dividend dates	Amount in issue	Amount in strip form (£) 2 April
Floating Rate 2001	GB0009997551	10-Jul-01	10 Jan/Apr/Jul/Oct	3,000	–
7% Treasury 2001	GB0008920588	06-Nov-01	06 May/Nov	12,750	–
7% Treasury 2002	GB0009997221	07-Jun-02	07 Jun/Dec	9,000	23
$9\frac{3}{4}$% Treasury 2002	GB0008986811	27-Aug-02	27 Feb/Aug	6,527	–
8% Treasury 2002-2006	GB0009028498	05-Oct-02	05 Apr/Oct	2,050	–
8% Treasury 2003	GB0000727205	10-Jun-03	10 Jun/Dec	6,999	–
10% Treasury 2003	GB0008986258	08-Sep-03	08 Mar/Sep	1,768	–
$6\frac{1}{2}$% Treasury 2003	GB0001633014	07-Dec-03	07 Jun/Dec	7,987	94
5% Treasury 2004	GB0006686579	07-Jun-04	07 Jun/Dec	7,408	11
$3\frac{1}{2}$% Funding 1999-2004	GB0003557229	14-Jul-04	14 Jan/Jul	543	–
$6\frac{3}{4}$% Treasury 2004	GB0008889619	26-Nov-04	26 May/Nov	6,500	–
$9\frac{1}{2}$% Conversion 2005	GB0008987777	18-Apr-05	18 Apr/Oct	4,374	–
$8\frac{1}{2}$% Treasury 2005	GB0008880808	07-Dec-05	07 Jun/Dec	10,373	32
$7\frac{3}{4}$% Treasury 2006	GB0008916024	08-Sep-06	08 Mar/Sep	3,857	–
$7\frac{1}{2}$% Treasury 2006	GB0009998302	07-Dec-06	07 Jun/Dec	11,700	26
$8\frac{1}{2}$% Treasury 2007	GB0009126557	16-Jul-07	16 Jan/Jul	5,930	–
$7\frac{1}{4}$% Treasury 2007	GB0009997114	07-Dec-07	07 Jun/Dec	11,000	24
$5\frac{1}{2}$% Treasury 2008-2012	GB0009032284	10-Sep-08	10 Mar/Sep	1,000	–
9% Treasury 2008	GB0009128371	13-Oct-08	13 Apr/Oct	5,441	–
$5\frac{3}{4}$% Treasury 2009	GB0003042636	07-Dec-09	07 Jun/Dec	8,827	16
$6\frac{1}{4}$% Treasury 2010	GB0008890161	25-Nov-10	25 May/Nov	4,750	–
9% Conversion 2011	GB0002215225	12-Jul-11	12 Jan/Jul	5,273	–
$7\frac{3}{4}$% Treasury 2012-2015	GB0009026674	26-Jan-12	26 Jan/Jul	800	–
9% Treasury 2012	GB0008938465	06-Aug-12	06 Feb/Aug	5,361	–
8% Treasury 2013	GB0008921883	27-Sep-13	27 Mar/Sep	6,100	–
8% Treasury 2015	GB0008881541	07-Dec-15	07 Jun/Dec	7,288	35
$8\frac{3}{4}$% Treasury 2017	GB0008931148	25-Aug-17	25 Feb/Aug	7,550	–
8% Treasury 2021	GB0009997999	07-Jun-21	07 Jun/Dec	16,500	35
6% Treasury 2028	GB0002404191	07-Dec-28	07 Jun/Dec	11,512	16
$4\frac{1}{4}$% Treasury 2032	GB0004893086	07-Jun-32	07 Jun/Dec	13,580	25
$2\frac{1}{2}$% Treasury	GB0009031096	Undated	01 Apr/Oct	474	–
$3\frac{1}{2}$% War	GB0009386284	Undated	01 Jun/Dec	1,909	–

Index-linked gilts	ISIN codes	Redemption date	Dividend dates	Amount in issue	Nominal including inflation uplift
$2\frac{1}{2}$% I-L Treasury 2001	GB0009065391	24-Sep-01	24 Mar/Sep	2,150	4,68
$2\frac{1}{2}$% I-L Treasury 2003	GB0009066365	20-May-03	20 May/Nov	2,700	5,84
$4\frac{3}{8}$ % I-L Treasury 2004	GB0009982686	21-Oct-04	21 Apr/Oct	1,300	1,63
2% I-L Treasury 2006	GB0009061317	19-Jul-06	19 Jan/Jul	2,500	6,13
$2\frac{1}{2}$% I-L Treasury 2009	GB0009071563	20-May-09	20 May/Nov	2,625	5,68
$2\frac{1}{2}$% I-L Treasury 2011	GB0009063578	23-Aug-11	23 Feb/Aug	3,475	7,94
$2\frac{1}{2}$% I-L Treasury 2013	GB0009036715	16-Aug-13	16 Feb/Aug	4,635	8,85
$2\frac{1}{2}$% I-L Treasury 2016	GB0009075325	26-Jul-16	26 Jan/Jul	4,965	10,3
$2\frac{1}{2}$% I-L Treasury 2020	GB0009081828	16-Apr-20	16 Apr/Oct	4,175	8,58
$2\frac{1}{2}$% I-L Treasury 2024	GB0008983024	17-Jul-24	17 Jan/Jul	4,820	8,41
$4\frac{1}{8}$% I-L Treasury 2030	GB0008932666	22-Jul-30	22 Jan/Jul	2,600	3,28

Rump gilts	ISIN codes	Redemption date	Dividend dates	Amount in issue	Central government holdings (DMO & NILO) at 3 March 2000
$9\frac{1}{2}$% Conversion 2001	GB0002215118	12-Jul-01	12 Jan/Jul	3	3
$9\frac{3}{4}$% Conversion 2001	GB0002213626	10-Aug-01	10 Feb/Aug	35	28
10% Conversion 2002	GB0009163782	11-Apr-02	11 Apr/Oct	21	11
$9\frac{1}{2}$% Conversion 2002	GB0002213733	14-Jun-02	14 Jun/Dec	2	2
9% Exchequer 2002	GB0003243242	19-Nov-02	19 May/Nov	83	66
$11\frac{3}{4}$% Treasury 2003-2007	GB0009050427	22-Jan-03	22 Jan/Jul	234	71
$9\frac{3}{4}$% Conversion 2003	GB0002214145	07-May-03	07 May/Nov	11	9
$12\frac{1}{2}$% Treasury 2003-2005	GB0009047936	21-Nov-03	21 May/Nov	152	49
$13\frac{1}{2}$% Treasury 2004-2008	GB0009052910	26-Mar-04	26 Mar/Sep	95	13
10% Treasury 2004	GB0009111021	18-May-04	18 May/Nov	20	5
$9\frac{1}{2}$% Conversion 2004	GB0002212982	25-Oct-04	25 Apr/Oct	307	90
$10\frac{1}{2}$% Exchequer 2005	GB0003270005	20-Sep-05	20 Mar/Sep	23	14
$9\frac{3}{4}$% Conversion 2006	GB0009021956	15-Nov-06	15 May/Nov	6	3
8% Treasury 2009	GB0009125369	25-Sep-09	25 Mar/Sep	393	62
12% Exchequer 2013-2017	GB0003252318	12-Dec-13	12 Jun/Dec	57	2
$2\frac{1}{2}$% Annuities	GB0000436070	Undated	5 Jan/Apr/Jul/Oct	3	0
3% Treasury	GB0009031211	Undated	05 Apr/Oct	55	5
$3\frac{1}{2}$% Conversion	GB0002212099	Undated	01 Apr/Oct	96	73
$2\frac{1}{2}$% Consolidated	GB0002163805	Undated	5 Jan/Apr/Jul/Oct	275	41
$2\frac{3}{4}$% Annuities	GB0000436294	Undated	5 Jan/Apr/Jul/Oct	1	0
4% Consolidated	GB0002163466	Undated	01 Feb/Aug	358	22

Source: Debt Management Office

Dividend dates: Conventional gilts pay dividends (also known as the interest or coupon) twice a year.

Amount in issue: This is a good indication of the liquidity of the market. Where there is only a small number in circulation the gilt may be difficult to sell.

Amount in strip form (conventional gilts only): This is where a gilt is split into its component parts so that you can buy the interest or the redemption payment elements separately.

Nominal including inflation uplift (index-linked only): This is the value of the amount in issue uplifted to take account of the retail price inflation increases that apply to this gilt.

Central government holdings: This is the amount of the gilt that is in issue but is actually held by the DMO or the National Investment and Loans Office (NILO). As you can see, in some cases the government holds virtually all of the remaining issue and in some cases it holds the lot.

Gilt jargon

Conversion: Table 16.1 shows a couple of 'conversion' gilts under the main 'Conventional gilts' heading but most appear under 'Rump gilts'. A conversion is where the Debt Management Office offers to exchange an existing gilt with a new issue. You don't have to accept the conversion but if you decide to hang on to your original issue it could end up as a rump and be hard to sell (see below). Don't confuse conversion with 'convertible'. There are no gilts with a convertible option in issue at present but this refers to a type of gilt that allows you to exchange one issue for another at a predetermined date.

Floating rate: The first entry in our table is the Floating Rate 2001, the only gilt of this type in circulation at present. This type of gilt, which is not considered suitable for private investors, is designed to mirror eurobond floating rate notes and tracks the London Interbank Bid Rate (Libid).

Gilt strips: Here gilts are divided or stripped into their component parts – that is, the interest and redemption payments. The interest payments can be bought and sold separately and can be treated as a gilt in their own right. Gilt strips are regarded as a particularly sophisticated product and are more volatile than conventional gilts.

Rump gilts: This refers to issues where there are very few gilts in circulation, perhaps following a conversion (see above). The point to note about rump gilts is that liquidity can be a problem owing to the small numbers.

Undated gilts: These gilts, also known as 'callable' gilts, have passed the redemption date set in the original prospectus. In most cases the DMO can give three months' notice to redeem undated gilts, so in many ways they behave like a three-month bond.

How to assess the income from conventional gilts and bonds

There are three important features of a bond or gilt to consider in this calculation:

■ The nominal value represents the amount you receive at redemption, when the borrower repays the loan. This might be different from the original purchase price (if the gilts were sold at auction) and almost certainly will be different from the price at which you buy during the life span of the gilt.

■ The coupon tells you the interest rate that applies to the nominal value throughout the loan period.

■ The market price is the current value if you buy or sell between the date of issue and the redemption date.

The coupon and nominal figures determine the level of interest, but the actual income return or yield will depend on the buying price. If the buying or market price of a gilt or bond goes up, the yield goes down because the coupon is a percentage of a higher price.

This see-saw effect is demonstrated in the following example. Suppose you buy a gilt which has a nominal price of 100 pence and the interest rate is 10 per cent. However, the price you pay is more than the nominal price at, say, 120 pence.

> The coupon and nominal figures determine the level of interest, but the actual income return or yield will depend on the buying price.

Remember, the interest is still only 10 per cent of 100 – that is, 10 pence. This means the yield on your investment is 8.33 per cent (10 pence as a percentage of 120p).

Now consider the reverse situation. If the nominal is 100 and the coupon 10 per cent and you buy at 80, you will still get 10 per cent of 100 pence, which is 10 pence – a yield of 12 per cent.

The safety of your investment

The important difference between gilts and other bonds is the nature of the guarantee. If you buy gilts, you are lending money to the UK government, which is the safest borrower in terms of creditworthiness. Other bonds might be guaranteed by banks, companies and foreign governments, so there is an element of credit risk. This is reflected in the slightly higher yield – often about 0.3 per cent above gilt yields – offered to compensate you for the higher risk.

One other point on the security of corporate bonds. Issuers and advisers may make much of the fact that in the event of a company's going bust, bonds rank before shares in the creditors' pecking order. Quite frankly, it is unlikely that a company in these circumstances could afford to repay bond holders but not shareholders. In most cases, therefore, it is wise to take this apparent additional security with a pinch of salt.

Price fluctuations

Gilts and bonds are traded during the loan period, and there are no guarantees on the return of capital if you sell before the redemption date. Prices tend to reflect the market's view on future interest rates. This means that although in general gilts and bonds are less volatile than shares, there have been many exceptions which prove that this is a flimsy rule to rely on. Over an exceptional period in 1994, for example, gilts fell by as much as 15–20 per cent.

Gilt interest is paid in arrears, so the price will also take into account whether a recent interest payment has been made to the holder – in which case the price is *ex-dividend*. If the interest is still to be paid, the price is *cum dividend*. The price quoted in the *Financial Times* is the mid-point between buying and selling prices.

Index-linked gilts

Many investors, particularly if they are retired, need to squeeze as much income as possible out of their assets and are reluctant to take any risks with the capital. Advisers usually recommend that even an income-orientated portfolio should contain at least some equity-based invest-ments. These, they argue, should provide some capital protection plus a rising income. (See Chapter 2 for the equity *v.* bonds argument and Chapter 10 for an example of the asset allocation of an income portfolio.)

If you are not comfortable with ordinary shares it may be worth consid-ering a halfway house, namely investments which offer a rising income plus some capital protection. The most common choice is index-linked gilts, which pay interest at a certain percentage above the rate of RPI. You might also consider index-linked corporate bonds (not many of these), *stepped preference shares* of *split capital investment trusts* (not many of these either), and escalator bonds, available from a few building societies, some of which were discussed briefly in Chapter 5. Here we just concen-trate on index-linked gilts.

Index-linked gilts guarantee to increase both the six-monthly interest payments and the 'nominal' or original capital investment due at redemption in line with increases in the retail price index.

Since the starting RPI used is eight months before the date of issue, the final value of the investment can be calculated precisely seven months before redemption (RPI figures are published a month in arrears).

Like conventional gilts, the index-linked variety is traded actively so the price and real value of the yield can fluctuate significantly between the issue and redemption dates. However, there is no inflation (RPI) risk for the investor in index-linked gilts other than the eight-month period without indexation at the end of each stock's life.

> **Many investors, particularly if they are retired, need to squeeze as much income as possible out of their assets and are reluctant to take any risks with the capital.**

Comparisons with other investments

So, how does this compare with the yields on equities? The income on index-linked gilts is guaranteed to grow in line with inflation over the years but cannot grow more quickly.

Equities, however, offer no guarantees, but historically have grown more quickly than the rate of inflation. However, under certain economic conditions, equities can lag behind inflation for a considerable period.

A similar comparison can be made with conventional gilts, which have a fixed income throughout their term.

Index-linked gilts have not offered particularly competitive returns compared with equities, conventional gilts or cash since they were first issued in 1981. They have provided a real return of 3.2 per cent in a period when the other two investment categories have provided real returns way above their long-term trend.

That said, index-linked gilts have provided their return for a much lower level of risk than the other two categories, and if you make adjustments for tax, their net return is a little more competitive.

Investors seeking absolute guarantees from their income-yielding portfolio may be tempted to put all their money in gilts. If you are in this position, go for a balance between conventional gilts, which offer a comparatively high fixed income but no index-linking of the capital value, and index-linked gilts, which offer a low initial income but protect the income and capital from rising inflation.

Corporate bonds

One of the most popular ways of holding corporate bonds is through a unit trust. Many corporate bond funds can be held in an individual savings account if you wish (see Chapter 7).

There is no reason why confident and experienced investors should not choose their own individual bonds provided you can achieve a sensible spread of risk.

For the bulk of bond funds which do not offer a guaranteed income it is important to view with caution the assumption made by some promoters that these funds offer investors absolute safety and security. With some funds your capital could be eroded to maintain high income payments.

> With some funds your capital could be eroded to maintain high income payments.

Rather like index-tracking funds, charges are a more significant factor in the corporate bond fund selection process than is the case with equity funds. With a bond fund the gap in performance between the best and the worst is small, so differences in charges are highly significant.

Charges and yields

The *Association of Unit Trusts and Investment Funds* (Autif) has co-ordinated the way corporate bond fund yields are calculated by its members so that managers show yields on a consistent basis.

The yield figures should not be examined without reference to the way the annual management charge is deducted. If this is taken out of capital, as opposed to the usual practice of deducting it from income, the yields will look artificially high. This may sound rather trivial but it is actually quite important. The argument goes something like this: it is not so unreasonable to deduct the annual charge from capital on an equity fund because the charge comes out of the capital growth (assuming there is some) rather than the original capital invested. However, for a bond fund there is usually no capital growth (unless it is partly invested in convertibles). This means that if the annual management charge is deducted from capital this will erode your initial lump sum investment. And if the manager wants to regain the capital base they have little choice but to take above-average risk even to achieve a reasonable return.

When it comes to the yield, there are two figures to consider: the gross redemption yield and the running yield.

- The *gross redemption yield* or 'projected total yield' takes into account both the income received and changes in the capital value of the bonds if they are held to maturity.

- The *running yield* or 'projected income yield' takes into account only the current rate of income received from the bonds. No allowance is made for any changes in the capital value, so this could mask capital erosion, for example if the annual charge is deducted from capital.

As a general rule the gross redemption yield is the better measure of the total expected investment return. A high gross redemption yield might be accompanied by a higher credit risk and often greater volatility in the capital value of the fund.

The running yield is important for investors concerned about the income they will receive. A high running yield is often associated with capital erosion.

Summary

- To assess the income of a conventional gilt or bond you need to look at the nominal value, which represents the amount you will receive at redemption, the coupon, which tells you the interest rate that applies to the nominal value, and the market or current price.

- Gilts are issued by the government and so represent the safest type of bond.

- Index-linked gilts provide an income which rises each year by a fixed percentage (e.g. 2 or 3 per cent) above retail price inflation.

- Consider the safety or creditworthiness of the borrower in order to assess the risk of bonds.

- If you are interested in corporate bonds, there is a good range of unit trusts which provide access to this market on a collective basis.

- If you buy a corporate bond unit trust find out whether the annual management charge is deducted from income or capital. Charges deducted from capital can lead to capital erosion.

Further information

Visit the Debt Management Office website at *www.dmo.gov.uk*. The site includes an online version of the informative *Private Investors' Guide*.

You can contact the Bank of England brokerage service on freephone 0800 818614 or go to the website at *www.bankofengland.co.uk*. A link appears on the DMO site.

Keeping your portfolio on track

Company reports and accounts

■ An accurate medical check

■ The format

■ Key ratios and statistics

■ Key questions

■ The balance sheet

■ The group cash flow statement/profit and loss account

■ Other financial information

■ Any questions?

Many new investors consider the annual report and accounts doubtless very worthy but nevertheless rather dull reading. In fact this can be one of the most important sources of information on a company's financial health. And in most cases it is free.

So, roll up your sleeves and have a go. Once you get a grip on the jargon, you will gain confidence in your abilities to interpret the key financial data.

Remember, though, by the time you see the annual report and accounts the information is already out of date. Regard it as a snapshot of the company's recent history. Clearly, you need to supplement it with more timely sources – for example from your stockbroker and from reports in the financial press.

An accurate medical check

Companies whose shares are traded on the Stock Exchange or the *Alternative Investment Market* must publish an annual report and accounts after the end of their financial year. (The financial year is not necessarily the same as the fiscal year, which runs from 6 April to 5 April.)

The report is sent to shareholders, who, as the owners of the company, want to see how well it is doing and whether it is meeting its stated targets. As a prospective investor you can also get a copy of the report either directly from the company or via the *Financial Times* share information service (see page 135 for details).

To guide you through a typical report this chapter uses examples from the retailer Boots. The choice is not in any way a recommendation – it merely helps you to see how the report is laid out. Not all of the references will appear in every annual report.

Two very useful guides to this topic are the ProShare *Introduction to Annual Reports & Accounts*, and *The Financial Times Guide to Using the Financial Pages* (see 'Further information' at the end of this chapter).

The format

Reports are divided into several sections.

■ *Chairman's statement:* Here the chairman draws attention to the positive achievements in the company's past year. This can be very helpful to the investor as it will highlight the major developments to date and opportunities which lie ahead. The chairman might comment on the dividend paid to shareholders and the company's strategic plans in terms of acquisitions.

As a general rule the chairman's statement will help you to gain a brief but important overview of the company's progress. Once you get past the first few paragraphs you are likely to find the stuff the chairman is less than pleased with. Watch out for expressions like 'in the face of very difficult trading conditions' and 'the strong pound currently affects the translation into sterling of overseas profits'.

The chairman may also take this opportunity to thank various key members of the board of directors and to announce important changes in personnel. If there are changes in the board's composition, find out why. (You receive the *Financial Times*' important news stories for the past 12 months when you request a report on a company – see page 135 for details.)

- *A mission statement:* This is not compulsory but companies find it helpful to remind shareholders what they are trying to achieve over the longer term. Although this can be rather woolly, it may help you make comparisons between similar companies and to set benchmarks against which you can measure a company's progress.

- *Chief executive's report:* This may not be written by the chief executive but there should always be a progress report on the company's or group's business operations and financial state of health.

- *Directors' report:* This is the regulatory and legal bit. The Companies Act requires the company to disclose a heap of information including – and this is of interest – who the directors are and their total remuneration including salary, profit shares, benefits and bonuses. More detail is provided in particular on their shareholdings and on their pensions – their most valuable company benefit after salary.

> The two most important sections of the report are the balance sheet and the profit and loss account.

- *Financial statements:* The two most important sections of the report are the balance sheet and the profit and loss account. For a snapshot view, focus on the following facts and figures: *size*; *profitability*; *ability to generate cash* (this indicates how lenders and investors view the company's strength and long-term financial health); *financial summary* (this shows whether the company is growing, treading water or shrinking).

Key ratios and statistics

The ratios analysts use to assess a company's financial strength were discussed in Chapter 14.

Some companies show certain key statistics in their reports and accounts. Otherwise it is quite easy to calculate them for yourself. Do remember, though, these are only useful in identifying trends and must be seen in the right context – for example in a comparison with other similar companies in terms of size and sector. Key ratios are:

- *The current ratio:* This is the value of the current assets divided by current liabilities and is used as a measure of liquidity – in other words, to show to what extent the company is solvent or up to its neck in debt.

A ratio of 1.0 simply shows that the company's books balance and that its assets are equal to its debts. If the ratio is less than 1.0 it shows that the company has more debts than it has assets to pay them. This is not always a bad thing, so do check the context. For example, a fast-growing company may have borrowed heavily but wisely to finance its expansion.

■ *The quick ratio:* This is the value of 'quick' assets (that is, easily converted to cash) divided by current liabilities and is similar to the current ratio but it takes a very short-term view. 'Quick' assets exclude comparatively illiquid assets such as stocks because they generally take time to turn into cash. Also excluded are trade debtors who are not expected to pay up within a month.

■ *The gearing ratio:* This is net borrowings divided by shareholders' funds and minority interests. The ratio is designed to indicate the extent to which the company relies on borrowings. If the ratio is low then the company profits are not vulnerable if there is a sharp rise in interest rates. A high ratio means that profits are at risk if interest rates rise sharply.

■ *Return on capital employed:* This is the profits before tax divided by the shareholders' funds and indicates the return the company is making on all the capital tied up in the business.

Key questions

The interpretation and importance of the above ratios will vary depending on the type of company and sector. As mentioned, in some cases it might be perfectly healthy for the company to have a high level of borrowing. So, check what is considered typical for the type of company and compare it with companies in the same sector.

> In some cases it might be perfectly healthy for the company to have a high level of borrowing.

You should also check past reports to identify important trends. For example, if the current ratio is falling this would indicate that the company's assets are falling in comparison with its liabilities and this should be investigated.

ProShare recommends that you consider the following five questions as you wade through company reports and accounts:

■ *Cash flow:* The cash flow refers to the funds available within the company that are generated by its operation rather than borrowed.

What you need to consider here is whether cash balances are rising or falling. This is very important because companies get into difficulties when they run out of cash and can even go bust, despite the fact they may appear to be making profits.

Does the ability of the company to generate cash from trading activities (this is shown as a separate line in the statement) indicate that it can convert profits into cash? If so, this indicates that the company can fund expansion and pay dividends to shareholders.

■ *Turnover and profit:* Is turnover rising or falling? How much of the change in turnover (compared with recent years) is due to the company's buying or selling businesses during the year in question? Are costs increasing or decreasing? If so, what particular overheads have changed? Are there any exceptional items in the sales or overheads this year which distort profit figures?

■ *Interest and borrowings:* Are interest charges up or down compared with last year? Is the change due to the size of the borrowings or to differences in interest rates? Are borrowings increasing or decreasing and what effect does this have on the company's gearing ratio?

■ *Taxation:* Is the tax charge rising or falling as a percentage of profits and why?

■ *Accounting policies:* Has the company changed its method of accounting and if so why? It is obliged to tell you and to show the effect of the change.

The balance sheet

Companies whose shares are traded on the stock market often own or control a number of other, subsidiary companies. They prepare group accounts which include a consolidated balance sheet showing the assets and liabilities of all the businesses combined, as well as the balance sheet of the parent company.

The style of presentation in annual reports and accounts differs between companies but they will all include a balance sheet which looks similar to the example shown for Boots (see page 216).

This is a snapshot of Boots at the end of its trading year. It shows you what the company owns – its *assets* – and what it owes – its *liabilities*. The figures are in £ millions. Negative figures are usually shown in brackets. The previous year's figures are shown for comparison purposes, although clearly you should look back over more than one year to identify any important trends.

The notes indicate that the company provides further explanations and a more detailed breakdown of the figures later in the report. 'FRS' indicates that the figures are provided in accordance with Financial Reporting Standards.

The balance sheet shows the following:

- *Assets:* divided into fixed or tangible assets (land and buildings, fixtures and fittings, equipment etc.) and current assets (money owed, investments and cash).

- *Current liabilities:* referring here to money the company owes and must repay within one year. It might also refer to bank overdrafts and any other debt, such as money owed to suppliers. A company's total assets should normally be greater than its liabilities – the surplus belongs to the shareholders, although part is also used to fund future expansion.

- *Net current assets:* this is the current assets minus the current liabilities.

- *Total assets less current liabilities:* this includes everything the company owns – not just the fixed assets.

- *Net assets:* several further items are deducted from the previous figures – in this case long-term borrowing and provision for any long-term liability. This calculation reveals the net assets figure – in other words, what the company is worth.

- *Capital and reserves:* this provides details about the shares allotted under the company's share schemes, and makes a reference to the profit and loss account.

- *Equity shareholders' funds:* this is the capital invested by shareholders, plus the profits built up over the years and not yet distributed as dividends.

- *Total capital employed:* this combines the shareholders' funds and equity minority interests.

The group cash flow statement/profit and loss account

This page of the company report and accounts (see page 214 for Boots) shows how much profit the company or group made and is no different in principle from totting up the costs of cakes and drinks and deducting this figure from takings on the door at the local school summer fair. If income exceeds expenditure, the company has made a profit.

Profit includes turnover, which is the total amount of goods and/or services sold throughout the financial year.

Losses include all the company's costs – labour costs, purchases and other overheads incurred in running the business.

Where the profit goes

Of course, not all of the net profit can be used by the company. First the Inland Revenue takes its share by charging, among other items, corporation tax, which is the company's equivalent of income tax on profits. Then there is National Insurance, which is effectively a form of taxation levied on salaries paid to employees.

> As a rule the FTSE 100 companies in particular try to maintain a sustainable dividend year in, year out.

Part of the remaining slice of profit is distributed to shareholders as *dividends* and the rest is ploughed back into the business. It is the directors of the company who decide how much of the profit should be paid out to shareholders, although their decision is subject to shareholder approval at the annual general meeting.

As a rule the FTSE 100 companies in particular try to maintain a sustainable dividend year in, year out. This is good news for investors who are looking for a regular stream of income, but the rule is not infallible.

Sources of turnover

Companies must also show how the turnover is divided between their different operations. To do this the group presents a consolidated profit and loss account which sets out the combined results of the parent company and all its subsidiaries.

Once again figures are in £ millions and negative figures are shown in brackets. This section includes:

- turnover;
- gross profit (turnover less costs);
- profit attributable to shareholders (the profit earned by and distributed to ordinary shares);
- undistributed surplus for the year (this is what the company intends to keep to build the business);
- earnings per share (the amount of dividend per share expressed as pence);
- headline earnings per share.

The last entry is an additional measure of earnings per share recommended by the Institute of Investment Management and Research (IIMR). It adjusts standard earnings to eliminate certain capital items – for example, loss on disposal of discontinued operations, sale of property and other fixed assets.

Other financial information

Auditor's report

This is the independent auditor's statement that the report and accounts comply with regulatory and legal requirements, in other words that they are honest and accurate.

Notes to the accounts

As mentioned earlier, there is a detailed breakdown of figures and further explanations in the notes to the balance sheet and profit and loss accounts. This is particularly useful in assessing the company's international operations – an important factor in its diversification and stability.

The notes may also include any contingent liabilities – for example a pending lawsuit.

Consolidated statement of total recognized gains and losses

This shows the total of all gains and losses made by the company, including exchange differences on foreign currency and re-evaluations of property.

Cash flow information

This shows how much cash has come into the business from customers, and suppliers, among others, and how much has gone out in payments to suppliers and employees, among others. This statement will also show such items as returns on investments, taxation, and capital expenditure.

Group financial record

This provides a summary of the most important figures for the past five years.

Shareholder information

This sets out the dates for key events such as the AGM, and the dates for dividend payments, interim results, interim dividend payments, and preliminary announcement of results.

Any questions?

If you have an advisory service with your stockbroker you could discuss any concerns or aspects of the report which you do not fully understand. But there is nothing to stop you going to the horse's mouth. Most companies have a special department for dealing with shareholder enquiries – just as they do for press enquiries – and they will be only too pleased to answer your questions, although if you are concerned about something you may well need to seek an independent analyst's view via your broker.

Whenever possible, do take advantage of your right to go to the annual general meeting. This can be an excellent source of information – particularly listening to the informed questions from the institutional investors and other private shareholders.

Summary

■ The annual report and accounts provide a wealth of information, but remember that by the time you see them this is already out of date.

■ The chairman's statement provides a good summary of past achievements and future strategic plans.

■ The two most important financial statements are the balance sheet and the profit and loss account.

■ In particular check cash flow, turnover and profits, interest and borrowings.

■ If you do not understand an entry ask the company directly (most large companies have a department for dealing with shareholders' queries) or ask your stockbroker.

Further information

ProShare's *Introduction to Annual Reports & Accounts* is available to private investors for £4.95 (for contact details see page 264).

Details for *The Financial Times Guide to Using the Financial Pages* are on page 265.

The Boots Company plc

Extract from the Annual Report and Accounts for the Year Ended 31 March 2000

Group Profit and Loss Account

For the year ended 31st March 2000	Notes	Before exceptional items 2000 £m	Exceptional items (note 3) 2000 £m	Total 2000 £m	Before exceptional items 1999 £m	Exceptional items (note 3) 1999 £m	Total 1999 £m
Turnover							
Continuing operations	1	5,189.4	–	5,189.4	4,912.4	–	4,912.4
Discontinued operation		–	–	–	132.2	–	132.2
Turnover: group and share of joint ventures	1	5,189.4	–	5,189.4	5,044.6	–	5,044.6
Less: share of joint ventures' turnover		(2.4)	–	(2.4)	–	–	–
Group turnover		5,187.0	–	5,187.0	5,044.6	–	5,044.6
Operating profit							
Continuing operations		573.3	(22.0)	551.3	561.4	(76.3)	485.1
Discontinued operation		–	–	–	2.7	–	2.7
Group operating profit		573.3	(22.0)	551.3	564.1	(76.3)	487.8
Share of operating loss of joint ventures		(8.4)	–	(8.4)	(1.7)	–	(1.7)
Total operating profit including joint ventures	1,2	564.9	(22.0)	542.9	562.4	(76.3)	486.1
Profit on disposal of fixed assets	3						
Continuing operations		–	12.9	12.9	–	4.6	4.6
Discontinued operation		–	–	–	–	0.3	0.3
Loss on disposal of business	4						
Discontinued operation		–	–	–	–	(318.9)	(318.9)
Profit on ordinary activities before interest		564.9	(9.1)	555.8	562.4	(390.3)	172.1
Net interest	5	5.9	–	5.9	(1.8)	–	(1.8)
Profit on ordinary activities before taxation		570.8	(9.1)	561.7	560.6	(390.3)	170.3
Tax on profit on ordinary activities	6	(168.8)	6.3	(162.5)	(169.9)	23.6	(146.3)
Profit on ordinary activities after taxation		402.0	(2.8)	399.2	390.7	(366.7)	24.0
Equity minority interests		(0.2)	–	(0.2)	(0.1)	–	(0.1)
Profit for the financial year attributable to shareholders	7	401.8	(2.8)	399.0	390.6	(366.7)	23.9
Dividends	8			(221.7)			(214.5)
Profit/(loss) retained				177.3			(190.6)
Basic earnings per share	9	45.4p	(0.4)p	45.0p	42.9p	(40.3)p	2.6p
Diluted earnings per share	9	45.1p	(0.3)p	44.8p	42.5p	(39.9)p	2.6p

Other primary statements of the group

Statement of Total Recognised Gains and Losses

For the year ended 31st March 2000	2000 £m	1999 £m
Profit for the financial year attributable to shareholders	**399.0**	23.9
Deficit on revaluation of properties	**(3.3)**	(1.4)
Impairment losses on revalued assets	**(1.1)**	(1.7)
Currency translation differences on foreign currency net investments	**(6.6)**	3.0
Other gains and losses	**–**	0.4
Total recognised gains and losses for the year	**388.0**	24.2

Currency translation differences include tax of £(0.4)m (1999 £(0.1)m)

Note on historical cost profits and losses For the year ended 31st March 2000	2000 £m	1999 £m
Reported profit on ordinary activities before taxation	**561.7**	178.8
Realisation of property revaluation surpluses	4.9	7.2
Difference between historical cost depreciation charge and actual charge for the year calculated on revalued amounts	0.5	1.3
Historical cost profit on ordinary activities before taxation	**567.1**	513.2
Historical cost profit/(loss) retained	**182.7**	(182.1)

Reconciliation of movements in shareholders' funds For the year ended 31st March 2000	2000 £m	1999 £m
Total recognised gains and losses for the year	**388.0**	24.2
Dividends	**(221.7)**	(214.5)
New share capital issued (net of expenses)	**0.5**	8.8
Repurchase of shares	**(95.4)**	–
Goodwill relating to acquisitions prior to 1st April 1998	**–**	(1.4)
Goodwill released on disposal of businesses	**–**	312.2
Net increase in shareholders' funds	**71.4**	129.3
Opening shareholders' funds	**1,780.2**	1,650.9
Closing shareholders' funds	**1,851.6**	1,780.2

Balance Sheets

31st March 2000	Notes	Group 2000 £m	Group 1999 £m	Parent 2000 £m	Parent 1999 £m
Fixed assets					
Intangible assets	10	**62.3**	64.4	**2.2**	2.8
Tangible assets	11	**1,799.0**	1,788.6	**609.9**	620.9
Investment in joint ventures – share of gross assets		**9.2**	7.1		
– share of gross liabilities		**(1.2)**	(0.9)		
	12	**8.0**	6.2	**14.8**	6.5
Other investments	12	**133.2**	106.2	**1,768.5**	1,717.4
		2,002.5	1,965.4	**2,395.4**	2,347.6
Current assets					
Stocks	13	**689.5**	722.0	**198.2**	200.1
Debtors falling due within one year	14	**404.5**	388.1	**229.8**	363.7
Debtors falling due after more than one year	14	**4.0**	14.1	**409.4**	273.2
Current asset investments and deposits	15	**379.2**	105.8	**357.9**	77.3
Cash at bank and in hand		**43.0**	32.2	**48.1**	10.6
		1,520.2	1,262.2	**1,243.4**	924.9
Creditors: Amounts falling due within one year	16	**(1,153.2)**	(1,191.0)	**(1,360.7)**	(985.9)
Net current assets		**367.0**	71.2	**(117.3)**	(61.0)
Total assets less current liabilities		**2,369.5**	2,036.6	**2,278.1**	2,286.6
Creditors: Amounts falling due after more than one year	17	**(489.2)**	(230.7)	**(767.5)**	(513.6)
Provisions for liabilities and charges	20	**(26.8)**	(25.3)	**–**	(4.8)
Net assets		**1,853.5**	1,780.6	**1,510.6**	1,768.2
Capital and reserves					
Called up share capital	21, 22	**224.8**	228.8	**224.8**	228.8
Share premium account	21	**252.5**	252.0	**252.5**	252.0
Revaluation reserve	21	**266.9**	276.2	**–**	–
Capital redemption reserve	21	**40.8**	36.8	**40.8**	36.8
Profit and loss account	21	**1,066.6**	986.4	**992.5**	1,250.6
Equity shareholders' funds		**1,851.6**	1,780.2	**1,510.6**	1,768.2
Equity minority interests		**0.5**	0.4	**–**	–
Non-equity minority interests		**1.4**	–	**–**	–
		1,853.5	1,780.6	**1,510.6**	1,768.2

The financial statements were approved by the board of directors on 31st May 2000 and are signed on its behalf by:

Lord Blyth of Rowington
Chairman

David Thompson
Deputy Chief Executive and Finance Director

Group cash flow information

Reconciliation of operating profit to operating cash flows		2000	1999
For the year ended 31st March 2000	Notes	£m	£m
Group operating profit before exceptional items		573.3	564.1
Depreciation, amortisation and impairments of fixed assets		154.4	140.1
Permanent diminution – QUEST		9.8	–
Loss on disposal of fixed assets, excluding properties		9.6	6.8
Decrease/(increase) in stocks, including property development stock		30.4	(78.3)
Increase in debtors		(8.3)	(55.3)
Increase in creditors		4.8	39.6
Other non-cash movements		(1.0)	(0.6)
Net cash inflow before expenditure relating to exceptional items		773.0	616.4
Exceptional operating cash flows	23	(19.3)	(14.5)
Cash inflow from operating activities		**753.7**	601.9

The cash inflow from operating activities includes £Nil (1999 inflow £0.4m) relating to discontinued operation.

Group cash flow statement		2000	1999
For the year ended 31st March 2000	Notes	£m	£m
Cash inflow from operating activities		**753.7**	601.9
Returns on investment and servicing of finance	23	**(9.8)**	(24.9)
Taxation		**(154.4)**	(112.4)
Capital expenditure and financial investment	23	**(221.0)**	(458.5)
Acquisitions and disposals	4	**(2.6)**	55.2
Equity dividends paid		**(216.3)**	(207.1)
Cash inflow/(outflow) before use of liquid resources and financing		**149.6**	(145.8)
Management of liquid resources	23	**(283.6)**	122.8
Financing	23	**172.8**	28.2
Increase in cash		**38.8**	5.2

Cash is defined as cash in hand and deposits repayable on demand, less overdrafts repayable on demand.

Reconciliation of net cash flow to movement in net debt		2000	1999
For the year ended 31st March 2000	Notes	£m	£m
Increase in cash		**38.8**	5.2
Cash outflow/(inflow) from change in liquid resources	24	283.6	(122.8)
Cash inflow from change in borrowings and lease financing	24	(267.7)	(19.4)
Movement in net debt resulting from cash flows		**54.7**	(137.0)
Loan notes issued as settlement for acquisition		–	(16.8)
Finance lease additions		(4.1)	(6.7)
Increase in value of investment in 10.125% bond 2017		18.2	16.5
Currency and other non-cash adjustments		(11.6)	(1.4)
Movement in net debt during the year		**57.2**	(145.4)
Opening net debt		(294.8)	(149.4)
Closing net debt	24	**(237.6)**	(294.8)

Net debt comprises cash, liquid resources, finance leases and all other borrowings.

Principal companies

	Principal activities	Percentage held by parent	Percentage held by subsidiary undertakings	Country of incorporation where operating overseas
Parent				
The Boots Company PLC	Manufacturing, marketing and distribution of healthcare and consumer products			
Subsidiary undertakings (incorporated in Great Britain)				
BCM Ltd.	Manufacturing pharmaceuticals and consumer products	100		
Boots Development Properties Ltd.	Property development		100	
Boots Healthcare International Ltd.	Marketing consumer products	100		
Boots Opticians Ltd.	Registered opticians		100	
Boots Properties PLC	Property holding	100		
Boots The Chemists Ltd.	Retail chemists	100		
Crookes Healthcare Ltd.	Marketing consumer products	100		
Halfords Ltd.	Retailing of auto parts, accessories and bicycles and car servicing	100		
Optrex Ltd.	Marketing consumer products	100		
Subsidiary undertakings (incorporated overseas)	Activities refer to healthcare and/or consumer products unless otherwise indicated			
Boots Healthcare Australia Pty. Ltd.	Marketing	100		Australia
Boots Healthcare Products (Austria) GmbH	Marketing	100		Austria
Boots Healthcare SA NV	Marketing		100	Belgium
Boots Healthcare SA	Marketing		100	France
BCM Cosmétique SA	Manufacturing and marketing (M&M)	100		France
Laboratoires Lutsia SA	M&M		100	France
Roval SA	Manufacturing		100	France
BCM Kosmetik GmbH	M&M	100		Germany
Hermal Kurt Herrman oHG	M&M		100	Germany
Boots (Retail Buying) Ltd.	Buying	100		Hong Kong
Boots Piramal Healthcare Ltd.	Marketing	60		India
Boots Healthcare Ltd.	Marketing	100		Ireland
Boots Healthcare S.p.A.	M&M	100		Italy
Marco Viti Farmaceutici S.p.A.	M&M	100		Italy
BCM Italia S.p.A.	Marketing		100	Italy
The Boots Company Japan k.k.	Marketing	100		Japan
Boots Investments Ltd.	Investment company	100		Jersey
Boots Trading (Malaysia) Sdn. Bhd.	Marketing	100		Malaysia
Boots Healthcare BV	Marketing		100	Netherlands
Boots Healthcare New Zealand Ltd.	Marketing	100		New Zealand
The Boots Company (Philippines) Inc.	Marketing	100		Philippines

	Principal activities	Percentage held by parent	Percentage held by subsidiary undertakings	Country of incorporation where operating overseas
Boots Healthcare Sp.z.o.o.	Marketing	100		Poland
Boots Healthcare Portugal – Produtos De Saúde LDA	Marketing		100	Portugal
The Boots Company (Far East) Pte. Ltd.	Marketing	100		Singapore
Boots Healthcare S.A.	Marketing	100		Spain
Boots Healthcare (Switzerland) AG	Marketing	100		Switzerland
The Boots Company (Thailand) Ltd.	Marketing	100		Thailand
Boots Retail (Thailand) Ltd.	Retail	49	51	Thailand
Joint ventures				
handbag.com Ltd. (Jointly controlled with Hollinger Telegraph New Media Ltd.)	Internet	50		UK
Boots MC Company k.k. (Jointly controlled with Mitsubishi Corporation)	Retail	51		Japan

Percentages relate to holdings of ordinary share capital.
All companies operate principally in the country of incorporation.
Minority shareholders have equity and non-equity holdings in certain subsidiaries incorporated in Thailand and India.

Group financial record

Profit and loss account	2000 £m	1999 £m	1998 £m	1997 £m	1996 £m
Turnover	5,187.0	5,044.6	5,021.9	4,578.0	4,124.7
Group operating profit before exceptional items	573.3	564.1	538.0	491.8	442.6
Share of operating loss of joint ventures	(8.4)	(1.7)	–	–	–
Total operating profit before exceptional items	564.9	562.4	538.0	491.8	442.6
Operating exceptional items	(22.0)	(76.3)	5.5	8.6	12.8
Total operating profit including joint ventures	542.9	486.1	543.5	500.4	455.4
Other exceptional items	12.9	(314.0)	(126.8)	26.3	1.4
Profit on ordinary activities before interest	555.8	172.1	416.7	526.7	456.8
Net interest	5.9	(1.8)	15.2	44.4	50.9
Profit on ordinary activities before taxation	561.7	170.3	431.9	571.1	507.7
Taxation	(162.5)	(146.3)	(169.2)	(178.3)	(167.1)
Profit on ordinary activities after taxation	399.2	24.0	262.7	392.8	340.6
Minority interests	(0.2)	(0.1)	1.3	0.5	–
Profit attributable to shareholders	399.0	23.9	264.0	393.3	340.6
Dividends	(221.7)	(214.5)	(203.4)	(586.1)	(176.4)
Profit/(loss) retained	177.3	(190.6)	60.6	(192.8)	164.2

Total recognised gains and losses	2000 £m	1999 £m	1998 £m	1997 £m	1996 £m
Profit attributable to shareholders	399.0	23.9	264.0	393.3	340.6
(Deficit)/surplus on revaluation of properties	(3.3)	(1.4)	(1.4)	27.1	16.0
Impairment losses on revalued assets	(1.1)	(1.7)	–	–	–
Currency translation differences	(6.6)	3.0	(13.7)	(10.4)	3.3
Other net gains	–	0.4	–	0.3	–
Recognised gains and losses for the year	388.0	24.2	248.9	410.3	359.9

Movements in shareholders' funds	2000 £m	1999 £m	1998 £m	1997 £m	1996 £m
Recognised gains and losses for the year	388.0	24.2	248.9	410.3	359.9
Dividends	(221.7)	(214.5)	(203.4)	(586.1)	(176.4)
New share capital subscribed	0.5	8.8	11.8	7.7	9.1
Repurchase of shares	(95.4)	–	–	(300.0)	–
Goodwill relating to acquisitions prior to 1 April 1998	–	(1.4)	(189.3)	(124.5)	(8.7)
Goodwill released on disposal of businesses	–	312.2	121.5	4.4	0.1
Scrip dividends	–	–	27.8	8.3	10.6
Increase/(decrease) in shareholders' funds	71.4	129.3	17.3	(579.9)	194.6

Shareholder information

Annual general meetings
The annual general meeting will be held at 11.00 am on Thursday, 27th July 2000 at the Royal Concert Hall, Theatre Square, Nottingham NG1 5ND. Each shareholder is entitled to attend and vote at the meeting, the arrangements for which are described in a separate notice.

The proposed date of the annual general meeting next year is 26th July 2001.

Dividend payments
The proposed final dividend (if approved) will be paid on 18th August 2000 to shareholders registered on 16th June 2000. Most shareholders excluding those in Canada and the USA) will have the opportunity to reinvest their cash dividend in existing shares bought on the London Stock Exchange through a dividend reinvestment plan. All applications to join that plan or amend existing instructions under it must be received by the company's registrars by 5.00 pm on 28th July 2000.

The expected dividend payment dates for the year to 31st March 2001 are:

Interim dividend	February 2001
Final dividend	August 2001

Results

For the year to 31st March 2001:

Interim results announced	November 2000
Interim statement circulated	November 2000
Preliminary announcement of full year results	May 2001
Annual report circulated	June 2001

Capital gains tax
For capital gains tax purposes, the market price of the company's ordinary shares of 25p each on 31st March 1982 was 112.5p.

Low cost share dealing services
Details of special low cost dealing services in the company's shares may be obtained from:
– **Hoare Govett Limited** (telephone 0207 678 8000) Hoare Govett is regulated by the Securities and Futures Authority.
– **Natwest Stockbrokers Limited** (telephone 0207 895 5489) a member of the London Stock Exchange and regulated by the Securities and Futures Authority.

Both Hoare Govett Limited and Natwest Stockbrokers Limited have approved the references to them for the purposes of section 57 of the Financial Services Act 1986.

Registrar and transfer office
Computershare Services PLC, PO Box 82, The Pavilions, Bridgwater Road, Bristol BS99 7NH. Telephone 0870 702 0148.

Company secretary and registered office
M J Oliver; The Boots Company PLC, Nottingham NG2 3AA. Telephone 0115 950 6111.
The Boots Company PLC is registered in England and Wales (No. 27657).

Analysis of shareholders at 31st March 2000

Shareholding range	Number	%	Total holding	%
1–500	55,293	38.54	13,545,739	1.51
501–1,000	34,977	24.38	26,706,869	2.97
1,001–10,000	50,243	35.02	127,837,540	14.21
10,001–100,000	2,372	1.66	58,353,312	6.49
100,001–1,000,000	449	0.31	135,842,703	15.11
Over 1,000,000	133	0.09	537,020,152	59.71
	143,467	100.00	899,306,315	100.00

Performance monitoring

- Portfolio measurement

- Collective funds

- Performance measurement services

- Periods of measurement

- A guide to reading the financial pages

To measure the progress of your portfolio and the individual shares and funds it contains, you need an appropriate benchmark or yardstick.

This chapter explains how to judge the performance of your portfolio in a realistic manner by comparing it with a range of suitable benchmarks, including recently launched model portfolios devised by performance measurement services.

Equally important is to set your own performance targets. These should be realistic and refer specifically to the objectives of your investment choice.

Don't feel daunted by the mass of detail in the *Financial Times*'s 'Company and Markets' section. This is the best starting point for any investor who wants to check the progress of a private portfolio of shares and provides a wealth of useful information once you learn to read the language. This chapter provides a quick course in how to interpret the pink pages.

An excellent book on this subject is Romesh Vaitilingam's *The Financial Times Guide to Using the Financial Pages*, published by FT Prentice Hall.

Portfolio measurement

Compare with 'safe' investments

Before you consider the performance of your choice of shares, it is always a good idea to check what returns you could achieve from comparatively 'safe' investments. For the purpose of comparisons with equities, a 'safe' benchmark would be one that offers a high degree of capital protection.

So, take a look at what the after-tax returns have been on 60 and 120-day building society postal deposit accounts and short-term and medium-term gilts. These benchmarks will reveal whether over these periods the returns from equities have been worth the additional risks to your capital.

Compare with inflation

There are several ways of evaluating the performance of your portfolio. The simplest measure also has the most serious drawbacks. This is an absolute benchmark. Let's say, for example, that retail price inflation is 3 per cent and your portfolio, which is designed to achieve a balance of income and growth, returns 6 per cent over the year. Considered in isolation you might be quite satisfied that your capital has grown by 3 per cent in real terms – that is, 3 per cent above the rate of inflation.

However, you might be less satisfied if you discovered that the FTSE All-Share (the main yardstick for the UK stock market as a whole) had risen by 12 per cent, or that many other investors with similar portfolio aims to your own had achieved 13 per cent.

The point to note here is that when markets are rising most professional investors and private amateurs can achieve what look like reasonable results. The real skill is in achieving above-average returns.

Compare with an index or peer group

> **T I P**
>
> To measure performance in this way you need a benchmark relative to an index or a peer group. As mentioned, the most relevant index for a portfolio of UK shares is the FTSE All-Share, which contains about 770 companies listed on the UK stock market.

If you specialize in medium-sized or smaller companies you might also measure against a more specific index such as the SmallCap (the companies in the All-Share which are outside the top 350) or the FTSE 250 (the largest 250 companies after the FTSE 100).

This is fine provided you keep the results in context. Whatever your specialization, it is always worth checking your progress compared with a broad benchmark. If you are in smaller companies and the best-performing shares are in the FTSE 100 you may decide that taking the extra risk associated with small companies isn't worth it.

For internet fans, the FTSE International website is packed with useful information about the FTSE indices (*www.ftse.com*).

Collective funds

With collective funds it is easy to measure against a peer group because the funds are categorized according to investment aim. For example, managed (a combination of equities, bonds and, sometimes, property), UK equity income, international fixed-interest and so on.

> Within the managed fund sector for life assurance and pension funds there is a wide range of different risk levels.

That said, within the managed fund sector for life assurance and pension funds there is a wide range of different risk levels, so check the asset allocation and the types of shares selected by the manager.

You might find, for example, that the manager has achieved an outstanding performance only because they took bigger risks than is typical for the fund sector as a whole. A good example is a managed fund where the manager invests almost wholly in equities when most of the other funds are, say, 70 per cent in equities with the rest in bonds and gilts to reduce risk.

It is also important to check performance on a discrete basis. Discrete results show year on year rather than cumulative performance. This is important because a good cumulative result over five years might hide an outstanding (possibly lucky) short-term performance followed by several years of mediocrity.

Unfortunately most published results for collective funds are cumulative, and discrete results are difficult to analyze without access to a major statistical database such as Standard and Poor's Micropal. However, your stockbroker or financial adviser certainly should have access to these statistics.

Performance measurement services

In the past private investors did not have any recognized scientific and independent performance measurement service comparable to what is available in the institutional market.

Recently, two independent services for private investors have been launched which both aim to provide a benchmark against which you can measure your portfolio. The first is the Private Investor Indices from FTSE International and the stockbrokers' association Apcims, and the second is from WM, one of the leading performance measurers in the institutional market.

The asset allocations for the three FTSE International indices (income, growth and balanced) were shown in Chapter 9. Two versions of each index are calculated. A capital-only index shows the growth in the value of the portfolio excluding income received; a total-return index assumes that gross income is reinvested in the portfolio.

You can use these indices, which are published in the *Financial Times*, in several ways:

■ to make a direct comparison with your own portfolio;

■ as the basis for a review of the asset allocation and structure of your portfolio with your investment adviser;

■ as a benchmark against which you can compare and assess the performance of discretionary stockbrokers.

The FTSE/Apcims indices show what happens to a portfolio which is run like a collection of index-tracking funds – each element representing the appropriate index for UK equities, various overseas equity indices, cash and so on. Clearly, the asset allocation of any 'model' portfolio is to some extent arbitrary, but given the expertise of the providers, this is as good a benchmark as any and will show whether your or your manager's deviations from the indices actually improved returns or undermined performance.

WM's service is slightly different. This shows whether you and/or your manager did better or worse than your peers, and is based on asset mix information from over 20 managers and brokers, combined with the returns on the appropriate investment indices over the quarter measured.

WM's choice of indices is as follows:

■ *UK equities:* FTSE All-Share.

■ *North America:* FT/S&P North America.

■ *Continental Europe:* FT/S&P Europe *ex* UK.

- *Japan:* FT/S&P Japan.

- *Pacific Basin ex Japan:* FT/S&P Pacific *ex* Japan.

- *Other international equities:* FT/S&P World *ex* UK.

- *UK bonds:* FTSE UK Gilts – All Stocks and Indexed All Stocks.

- *Overseas bonds:* JP Morgan Global (Non-UK) Traded Index (Unh'd).

- *Cash/Other:* LIBID 7-Day.

Both services are very useful, but remember that benchmarks are only intended to provide guidelines and should not be regarded as an absolute measure of performance. The FTSE indices, for example, are designed to relate to the average UK-based investor with a sterling-denominated pool of savings.

FTSE International point out that investors may have potential capital gains tax liabilities which must be taken into account, as must any advisory fees. Also, investors may hold particular stocks for a variety of reasons.

Details of both services are provided in 'Further information' at the end of the chapter.

Collective funds

The websites that provide useful information on funds are listed on page 174. Chase de Vere publishes an annual guide to Isas and updates its performance supplement every six months (*www.chasedevere.co.uk*).

> If you have the time, you could build up a more detailed record of performance fluctuations by monitoring your fund's price changes.

Another excellent source of informed commentary on Isa performance is Bestinvest. In addition to its recommendations, in a refreshingly brisk manner the company also publishes a *Spot the Dog* guide which lists all the funds you should consider avoiding or selling (see page 174).

For investment trusts probably the most useful source of performance data is the monthly information sheet (MIS) from the Association of Investment Trust Companies, which shows the results of £100 invested in each investment trust share and the performance of the underlying net assets. The latter is considered a far better measure of the company's investment expertise because it disregards the impact of market forces on the company's share price.

If you have the time, you could build up a more detailed record of performance fluctuations by monitoring your fund's price changes, although this would not show the impact of dividend reinvestment. With unit trusts, for example, your unit trust manager should send you a quarterly or six-monthly valuation which will show the unit price. For more frequent updates you can check the price in the authorized unit trusts pages in the *Financial Times*. On Saturdays the information appears in the 'Weekend Money' section, while on weekdays you will find these figures in the 'Companies and Markets' section.

Compare percentage price changes with changes in an appropriate benchmark. Again, the FTSE All-Share is the best general index for UK equity-based unit trusts.

If you find reading the pink pages rather daunting, a basic description of the column headings is provided in the *FT* itself, but a more detailed source is the *Financial Times Guide to Using the Financial Pages* (see 'Recommended reading' on page 265).

Personal pension plan performance is covered by surveys in *Money Management*, among other specialist publications. Your adviser will probably also subscribe to one of the top consultants' annual surveys, which provide detailed analysis of performance and how that performance was achieved and record whether the team responsible is still in place. The surveys also consider the strength of the company and the flexibility of the contract.

Periods of measurement

The cost of buying shares, whether direct or through a unit or investment trust, combined with the short-term volatility of markets, has meant that performance tends to be measured over the medium to long term – typically over a minimum period of five years.

While this is a sensible approach for private investors it should be backed up by more regular monitoring, which will pick up on changes in fund management style or personnel.

With equity investments clearly past performance is an imperfect guide to the future – whether you hold them directly or through collective funds. However, performance can give a good indication of a share's prospects where it is examined in conjunction with other essential data about the company and its investment processes.

Once you have identified the funds that are appropriate in terms of asset class and allocation, it is important to assess different managers' investment styles. For example, was the performance achieved through a consistent ability to pick the right stocks or did the total returns rely on occasional periods of outperformance based on a high-risk strategy?

It is also important that you or your adviser keep track of the actual management team responsible for the performance. Investment teams have a nasty habit of defecting to rival companies, and, if this happens in an investment house where star managers rule the roost, you might consider a similar move. Very sensibly, some investment houses keep a tight lid on individual managers and insist on a team mentality which provides a more stable environment.

A guide to reading the financial pages

The sections below on 'How to read the figures' were drawn from *Using the Financial Pages* and other guides mentioned at the end of this chapter, plus details provided in the *Financial Times* 'Guide to The London Share Service', which is published at the end of the share prices in the 'Companies and Markets' section. For investment trust performance data, the AITC was the main source.

Financial Times services

The *Financial Times* London Share Service includes various investor services indicated by a symbol after the company name. A club symbol indicates you can obtain the current annual or interim report free of charge. All you have to do is phone a 24-hour number quoting the reference number provided in that edition of the *Financial Times*.

Up-to-the-second share prices are available from the *Financial Times* Cityline service: *www.ftcityline.com* or call 020 7873 4378.

Share price information: the London Share Service

Share prices, including investment trusts, are quoted each day in the *Financial Times* 'Companies and Markets' section. This includes companies in the All-Share, the Alternative Investment Market (the market for new, smaller companies) and the foreign companies.

How to read the figures The column headings used in the *Financial Times* are shown in brackets (Figure 18.1).

- *Name and notes (Notes):* The first column lists the company name or its abbreviation. The various symbols represent particular features of its shares. For example, a diamond indicates a merger, bid or reorganization in progress. A club symbol indicates that there is a free annual or interim report available. A heart symbol indicates a stock not officially listed in the UK. Many shares of overseas mining companies fall into this category. A spade symbol indicates an unregulated collective investment scheme.

These are some of the main symbols used but for a comprehensive list refer to the 'Guide to The London Share Service' in the 'Companies and Markets' section of the *Financial Times*.

■ *Market price (Price):* The second column shows the average (or mid-price) of the best buying and selling prices in pence quoted by market makers (the financial institutions that actually buy and sell shares) at the 4.30pm close of the market on the previous trading day. If trading in a share has been suspended, perhaps because the company in question is involved in a takeover, the figure shown is the price at suspension and this is indicated by a hash symbol (#). The letters 'xd' following a price mean ex-dividend and indicate that a dividend has been announced recently but buyers of the shares will not be entitled to receive it.

■ *Price change (+ or –):* The third column gives the change in the closing price compared with the end of the previous trading day.

■ *Previous price movements (52 week high/low):* Columns four and five show the highest and lowest prices recorded for the stock over the past year.

■ *Trading volume (Volume '000s):* This shows the trading volume at the end of each day and is a good indication of a share's liquidity. Both buying and selling figures are counted, so divide by 2 to get the number of shares which changed hands.

■ *Dividend yield (Yield):* Column seven shows the percentage return on the share. It is calculated by dividing the dividend by the current share price.

■ *Price/earnings ratio (P/E):* The final column is the market price of the share divided by the company's earnings (profits) per share in its latest 12-month trading period. In effect this is a measure of investor confidence, since it compares the price of a stock with the amount the company is earning in profits. Generally, the higher the figure, the higher the confidence, but you should only measure against companies in the same sector.

Yields and p/e ratios move in opposite directions. If the share price rises, since the dividend remains the same, the dividend yield falls. Also, if the share price rises, since the earnings per share are constant, the p/e ratio increases. Expect a big change in these figures when important company announcements are made on earnings and dividends.

Figure 18.1 Example share price

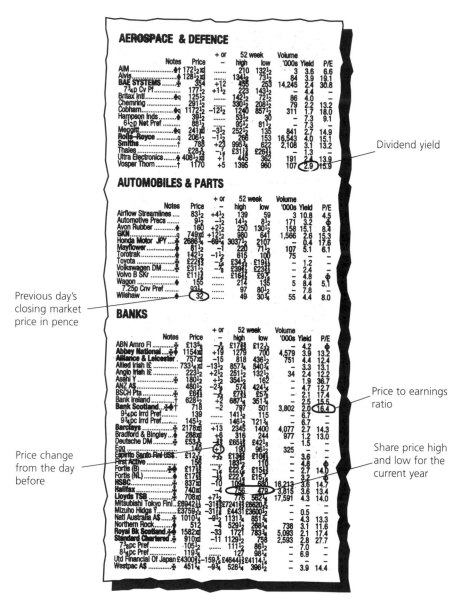

Dividend yield

Previous day's closing market price in pence

Price to earnings ratio

Price change from the day before

Share price high and low for the current year

Source: Financial Times, April 18, 2001

Weekly summary

Figure 18.2 Example Monday share prices

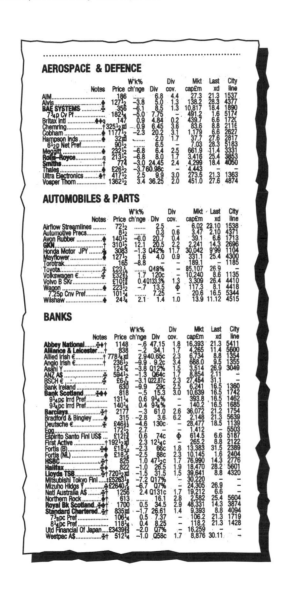

Source: Financial Times, August 13, 2001

On Mondays the *FT* provides information on the following (Figure 18.2):

- *Price change:* The weekly percentage change in the share price.

- *Dividend:* The dividends paid in the company's last full financial year. A double dagger symbol indicates that the interim dividend has been cut in the current financial year, while a single dagger indicates an increase.

- *Dividend cover:* This shows the number of times the dividend could have been paid out of net profits. The figure is a ratio of profits to dividends, calculated by dividing the earnings per share by the dividend per share. Analysts regard this as a key figure in assessing the security of the company and its ability to maintain the level of future dividend payments.

- *Market capitalization:* This is an indication of the stock market value of the company in millions of pounds sterling. It is calculated by multiplying the number of shares in issue by their market price. In order to calculate the number of shares in issue from the figures listed you can divide the market capitalization figure by the market price. However, if there are other classes of share capital in issue, their value would also need to be added in order to calculate the company's total market capitalization.

- *Ex-dividend date:* The last date the share went ex-dividend.

- *Cityline:* For up-to-the-second share prices call FT Cityline on 0906 003 or 0906 843 followed by the four-digit code in this column.

Unit trust and open-ended investment company (Oeic) prices

Unit trust and Oeic prices appear under the 'Managed Funds Service' section (Figure 18.3). These are funds authorized by the Financial Services Authority and can be marketed direct to the public. Unauthorized funds are not sold to the public but are used as internal funds by the financial institutions.

Unit trust and Oeic management groups are obliged to provide certain information to unit holders and the accepted practice is to publish unit prices, together with other important information in the *Financial Times* and other national newspapers.

> Unit trust and Oeic management groups are obliged to provide certain information to unit holders.

Figure 18.3 Example unit trust and Oeic prices

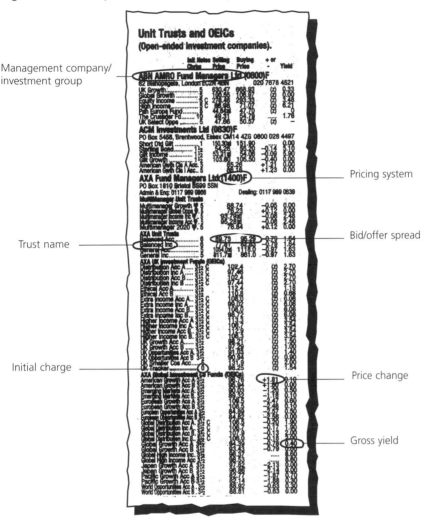

Source: *Financial Times*, April 18, 2001

How to read the figures

■ *Name of the investment group, its pricing system and trust names:*
this is shown as, for example, 'AIB Govett Unit Trust Managers Limited
(1000)F' followed by the company's address and telephone number
for dealing or enquiries. (Use this number if you want to get a free
copy of the management group's most recent report and scheme
particulars.) Under each company heading are listed its authorized unit
trusts.

The figure in brackets in the heading is the basis of the company's pricing system. The figure refers to the time at which the price was measured (using a 24-hour clock) and the basis of calculation. 'F' refers to forward pricing, which means orders are taken from investors and the price of units is determined by the next valuation. All larger groups have a valuation point each day, often at noon. So, if an investor phones through their order at 10am, the price will be struck at noon that same day. An investor who phones at 1pm will have to wait for a price until the following midday valuation.

Some groups still deal on an historic price basis, indicated by 'H'. This means they buy and sell using the price agreed at the last valuation point.

- *Initial charge (Init chrge):* Column two indicates the percentage charge deducted from your investment to cover certain costs – for example administration and the sales commission paid to advisers, if applicable. If the charge is 5 per cent then £95 out of every £100 will actually be available to be invested in your chosen fund.

- *Notes:* The symbols and letters in column three indicate particular features of a unit trust. For example, 'E' indicates there is an exit charge when you sell your units. A full list of notes, some of which may appear against figures in other columns, can be found at the end of the *FT* 'Managed Funds' section.

- *Selling price:* Given in column four, this is also called the bid price. This is the price at which investors sell units back to the manager.

- *Buying price:* Given in column five, this is also called the offer price. This is the price at which investors buy units.

- *Price change (+ or –):* The sixth column compares the mid-point between the bid and offer prices with the previous day's quotation.

- *Yield:* The last column shows the gross income paid by the unit trust as a percentage of the offer price. The quoted yield reflects income earned by the fund during the previous 12 months and therefore relates only to past performance.

Investment trust prices

As quoted companies, investment trusts are quoted in the London Share Service section (Figure 18.4). Most of the information is the same as for other companies, with the exception of the last two columns.

■ *Net asset value (NAV):* This is the approximate value of the underlying assets owned by the company. As with the share price, the NAV is shown in pence.

■ *Discount or premium (Dis or PM(–)):* The premium is shown as a minus sign. If the value of the underlying assets is higher than the share price, then the trust is said to be at a discount. In other words, assuming there is nothing untoward about the trust, the shares are likely to be good value because their underlying value is worth more than the price you pay. If the NAV is lower than the share price, the shares are at a premium and generally should be avoided.

Figure 18.4 Example investment trust prices

Source: Financial Times, August 13, 2001

AITC Monthly Information Service   For a more detailed guide to investment trust performance, use the AITC's Monthly Information Service (MIS: see page 264). If you are new to the service you will find it helpful first to read the user's guide, which explains how the MIS is organized and what the various figures represent.

The monthly service shows the performance of all the trusts over several time periods and includes a comparison of trust performance measured against various indices and other important benchmark figures such as unit trusts, building societies and the retail price index.

Bear in mind that with the AITC it is the trust itself, not the management group, that is the member. The AITC covers most of the investment trust market by volume but there are several important omissions. In particular, four trusts run by M&G are not members, nor is the British Investment Trust, which is run by Edinburgh Fund Managers.

Summary

- In order to measure anything you need an appropriate benchmark with which to make comparisons.

- An absolute benchmark is useful and tells you the real growth achieved by your fund after taking into account the effects of inflation.

- A better benchmark, however, is to measure against an appropriate index or, in the case of collective funds, a peer group (for example UK equity income).

- A third benchmark is to measure against a similar portfolio to your own. There are two such services, from the FTSE International/Apcims and WM.

- Share prices, including investment trusts, and most collective funds are quoted daily in the *Financial Times*.

Further information

For shares, the *Financial Times* and *Investors Chronicle* are the best sources of information. The *FT* also covers collective funds but there are several additional sources of reference, for example the useful articles, surveys and statistics which appear in specialist publications such as *Money Management*, *Planned Savings*, *Bloomberg Money* and *Moneywise* – all of which are available from newsagents. The Consumers' Association publishes best buys for personal pensions, among other savings and investment plans, in its *Which?* magazine.

Details about the Private Investor Indices, including their construction and management and back histories, are available free of charge from FTSE International's internet site at *www.ftse.com*. Details about WM's Private Client Indicators are available from WM, World Markets House, Crewe Toll, Edinburgh EH4 2PY. Tel: 0131 315 2000. Fax: 0131 315 2999.

For a free sample copy of the AITC Monthly Information Service write to the Association of Investment Trust Companies, Durrant House, 8–13 Chiswell Street, London EC1Y 4YY. Tel: 020 7431 5222. The association's website is at: *www.aitc.org.uk*.

Performance measurement: private client indices

The FTSE-Apcims indices are shown in the 'Weekend Money' section of the *Financial Times* on Saturday, or go to *www.ftse.com*.

WM indices are shown on the website, *www.wmcompany.com*.

Shareholders' rights

■ Your rights as a part owner of a company

■ Dividends

■ Rights issues

■ Scrip issues

■ Company literature

■ The annual general meeting

■ Voting rights

■ Good corporate governance

■ A change in management

■ What if the company goes bust?

This chapter explains the significance of major events throughout the company's financial year, such as results and dividend announcements. We also examine important but *ad hoc* events such as a rights or scrip issue, a merger, takeover or acquisition.

Fortunately, even a seemingly hostile takeover bid has to conform to the equivalent of the Queensberry rules for corporations. Boxing gloves are mandatory, foul holds and blows are not permitted, and the whole match must be over within a sensible period. If you know what to expect you can consider your options in principle long before it gets to voting time.

Of course if you have a discretionary manager they will be responsible for taking any necessary action. But if you want to check your investments yourself, and particularly if you are using an execution-only stockbroker, then you need to know your rights.

With modern technology and the internet for communications, you would imagine that private investors are snowed under with information. Unfortunately you would be wrong. To speed up settlement of sales and purchases, increasingly private investors are being asked to hold shares in a nominee account. This can have a devastating effect on the information you receive – either because the nominee does not offer the facility to distribute reports and accounts, among other items, or the company itself refuses to treat shareholders in nominees as real people. (See Chapter 15 for details of nominees.)

This chapter will help you identify the information you need to monitor the progress of the companies in which you invest.

Your rights as a part owner of a company

When you buy shares in a company you become a part owner of the business and under company law this confers, for example, the right to be told certain information about the company and to communicate your views to the board.

The most important shareholders' rights are explained in a useful guide from ProShare (contact details on page 264).

How you hold your shares

As a shareholder you can opt to hold your shares in one of three ways:

- *Nominee account:* This method enables fast and efficient settlement through Crest (see page 178). However, in a nominee account you lose certain automatic rights of ownership such as access to annual reports and accounts and voting rights. You may also lose any shareholder perks. Some nominees do make special provision to allow you to maintain these rights so, if you value them, it is worth shopping around.

- *Sponsored membership of Crest:* If you want to continue to get the advantages of speedy settlement and to continue to receive all information from the companies whose shares you own, you can choose sponsored membership of Crest.

- *Share certificates:* You are entitled to have your name added to the register of members of the company which will show how many shares you own. You are also entitled to a share certificate.

> **T I P**
>
> If you choose to retain your share certificate, you keep your automatic rights of ownership, but you may experience delays or possibly extra costs when you trade your shares.

Dividends

As a shareholder you have a right to a share of the company's earnings, known as dividends. These are generally paid twice a year. The first payment in a company's financial year is known as the 'interim' dividend and the second payment is known as the 'final' dividend. Along with the dividend payment you should receive a note setting out the number of shares you hold and the dividend rate payable per share.

If you hold preference shares you will usually receive a fixed dividend which will take priority over payments to ordinary shareholders if a company has any difficulty paying out the full range of dividends.

Rights issues

> The issue of new shares may cause the price of your existing shares to fall because an increase in the total number in circulation dilutes the value per share.

From time to time a company may wish to raise more money. As a shareholder you may be offered the chance to participate in a rights issue. This is where the company asks existing shareholders whether they want to buy new shares in the company, usually at a discount to the current market price. However, the issue of new shares may cause the price of your existing shares to fall because an increase in the total number in circulation dilutes the value per share.

Scrip issues

Quoted companies in the UK do not like the price per share to get too large as this can affect liquidity and hence slow dealing activity. To dilute the share price a company will sometimes offer you 'free' shares. This increases the number of shares in circulation but the price per share falls in proportion to the total number in issue, so the value of your holding remains the same.

Scrip dividend

Occasionally a company may ask you to take your dividends in the form of shares. This is an easy way of saving and adding to your portfolio but it can complicate the administration in terms of the number of shares you own, the price at which you purchased them and the calculation of the capital gains tax liability when you eventually come to sell.

Company literature

All shareholders who have their name on the register of shareholders are entitled to certain documents that the company issues from time to time. These include the annual report and accounts (see Chapter 17) and other notices about important events, such as major acquisitions, disposals, or very significant changes in the structure of the company – a demerger, for example.

It is important to remember that if you hold shares through a nominee account, it will not be your name but the nominee's name which appears on the register of the company shareholders. If you want company literature, check whether your nominee will send it to you.

The annual general meeting

Every company must hold an annual general meeting once a year. Shareholders whose names are on the register have the right to attend and speak at the meeting and they must be given at least 21 days' notice of the time and the venue. Clearly, the same point applies here as for the company literature. If you want to attend AGMs, check this point with your nominee.

Voting rights

Companies must ask shareholders to vote on important matters that affect their future. You can either vote in person at the AGM or use a proxy card sent by the company, which allows you to vote by post.

By law the company must ask the shareholders their view on the following:

- A decision which would dilute shareholdings such as the issue of more company shares – for example a rights issue or the establishment of an employee share option scheme.

- The appointment or dismissal of the auditors. Auditors are external accountants used by the company to check their financial statements. Their role is important because they protect the shareholders from the actions of irresponsible directors.

- The appointment and dismissal of directors. Shareholders must approve any such change because, as owners of the company, they have the right to elect the directors to run the business on their behalf and hold them accountable for its progress.

Proposed resolutions at the AGM

Under company law, shareholders can put forward motions only if they can muster 5 per cent of the company's total voting rights or 100 shareholders with at least £100 worth of shares. The company must submit resolutions no later than six weeks before the meeting and send a copy to all shareholders.

Extraordinary general meetings

These are company meetings other than the AGM. Directors often have to call an extraordinary general meeting to transact special business which cannot wait for the next AGM.

Shareholders concerned about a company's progress also have the right to force the board to call a meeting. To do this they must have the support of 10 per cent of the company's overall share capital, so this would involve rallying a large number of individual shareholders and almost certainly some of the big financial institutions such as life assurance and pension funds.

Good corporate governance

Several important committees – Cadbury, Greenbury and Hampel – have established what is accepted as good corporate governance and in due course the London Stock Exchange is expected to take charge of a new 'supercode' on corporate governance which will set out to directors and shareholders how companies should be run.

This topic covers several important issues, including the following points provided in the Gartmore guide (see 'Further information'):

- The chairman and chief executive should be separate roles in most cases.

- Non-executive directors should bring outside experience and independent judgement to the company's strategy.

- There should be appropriate remuneration and incentive schemes, with the chairman of the remuneration committee answerable to shareholders at the AGM.

- Service contracts for members of the board should be of two years or less.

- Directors normally stand for re-election after three years, though in some companies executives have been insulated from this requirement, which prevents shareholders from passing judgement on a director.
- Raising new capital should be supported where it is in the long-term interests of the shareholders. Existing shareholders should be given a right of first refusal to subscribe for such new shares.
- A proposed takeover should go ahead only if it is in the interests of shareholders.

A change in management

One of the most worrying times for private investors (apart from when their shares are plummeting) is when a company in which they invest is the target of a takeover or a partner to a merger.

This is the type of action that makes newspaper headlines and raises the profile of institutional investors, who carry a lot of clout in these battles. (Remember, pension funds and life assurance funds between them own about two-thirds of the UK stock market.) But these events can be far from thrilling for the individual investor, who may feel rather powerless.

It is possible for private investors to do well out of a takeover because the acquiring company is usually so keen to build up a controlling stake that it will pay over the odds for your shares.

If you own shares in the target company, you have two basic choices. You can grab the money and run (but only after checking your capital gains position first

> As always, information is your best friend and as a shareholder you are entitled to receive details of the proposed deal.

– see page 255). Alternatively, you can hang on and see if a white knight (a supporter of the takeover target company) or the aggressor will turn what might have been hitherto a rather stagnant investment into a growth stock.

If you hold shares in the acquiring company, the takeover could be a good boost to the business, but if the management team are forced to pay dearly for their acquisition it will absorb any spare cash sloshing around in the company's coffers which otherwise might have been distributed to shareholders as dividends. Even if the acquired company is a good fit, it could take some time for the new structure to work well and to put profits and dividends back on track.

Clearly there are no easy answers in these situations. As always, information is your best friend and as a shareholder you are entitled to receive details of the proposed deal. In addition you should trawl the financial press for useful facts and opinions.

What if the company goes bust?

This is the worst possible scenario because ordinary shareholders are just about last in the queue of unsecured creditors, so unless it is an unusual situation – for example the winding up of an investment trust – there is rarely anything left after the taxman and the government have taken their share and the secured creditors (mortgage lenders, for example, who have a claim on the property) and banks have had theirs.

Remember, in the pecking order, bond holders come before share-holders, although stockbrokers suggest that this is no great deal and that in the majority of cases bond holders will not get anything either.

In practice very few quoted companies go bust in the UK. If you are unfortunate enough to be left holding dud shares, there is a procedure for claiming the losses under the capital gains tax rules (see page 256).

Summary

- As a shareholder you are a part owner of the company and under company law this confers certain rights.
- Your rights are affected by the way you hold your shares – if you use a nominee account you may not be sent the annual report and accounts or benefit from any perks, for example.
- Dividends are usually paid twice a year. The first payment is the interim dividend and the second is the final dividend.
- Companies can raise extra money through a rights issue. Usually, as an existing shareholder you would be offered the shares at a discount to market price.
- A scrip issue simply increases the number of shares in circulation and reduces the per price share proportionately. This is to aid liquidity by keeping the share price within acceptable limits.
- The annual general meeting is an informative event and as a shareholder you have the right to attend or to vote by proxy on any important issues.

Further information

ProShare *Shareholders' Rights* information sheet (see page 264 for contact details).

The information on corporate governance was reproduced from a guide published by Gartmore, the *Guide to Corporate Governance*.

Tax and your investments

- Keep it legal

- Your tax allowances and exemptions

- Income tax

- Capital gains tax

- Reduce your inheritance tax bill

AT A GLANCE

Smart tax saving begins at home. Here you can redistribute income and assets to make best use of each family member's annual personal allowances and exemptions. You might also consider making appropriate inheritance tax arrangements to help retain your wealth within the family when you die.

Keep it legal

The hallmark of good tax planning is that it will pass the Inland Revenue's scrutiny with flying colours, even where complicated family trust arrangements and considerable wealth are involved.

> The hallmark of good tax planning is that it will pass the Inland Revenue's scrutiny with flying colours.

As you read this chapter, keep in mind the way the Inland Revenue distinguishes between our various attempts to minimize our tax liability. In particular you need to understand the terms 'evasion', 'avoidance' and 'mitigation'. Although these tend to be used indiscriminately, their meanings are very different.

T I P

If you deliberately omit something from your tax return, or give a false description, that's evasion. You have not just been dishonest – you have acted criminally and could be fined or imprisoned.

Tax evasion is illegal. Avoidance and mitigation are on the right side of the law but, again, there is an important distinction. If your tax saving has been encouraged by the government – for example you put your investments in an Isa – that is mitigation. This is definitely on the right side of the Revenue.

Avoidance is where you use more complicated – but legal – methods to avoid paying tax. If too many people use a loophole that enables them to avoid tax, the government tends to put a stop to it by closing the loophole.

Among other services, your accountant will help you to mitigate and avoid tax.

Your tax allowances and exemptions

Successful tax planning requires common sense and expert advice in equal measures. So, before you change anything, check that the particular use of an allowance or exemption has a genuine benefit.

Unless you are very experienced, you should consult a qualified accountant. All transactions must comply with current tax law and be carefully documented.

There are three main personal allowances and exemptions. A full set of figures is provided in Table 20.1, but briefly, for the 2001–2002 tax year, each member of your family has:

- the income tax annual personal allowance of £4,535 (more if you qualify for the age allowances);
- the *capital gains tax* annual exemption of £7,500;
- the *inheritance tax* annual exemption for gifts of £3,000. The main exemption on death is £242,000.

Income tax

Most families are not tax-efficient because their combined wealth – in terms of both earned income and assets – tends to be concentrated in the hands of the main breadwinner. He or she, therefore, is also responsible for paying most of the tax, often at the top rate.

One of the best ways to save on income tax is to share income between spouses, whether the source is earnings, investments or a combination of the two. This makes use of the non-working or lower-earning spouse's allowance and, where the income exceeds the personal allowance, the lower and basic tax rates. The two most common redistribution techniques are to give income-generating assets to your spouse and, where you run your own business, to pay your spouse a salary.

Table 20.1 Your main tax allowances and exemptions for 2001–2002

Income tax allowances	£
Personal allowance under 65	4,535
Personal allowance 65–74*	5,990
Children's tax credit at 10%	5,200
Income tax rates	
Lower rate 10% on first	1,880
Basic rate 22% on next	27,520
Higher rate 40% over	29,400
Annual CGT exemption	7,500
Inheritance tax 40%	over 242,000

* 20% on interest and dividends.
Source: Inland Revenue

It is also possible to give income-producing assets to children who can make use of their own allowances and, where necessary, their lower and basic rates of taxation.

However, this requires great care. If you give this type of asset to your children and the income exceeds £100 per annum, you, as the parents, will be taxed on the entire amount. For this reason it is usually necessary to hold the assets in a 'bare trust' under which the parents are the registered owners but hold them as nominees for the children and the income is accumulated until they are 18. This would not be necessary in the case of gifts from other family members – grandparents, for example.

Finally on this point, remember that if you give a gift of assets this has to be unconditional; otherwise the Revenue will see through the arrangement and continue to tax you on the asset's value. Think carefully before you give your favourite shares to your spouse or children!

Capital gains tax

The annual exemption of £7,500 for the 2001–2002 tax year is the amount of capital gains you can make before you pay capital gains tax at your top rate of income tax. As gifts between spouses are exempt from CGT the tax-efficient couple should consider sharing assets in order to make use of both exemptions.

CGT and your shares

In practice most investors manage to avoid CGT without making any special arrangements, simply because their liability regularly falls within the annual CGT exemption. Even if you have a very large portfolio and you are an active investor, you may still be able to avoid or reduce your liability, but this will require some careful planning.

CGT is payable when you sell an asset and make a 'chargeable gain', that is, where the value of an asset you sell has increased since you acquired it, after taking into account the effect of inflation (see below – this figure is frozen). Remember, CGT is not charged on the asset itself but on its gain in value.

> Remember, CGT is not charged on the asset itself but on its gain in value.

Investors who have received free *windfall* shares from demutualized building societies and life assurance companies should bear in mind that the proceeds of any sales will be classed as a pure capital gain unless they are held in a tax-exempt investment such as an individual savings plan.

CGT 'tapering' relief

In the March 1998 budget, the chancellor froze indexation relief and introduced 'taper relief'. He also scrapped 'bed and breakfasting' of shares so you can no longer sell and repurchase the following day to crystallize a gain or loss. Instead you can sell and your spouse can repurchase them – a procedure known as 'bed and spouse' or you can purchase shares in a similar company.

Under the new 'taper relief' rules, gains on assets held for three years or more will be taxed at a lower rate according to how long you have held them. The rate falls from the top level of 40 per cent on gains realized before year three to the lowest rate of 24 per cent on assets held for ten years.

However, the 'taper' for business assets, which is much more favourable than for personal assets, now includes shares held through company share schemes. Even if you are a higher-rate taxpayer, your CGT rate could be as low as 10 per cent on gains in excess of the exemption when you sell these shares.

Small business owners who sell up will also be taxed at a lower rate, again depending on how long they owned the business, with a minimum rate of 10 per cent.

Shares in companies that go bust

Once a company officially ceases to exist, the tax rules automatically treat this as the date you disposed of your shares (for nothing).

However, fortunately you don't have to wait for this official extinction date to make a claim on dud shares and to use the loss to offset gains during that tax year. Instead, the purchase cost (or the March 31, 1982 value if appropriate) of shares declared by the Inland Revenue to be of 'negligible value' is regarded as an allowable capital loss. This loss is treated as taking place on the date you enter your claim (within certain limits).

It is also possible to check whether a company in which you hold shares is in receivership or liquidation. It may help you decide what to do if your shares clearly are worthless but have not yet been declared of 'negligible value' by the Inland Revenue.

A comprehensive list is published in Extel's *CGT Capital Losses* (see 'Further information'; your accountant or investment adviser should have a copy). Most of these shares will eventually end up on the 'negligible value' list, but if the Inland Revenue appears to be taking its time in listing your dud shares, do seek advice. If you put in a claim on your tax return as soon as you believe that the company faces ruin, the timing of your claim may not be appropriate from a tax planning point of view. First check your chargeable gains and other allowable losses to make sure you can fully utilize the loss.

Finally, bear in mind that not all of the shares listed are duds. Some belong to companies such as *investment trusts* that are being reorganized or voluntarily wound up.

Reduce your inheritance tax bill

Inheritance tax is a tax on your wealth at death and the exemption (£242,000 in 2001–2002) is deducted from your estate before it can be passed on to your heirs. There is no IHT liability on the assets you leave to your spouse, but once he or she dies, the value of the estate in excess of the exemption is taxable.

There are several ways to mitigate your inheritance tax bill. Each year you can give away up to £3,000 free of CGT. If you didn't use last year's exemption you can add it to this year's, giving a total gift of £12,000 per couple.

It is possible to give away any amount in excess of this, but at present, if you die within seven years, you pay tax on a sliding scale based on when you made the gift and when you die. This arrangement, known as a 'potentially exempt transfer' (PET), may be abolished in a future budget along with other IHT-avoidance measures.

One option worth considering if you anticipate a large IHT liability is to take out a life assurance policy which will cover the costs when you die. This should be written in trust for the successors (the children, for example) to make sure the policy does not form part of your taxable estate on death.

Summary

- Make sure your tax arrangements are not so complicated that they eliminate any tax savings in administration costs.
- Where possible, married couples should share assets to make use of both partners' personal income tax allowance and capital gains tax exemption. This is particularly tax-efficient if one partner is a non-taxpayer or pays tax at the lower or basic rate.
- A capital loss can be offset against any capital gains in excess of the exemption.

Further information

Readers interested in doing their own CGT calculations will find more detailed information in a recently updated Inland Revenue booklet, CGT 14 *Capital Gains Tax: an introduction*, available from tax offices.

Extel CGT Capital Losses Service – tel: 020 7970 0210, website: *www.ft.com* (look on the left-hand side for 'Ask FT').

Getting help

■ Investment clubs

■ Financial advice

■ Complaints

■ Recommended reading

In this chapter we cover a variety of information which private investors will find useful. This includes:

■ *Investment clubs:* these are an excellent way to build up experience and share ideas with other private investors.

■ *Your guide to financial advisers and stockbrokers:* if you want to delegate the task of running your portfolio, clearly your choice of adviser is critical. Use our guide in conjunction with Chapter 3.

■ *How to complain:* if you are lucky you may never need this section, but keep it handy, just in case.

■ *Recommended reading:* this is not a comprehensive reading list but is unashamedly selective and represents the author's choice of the most helpful books available.

■ For a guide to internet services, see page 173.

Investment clubs

There are over 8,500 investment clubs in Britain. These clubs are beginning to take off in a big way and can be an ideal environment in which new investors – as well as the more experienced – can learn the art of investing successfully without having to risk a large amount of capital.

Many of these clubs belong to ProShare, the organization dedicated to increasing the public's knowledge of the benefits of equity investment.

Not surprisingly, an excellent source of information on this topic is the *ProShare Investment Club Manual* (see page 264 for contact details), which gives detailed information on setting up and running a club, explains how to use a stockbroker and how to register investments, and covers all the necessary accounting, tax and other administration. The ProShare website also has a lot of information to get you started.

Also very informative is the guide from Barclays Stockbrokers, which helps set up clubs and has about 3,000 around the country (details on page 262).

How they work

The principle of an investment club is simple. A group of friends, family or work colleagues pool a regular amount of money each month to invest in equities. The group meets monthly to discuss its portfolio and its decisions to buy or sell are made democratically.

Inexperienced investors learn from fellow members who already own shares, but everyone benefits from the general pooling of knowledge and experience.

> Inexperienced investors learn from fellow members who already own shares, but everyone benefits from the general pooling of knowledge and experience.

By far the best way to get involved is to start up a new club. Rather like running a private business, it is much more fun and reassuring if you can invest with people you know and trust, whose company you enjoy and whose opinions you respect.

The maximum number of members for a ProShare club is 20 – otherwise it can become unwieldy. You and your fellow members decide how much the monthly subscription should be. Some clubs start off with as little as £10 per member but more typically the subscription is around £25–£30. According to ProShare, there are clubs in the UK with stocks and shares valued at £500,000.

Experienced investors can and do mirror the decisions taken by the club in their private investment portfolio. However, ProShare warns that substantial investors should not use the club for anything other than a small portion of their total portfolio.

Contacts

For further information write to ProShare Investment Clubs, Library Chambers, 13 & 14 Basinghall Street, London EC2V 5BQ, phone 020 7394 5200 or visit the website at *www.proshare.org*.

For details about Barclays Stockbrokers investment clubs phone 0845 777 7800 or go to *www.barclays-stockbrokers.co.uk*.

Financial advice

Before you appoint a firm to act on your behalf, you can check with the chief regulator, the Financial Services Authority, that the firm is authorized and registered with the appropriate regulator. To contact the **FSA central register**, phone 020 7929 3652, website: *www.fsa.gov.uk*.

Stockbrokers and investment managers

The Association of Private Client Investment Managers and Stockbrokers (Apcims) publishes a free directory of member firms, many of which provide a full financial planning service. Contact Apcims, 112 Middlesex Street, London E1 7HY. The Apcims directory is available at *www.apcims.co.uk*. E-mail: *info@apcims.co.uk*.

Financial planners and advisers

The Institute of Financial Planning (IFP) is multi-disciplinary and its members are well qualified in giving independent planning advice. Contact the IFP at Whitefriars Centre, Lewins Mead, Bristol BS1 2NT. For the register of fellows of the institute, phone 0117 930 4434 or go to the website at *www.financialplanning.org.uk*.

The Society of Financial Advisers (SOFA) is part of the Chartered Insurance Institute and is a major examiner of independent advisers and life assurance company sales staff. Contact SOFA at 20 Aldermanbury, London EC2V 7HY. Tel: 020 7417 4419 (*www.sofa.org.uk*).

Independent advisers: For a list of local independent advisers, contact **IFA Promotion** on 0117 971 1177 or at *www.ifap.org.uk*. For fee-based independent advisers contact the **Money Management Register** on 0117 976 9444.

Accountants

About 700 members of the Institute of Chartered Accountants are qualified to offer a full advisory service, but members of other taxation bodies can also help.

The Institute of Chartered Accountants in England & Wales, Moorgate Place, London EC2P 2BJ. Tel: 020 7920 8100/8711. Website: *www.icaew.co.uk*.

The Institute of Chartered Accountants in Scotland, 27 Queen Street, Edinburgh EH2 1LA. Tel: 0131 225 5673.

The Association of Chartered Certified Accountants (ACCA), 29 Lincoln's Inn Fields, London WC2A 3EE. Tel: 020 7242 6855. Website: *www.acca.org.uk*.

The Chartered Institute of Taxation and Association of Tax Technicians, 12 Upper Belgrave Street, London SW1X 8BB. Chartered tax advisers and members of this institute specialize purely in tax work for companies and for individuals. Tel: 020 7235 9381. The Institute's website is at *www.tax.org.uk*.

Solicitors

The Law Society of England & Wales, 113 Chancery Lane, London WC2A 1PL. Tel: 020 7242 1222 Website: *www.lawsociety.org.uk*.

The Law Society of Scotland, 26 Drumsheugh Gardens, Edinburgh EH3 7YR. Tel: 0131 226 7411.

The Law Society of Northern Ireland, Law Society House, 98 Victoria Street, Belfast BT1 3JZ. Tel: 01232 231 614.

Solicitors are strongly represented in the financial services market. Two organizations dedicated to professional independent advice are:

Solicitors for Independent Financial Advice (SIFA): phone the helpline 01372 721172 or go to *www.solicitor-ifa.co.uk*.

The Association of Solicitor Investment Managers (ASIM), Chiddingstone Causeway, Tonbridge, Kent TN11 8JX. Tel: 01892 870065. Website: *www.asim.org.uk*.

Pension specialists

The Association of Consulting Actuaries: Number 1 Wardrobe Place, London EC4V 5AH. Tel: 020 7248 3163. *www.aca.org.uk*.

The Association of Pension Lawyers (APL)**:** c/o Eversheds, Senator House, 65 Queen Victoria Street, London EC4V 4JA. Tel: 020 7919 4500.

Other useful organizations

The Association of Investment Trust Companies (AITC) publishes a range of booklets on how to use investment trusts for long-term investment plans. AITC, Durrant House, 8–13 Chiswell Street, London EC1Y 4YY. Tel: 020 7431 5222. Website: *www.aitc.org.uk*.

The Association of Unit Trusts and Investment Funds (Autif) publishes a range of free fact sheets that explain how these investments work. Autif, 65 Kingsway, London WC2B GTD. Tel: 020 7831 0898. Website: *www.investmentfunds.org.uk*.

The Department of Social Security has a wealth of information on its website: *www.dss.gov.uk*.

The Occupational Pensions Regulatory Authority (Opra) runs the stakeholder scheme register. Website: *www.opra.gov.uk*.

ProShare publishes a useful guide to employee share ownership. Contact ProShare, Library Chambers, 13–14 Basinghall Street, London EC2V 5BQ. Tel: 020 7220 1730. The website covers all the main arrangements and is at *www.proshare.org*.

The Stock Exchange publishes useful leaflets on buying and selling shares and on rolling settlement and nominee accounts. The Stock Exchange, London EC2N 1HP. Tel: 020 7797 1000. The Exchange's website can be found at: *www.londonstockexchange.com*.

Complaints

Under the Financial Services Act, if a company has sold you an inappropriate product for your needs you may be able to claim compensation.

If you have an investment complaint, write to the compliance officer at the company that sold you the product. You should receive an acknowledgement of your letter within seven days, but allow two months for the actual investigation before taking the case to the ombudsman or regulator.

The company's letterhead should show the details of the regulator but if not, contact the Financial Services Authority central register (see page 262) or write to: **The Financial Services Authority**, 25 The North Colonnade, Canary Wharf, London E14 5HS. Consumer helpline: 0845 6061234. The FSA publishes a wide range of information leaflets on financial advice, pensions, investments and complaints. Website: *www.fsa.gov.uk*.

The Financial Ombudsman Service is on 020 7964 1000.

Recommended reading

For a guide to useful websites, see pages 173–5.

A good source of reading matter is the ProShare website, which lists top publications and offers a discount on the retail price. Go to *www.proshare.org*.

An excellent guide to online services is *E-cash* by Marianne Curphey (published by Prentice Hall). This includes a run-down on the main online trading and information services. Marianne runs The Guardian Unlimited Money site at *www.guardian.co.uk*.

Also useful to the dedicated online trader is *The UK Guide to Online Brokers* by Michael Scott (Scott IT, 2000). There is an online version of the book at *www.investment-gateway.com*.

Two books on interpreting financial pages in the *Financial Times* are *How to Read the Financial Pages* by Michael Brett, published by Random House, and *The Financial Times Guide to Using the Financial Pages* by Romesh Vaitilingam, published by FT Prentice Hall.

For a good basic guide to investment, try *The Motley Fool UK Investment Guide*, published by Boxtree. Also excellent is Bernard Gray's *Beginners' Guide to Investment* published by Century. For the more advanced reader, try Gillian O'Connor's *A Guide to Stockpicking*, published by Century. For the more advanced reader, try Gillian O'Connor's *A Guide to Stockpicking*, published by Century.

Finally, don't be without *The Investor's Guide to Information Sources* published by ProShare.

Glossary

Accumulation unit: Units in a *unit trust* where the income is reinvested automatically, increasing the unit price. The alternative is *income units* where the income is distributed to the unit holders.

Acid test: The ratio of a company's current assets (excluding stock) to its current liabilities.

Active management: Unlike passive investment management or *index tracking*, the active manager selects sectors in the light of expected economic conditions and individual stocks on the basis of research into a company's prospects.

Additional voluntary contributions (AVCs) or 'free-standing' AVCs (FSAVCs) can be used to top up your company pension. If you earn less than £30,000 p.a. you could also use a *personal pension* or *stakeholder* plan. An *individual savings account* (Isa) also makes a good and more flexible retirement savings plan.

Advisory management: An advisory stockbroker service allows you to discuss investment opportunities with your broker and receive tips, but no action can be taken without your approval. Under a *discretionary management* arrangement the broker makes all the decisions for you. An *execution-only* service is where your broker acts on your instructions but gives no advice or opinion.

Alternative investment: One that does not follow the risk/return profile and pattern of traditional equity and bond markets.

Alternative Investment Market: AIM is for small, fast-growing companies. Can be a springboard to the *Official List* (main stock market).

Annual charge: The annual management charge made by your stockbroker or collective fund manager. For collective funds, this can be anything from 0.5 per cent for the low-cost tracker unit trusts and investment trusts, to 1.5 per cent (higher for the more specialist funds). This covers the cost of investment management, administration and any ongoing sales *commission* to your adviser.

Annual report and accounts: Companies that trade on the Stock Exchange or Alternative Investment Market must provide shareholders and the Exchange with an annual report and accounts which include financial details of the past trading year.

Annuity: This provides a guaranteed regular income in return for a lump sum. With an investment-linked annuity your income is dictated partly by stock market returns.

Arithmetic average: This is a simple arithmetic calculation – the sum of the total returns for a given category of shares divided by the number of companies within the category. (See *size-weighted average*)

Assets: A catch-all term which refers to the fundamentally different types of investments, for example, UK *equities*, overseas equities, property, fixed-interest securities (*gilts* and *bonds*), and *cash*.

Association of Investment Trust Companies (AITC): The main trade body for *investment trusts*.

Association of Unit Trust and Investment Funds (Autif): The main trade body for *unit trusts* and *open-ended investment companies*.

Authorized unit trust: Unit trusts sold to the public must be authorized by the *Financial Services Authority* (FSA), the chief regulator for financial services in the UK.

Balance sheet: Produced with the *annual report and accounts*. Shows what the company owns and owes.

Band earnings: National Insurance is levied on earnings between £87 and £575 per week in 2001–2002.

Bargain: The term used when a purchase or sale agreement is struck.

Bear market: This is where share prices are falling over a prolonged period.

Bed and spouse: At the end of the tax year you can sell shares and your partner can repurchase them (usually the following day) in order to crystallize a capital gain, which you could write off against your annual capital gains tax exemption, or a capital loss which you can offset against a CGT liability in excess of the exemption.

Beneficial owner: The real owner of shares held in a *nominee account*.

Beneficiaries: Those who benefit from a trust. With a unit trust, the trustees run the fund on behalf of the beneficiaries – in this case, the unit holders. With a pension fund the beneficiaries are the scheme members and their dependants.

Bid/offer spread: The full initial cost of your investment in a fund. This includes administration, sales commission if applicable, dealing costs and *stamp duty* among other items. Typically the spread is about 6 per cent but where the initial charge is reduced or abolished it could be as low as 0.5 per cent.

Bid price: The price at which you sell units in a unit trust back to the manager. You purchase at the *offer price*.

Big Bang: Major changes which opened up the Stock Exchange to greater competition, including foreign ownership of member firms and the abolition of minimum commissions.

Blue chip: A large, well-established company, e.g. a *FTSE 100* company.

Bonds: UK bonds are issued by borrowers, for example the government and companies, which undertake to repay the principal sum on a specified date, rather like an IOU. During the time the bond is outstanding a fixed rate of interest is paid to the lender, which might be an individual or a financial institution. Not to be confused with insurance company bonds, which are collective investments sold by insurance companies.

Brokers: Shortened term for *stockbrokers*. Also, the original traders who bought and sold shares on behalf of clients. (See *jobbers*)

Bull market: A market where share prices are rising over a prolonged period.

Cancellation price: The lowest possible valuation in any one day of your unit trust units. The actual selling or bid price is usually higher.

Capital gains tax: The tax on the increase in the value of an asset when it is sold, compared with its value at the time of purchase adjusted partly to take account of inflation and partly according to the length of time you held the asset. (See *taper relief*)

Capital growth: An increase in the value of shares or assets in a fund.

Cash: As an asset class, cash usually refers to deposit accounts.

Chartist: An investor who uses charts of company price movements to determine investment decisions.

Commission: (1) The fee that a stockbroker charges clients for dealing on their behalf. (2) The remuneration an adviser receives from a financial institution for selling you one of its products. (See *fee-based adviser*)

Company share option scheme: Run by an employer to allow employees to buy shares in the company at a discount. (See *Save As You Earn*)

Contract note: Confirmation of your share purchase.

Convertibles: Fixed-interest securities which may be converted to equities on a predetermined future date.

Corporate bond: An IOU issued by a public company. In return for borrowing your money, the company pays a fixed income (*coupon*) for a specified period and guarantees to return the original capital (nominal) on a predetermined future date.

Coupon: The rate of interest as a percentage of the nominal price which is paid by a bond or gilt. The purchase price may be different from the nominal price.

Creation price: The highest possible purchase price for your units in a unit trust. The actual buying or offer price is usually lower.

Crest: An electronic service that handles the mechanics of settling share transactions.

Cum dividend: The purchase price includes the value of the dividend. *Ex-dividend* means that the dividend will be paid to the previous owner.

Current ratio: The value of a company's current assets divided by current liabilities. Used as a measure of liquidity.

Custodian: Usually a bank whose primary function is to look after the assets of a trust (e.g. unit trust or pension fund), among other functions.

Debentures: Bonds issued by UK companies which are secured on the company's underlying assets – for example property. Unsecured bonds are known as loan stocks.

Demutualization: The process by which a mutually owned building society or life office becomes a public limited company. Members of the former mutual usually receive *windfall* or free shares.

Derivatives: Financial instruments are referred to as derivative securities when their value is dependent upon the value of some other underlying asset. (See *future, option* and *warrants*)

Designated account: An account held in one name (often a child's) with a second name as additional identification.

Discount: If the share price of an *investment trust* is lower than the value per share of the underlying assets (net asset value), the difference is known as the discount. If it is higher, the difference is known as the *premium*. As a general rule a share trading at a discount often represents good value.

Discretionary management: This is where your stockbroker makes all the investment service decisions for you. (See *advisory management* and *execution-only*)

Distributions: Income paid out from an equity or bond fund.

Dividend: The owner of shares is entitled to dividends – usually a six-monthly distribution to shareholders of part of the company's profits.

Dividend cover: The number of times a company could pay its annual dividend out of earnings.

Dividend yield: See *gross yield*.

Earnings per share: The amount of profit earned for each ordinary share of the company.

Endowment: Combines life assurance and investment. Sold by life offices, usually to build up a fund to repay an interest-only mortgage.

Equities: The ordinary share capital of a company.

Equity risk premium: The higher risk/reward characteristic of equities when compared with, for example, *cash* and *bonds*.

Eurosterling bond: A *corporate bond* issued in sterling by a company which wants to borrow money on the international markets rather than just in the UK.

Ex-dividend: The period of about six weeks before a fund or equity pays out its dividend/income. If you buy during this period you are not entitled to that dividend. (See *cum dividend*)

Execution-only: The investment manager/stockbroker simply buys and sells at your request without offering any advice. (See *advisory* and *discretionary*)

Exit charges: A charge deducted from some collective funds if you pull out early – usually within the first five years.

Fee-based adviser: Professional advisers do not accept sales *commission*. Instead they usually charge a fee calculated on an hourly basis and/or an annual percentage of your fund.

Final dividend: Paid at the end of a company's financial year when the final report is made which sets out its financial position. (See *interim*)

Financial gearing: The ratio between a company's borrowings and its capitalization – i.e. a ratio between what it owes and what it owns.

Financial Services Act 1986: The Act which established the system of self-regulation for financial services. The *Financial Services Authority* regulates different types of financial institutions and the advisers and representatives who sell their products.

Financial Services Authority (FSA): The chief regulator for financial services in the UK under the *Financial Services Act 1986*.

Fixed-interest securities: Another term for bonds. (See *bonds, corporate bond*)

Flotation: The initial offering in the *primary market* of a company coming to the Stock Exchange for the first time.

Free-standing additional voluntary contribution: You can top up your company pension either by paying into your employer's *additional voluntary contribution* scheme or by an individual contract with a financial institution, known as a free-standing AVC (FSAVC). You can also use a personal pension or stakeholder plan if you earn less than £30,000 p.a.

FTSE 100 Index: The index which covers the top 100 companies on the UK Stock Exchange measured by market capitalization (the number of shares times the share value).

FTSE All-Share Index: The yardstick for professional investors. The All-Share contains about 770 companies listed on the UK Stock Exchange.

FTSE Mid-250 Index: The index which measures the 250 companies below (by market capitalization) the FTSE 100.

FTSE SmallCap: The All-Share minus the top 350 companies.

Fund of funds: Unit trusts which can only invest in other authorized unit trusts.

Future: A type of *derivative*. A futures contract is a legally binding agreement to buy or sell a number of shares (or other instruments) at a fixed date in the future at a fixed price.

Gearing: In company terms, the ratio of long-term borrowing to assets. High gearing means that there is a large proportion of debt in relation to the assets held.

Gilts: The most secure type of bonds because they are issued by the UK government. Conventional gilts pay a fixed percentage of the nominal price. *Index-linked* gilts rise each year by a fixed percentage above the rate of inflation.

Gross yield: A method of assessing the income from an investment. It is the annual gross dividends (as currently declared or forecast by the directors of the investment trust) as a percentage of current market price. This shows the rate of gross income return a shareholder would receive on an investment at the share price on the date specified – much as one might describe the interest received on a deposit account.

Hedge funds: These aim to generate 'absolute returns' – that is, positive returns throughout all market cycles.

Income drawdown: Allows you to defer buying an annuity at retirement and to keep your fund fully invested while drawing an income.

Income unit: If you buy income units in a unit trust you receive automatically your share of the income generated by the fund. However, you can opt to have the income reinvested within the fund. (See *accumulation unit*)

Index-linked: An investment (e.g. a *gilt*) whose value increases each year in line with retail price inflation or by a fixed percentage above the RPI.

Index tracking: With a tracker fund, the investment manager uses a computer model to select stocks to simulate the performance of a specific stock market index. In some cases all the shares in an index will be held. Index tracking is also known as passive management.

Individual savings account (Isa): The Isa replaced personal equity plans (Peps) after April 1999 as the main tax-efficient investment apart from pensions.

Inflation: An increase in the general level of prices over a prolonged period, which forces down the real value or purchasing power of money. There are various measures of inflation, the most common being the *Retail Price Index (RPI)*.

Inheritance tax (IHT): A tax on the value of your estate above £242,000 (in 2001–2002) when you die.

Initial charge: A charge, typically 5 per cent, levied by a fund manager to cover administration and sales commission. However, the full upfront cost of your investment is shown in the *bid/offer spread* which includes additional charges such as stamp duty.

Interest cover: The number of times profits can cover the interest payments on a company's debts.

Interest rates: The Bank of England is responsible for setting short-term interest rates – the premium borrowers charge for lending their money.

Interim: A statement by a company which sets out its financial position halfway through its financial year. An interim dividend is also paid. (See *final dividend*)

Investment club: A group of private investors who pay a small subscription which is collectively invested in shares.

Investment trust: A UK company, listed on the Stock Exchange, which invests in the shares of other companies in the UK and overseas. (See *discount* and *premium*)

Jobbers: The original traders through whom *brokers* made their sales and purchases. Replaced by *market makers* in 1986.

Joint stock company: The forerunner of today's public limited company.

Liabilities: What a company owes to suppliers and lenders.

Liquidation: When a company is wound up and its assets, if any, are distributed to its creditors.

Loan stocks: Unsecured *bonds* issued by UK companies. Bonds secured on a company's underlying assets (property, for example) are known as *debentures*.

Long-dated bond: A bond or gilt with 15 years or more to go to *redemption*, when the nominal capital is repaid to the holder.

Market maker: A dealer who can buy and sell shares. Replaced earlier system of *brokers* and *jobbers*.

Maturity: Another word for *redemption*, when the investment period ends and, in the case of a *bond*, the nominal capital is repaid.

Medium-dated bond: A bond or gilt with 5–15 years to go to *redemption*, when the nominal capital is repaid to the holder.

National Insurance: A form of taxation levied on 'band' earnings – that is, weekly earnings between £87 and £575 in 2001–2002.

National Savings Certificates: Tax-free investments from the government.

National Savings Stock Register (NSSR): Postal facility for the public to buy *gilts*.

Negligible value: Shares in companies which have gone bust and which the Inland Revenue recognizes as a capital loss.

Net asset value (NAV): The market value of an *investment trust*'s underlying assets. This may be different from the share price, since the latter is subject to market forces and supply and demand. (See *discount* and *premium*)

Net yield: The return on an investment after tax has been deducted. (See *gross yield*)

Nominee account: To speed up transactions a stockbroker might recommend you hold your shares in its nominee account. You remain the *beneficial owner* but the nominee company is the registered shareholder.

Offer price: The price at which you buy units from the unit trust or Isa manager. You sell back to the manager at the 'bid' price. (See *bid/offer spread*)

Official List: The daily report of all the transactions in the main 'secondary' market.

Offshore funds: For UK investors this usually refers to funds in the Dublin International Financial Centre, the Isle of Man, the Channel Islands and Luxembourg. Offshore locations are not subject to UK tax law, although usually if you are a UK resident, when you repatriate money to the UK you must pay the appropriate income and capital gains tax.

Open-ended investment companies (oeics): These are a type of investment fund launched in 1996. They are similar to unit trusts but have a corporate structure and a single price rather than a *bid/offer spread*, so in some respects also resemble *investment trusts*.

Options: A type of *derivative*. A call option gives the buyer the right (but not the obligation – hence *option*) to buy a commodity, stock, bond or currency in the future at a mutually agreed price struck on the date of the contract. 'Put' options give you the right, but not the obligation, to sell.

Passive investment management: See *index tracking*.

Personal equity plan (Pep): A Pep is a wrapper or basket which shelters Inland Revenue-approved stock market investments from the taxman. Both income and capital gains are tax free for the lifetime of the investor. Peps were replaced in April 1999 by *individual savings accounts* (Isas) but funds built up in a Pep can be left in the plan.

Placing: A new issue of shares sold privately through a group of financial institutions.

Pooled funds – Another term for collective or mutual funds which invest in a range of shares and other instruments to achieve diversification for the smaller investor who buys units in these funds.

Portfolio: A collection of assets.

Preference shares ('prefs'): These are similar to bonds in that they pay a fixed rate of interest, although its payment depends on company profits. Preference shares are first in the pecking order of payouts when an investment trust is wound up. (See *stepped preference shares* and *zero-dividend preference shares*)

Preliminary results: A report to the Stock Exchange on the company's annual results. This is issued about six weeks before the annual report and accounts are published.

Premium: If the share price of an investment trust is higher than the value of the underlying assets, the difference is known as the premium. Normally investors are advised not to buy under these circumstances. If the price is lower than the net asset value, the difference is known as the discount.

Pre-tax profit margin: A company's trading profit (before the deduction of depreciation, interest and tax) as a percentage of turnover.

Price/earnings ratio (p/e): The market price of a share divided by the company's earnings (profits) per share in its latest 12-month trading period.

Primary market: Used for flotations of new companies and for further raising of capital under a *rights issue*.

Profit and loss account: This is contained within a company's annual report and accounts, together with the *balance sheet*. It sets out what the company has sold (turnover) during the past 12 months and its expenses in terms of salaries, raw materials, etc.

Protected funds: These funds limit your exposure to the downside of an index and so protect your capital from severe loss. However, as largely cash funds which use a *derivative* to provide the capital protection, they do not benefit from reinvestment of dividends.

Public-sector borrowing requirement (PSBR): The amount by which government spending exceeds the income from taxation and other revenues.

Purchased life annuity: PLAs offer a guaranteed regular income in return for a lump sum investment. Sold by insurance companies.

Redemption: The date at which a bond becomes repayable. Also known as the maturity date.

Redemption yield: The current dividend or interest rate increased or decreased to take into account the capital value if the bond is held to maturity.

Retail Price Index (RPI): The main measure of consumer inflation.

Return: The amount by which your investment increases as a result of interest or dividend income and capital growth.

Rights issue: An issue of shares to raise additional capital. Usually offered to existing shareholders at a discount.

Risk: A measure of the probability that the value of your savings and the income they generate will fall as well as rise.

Running yield: The current dividend or interest payments on a fund.

Save As You Earn (SAYE): Schemes run by employers to allow employees to buy shares in the company, usually at a discount.

Scrip dividend: Dividends paid in the form of shares.

Scrip issue: 'Free' shares given to shareholders to dilute the share price to aid liquidity.

Secondary market: Where shares are bought and sold on the Stock Exchange after the initial *flotation* in the primary market.

Securities: The general name for all stocks and shares. Broadly speaking stocks are fixed-interest securities and shares are the rest. The four main types of securities listed and traded on the UK Stock Exchange are UK *equities*, overseas equities (i.e. issued by non-UK companies), UK *gilts* (bonds issued by the UK government) and *corporate bonds/fixed interest securities* (issued by companies and local authorities).

Self-select: A plan that does not restrict you to the funds of one Isa manager but instead allows you to hold a range of assets, including individual shares and bonds as well as unit and investment trusts.

Settlement: The transfer of shares from the existing owner to the new owner and the corresponding transfer of money.

Share exchange: A facility offered by plan managers whereby they take your shares, sell them and invest the cash in an Isa. In some cases they may be able to absorb the shares into their funds and reduce dealing costs.

Short-dated bond: A *gilt* or *bond* with up to five years to go to *redemption*. See *long-dated bond* and *medium-dated bond*.

Size-weighted average: The average return after weighting each company in the category or index by size of market capitalization at the start of the period. This means that the performance of really small shares or trusts does not have a disproportionate impact on an index. Size-weighted average is the preferred method used by the independent measurers of the big institutional pension funds. (See *arithmetic average*)

Split capital trust: An investment trust which has different types of shares – for example, some offer a high income but no capital growth and some offer pure capital growth but no income.

Stakeholder pension scheme: These were launched in April 2001. A stakeholder is a type of *personal pension* which must offer low cost, low minimum contributions and penalty-free entry and exit terms. Anyone under 75 can invest up to £3,600 p.a. irrespective of earnings.

Stamp duty: A tax on the purchase (but not the sale) of shares, currently 0.5 per cent.

Stepped preference shares: Shares in a *split capital trust* paying dividends that rise at a predetermined rate and have a fixed redemption value paid when the trust is wound up.

Stockbroker: A member of the London Stock Exchange who buys and sells shares on behalf of clients.

Stock Exchange Automated Quotations (SEAQ): A computer-based system which allows stockbrokers to see share price information anywhere in the UK. The Stock Exchange Alternative Trading System (SEATS) was introduced in 1993 for less liquid securities.

Stock Exchange Trading Services (SETS): Introduced in October 1997 to speed up order-driven trading, initially in the FTSE 100 companies. Allows sales and purchases to be matched electronically.

Stock market: The place where shares, bonds and other assets change hands.

Stock market indices: An index is a specified basket or portfolio of shares and shows how these share prices are moving in order to give an indication of market trends. Every major world stock market is represented by at least one index. The FTSE 100 index, for example, reflects the movements of the share prices of the UK's largest 100 quoted companies by market capitalization.

Taper relief: Reduces the capital gains tax liability on the sale of an asset according to the length of time you have held it.

Tax avoidance: Saving tax by using loopholes in the law. This is legal but may be frowned upon by the Inland Revenue.

Tax-efficient investments: Investments which offer an element of tax exemption, reduction or deferral. The main UK investments that fall into this category are:

■ *Pensions:* available from a range of financial institutions and also provided by many employers in the form of an occupational pension scheme. Pension schemes and plans approved by the Inland Revenue offer tax relief on contributions, virtually tax-free growth of the fund and, in some cases, a tax-free lump sum at retirement. The pension income is taxed.

■ *Personal equity plans (Peps):* investments made in a Pep before April 5, 1999 can remain in the plan.

■ *Individual savings accounts:* ISAs replaced Peps and Tessas in April 1999. The annual maximum is £7,000. The investment range includes up to £3,000 per annum in deposits and £1,000 per annum in life assurance funds.

■ *National Savings Certificates:* available direct from National Savings or via the Post Office. NS certificates offer a tax-free return.

■ *Enterprise zone trusts (EZTs):* available by direct subscription. EZTs are designated areas where tax reliefs and reduced administrative controls are used to attract new business, providing investment in property with income tax relief on most of the cost.

■ *Enterprise investment schemes (EISs):* available by direct subscription. EISs offer a range of tax reliefs if you invest in the shares of mainly unquoted trading companies.

■ *Venture capital trusts (VCTs):* available from a range of financial institutions and by direct subscription. VCTs allow you to participate in EIS-type investments on a collective basis.

■ *Timber:* available by direct subscription. Timber offers an 8–10-year investment for tax-free income through felling or a very long-term investment for the next generation.

Tax evasion: A deliberate attempt to reduce your tax bill by withholding information or lying. This is illegal.

Tax-exempt special savings account (Tessa): A deposit account where the fund accumulates tax free provided the capital is not withdrawn for a minimum of five years. Replaced by cash Isas in April 1999.

Tax mitigation: Tax saving encouraged by the law, for example by investing in a pension plan.

Tax year: Tax and investment allowances apply to the 12 months from April 6 to the following April 5.

Tracker funds: See *index tracking*.

Trust deed: The legal document on which a unit trust or pension is based, for example. The use of a trust separates the fund from the management or sponsoring company's assets.

Trustee: You cannot have a trust without a trustee, who, as legal owner of the fund, looks after the assets on behalf of the beneficiaries. UK pension funds are established under trust, as are unit trusts.

UCITS (Undertaking for Collective Investments in Transferable Securities): A European Union term for a collective fund such as a *unit trust* or *oeic* which can be marketed in all the Union's markets.

Unit trust: A collective investment. Your money purchases units, the value of which rises and falls in line with the value of the underlying assets.

Warrants: Risky and volatile investments which give the holder the right but not the obligation to buy investment trust shares at a predetermined price within a specified period. This type of share has no voting rights and holders do not normally receive dividends.

Windfalls: Free shares given to members of a building society or mutual life office when it demutualizes to become a public limited company.

Yield: The annual dividend or income on an investment expressed as a percentage of the purchase price. (See *gross yield*)

Zero-dividend preference shares ('zeroes'): A lower-risk and predetermined investment. They offer a fixed capital return in the form of a redemption value paid when the trust is wound up. These shares are not entitled to income and therefore there is no income tax liability.

Index